Paschal Beverly Randolph

**Dealings with the Dead**

The human soul, its migrations and its transmigrations

Paschal Beverly Randolph

**Dealings with the Dead**
*The human soul, its migrations and its transmigrations*

ISBN/EAN: 9783337038045

Printed in Europe, USA, Canada, Australia, Japan

Cover: Foto ©Thomas Meinert / pixelio.de

More available books at **www.hansebooks.com**

# DEALINGS WITH THE DEAD:

## THE HUMAN SOUL,

### ITS MIGRATIONS AND ITS TRANSMIGRATIONS.

#### Penned by the Rosicrucian.

---

"I have stolen the golden keys of the Egyptians; I will indulge my sacred fury."—KEPLER.

"What is here written is truth, therefore it cannot die."—POE.

"I have found it! This night have I read the Mystic Scroll. The GRAND SECRET OF THE AGE stands revealed. It is mine! Alone I delved for it, alone I have found it! Now let the world laugh! I am immortal!"—P. B. RANDOLPH.

---

UTICA, N. Y.:

## PUBLISHED BY M. J. RANDOLPH.

1861-'62.

DEALINGS WITH THE DE

# DEDICATION.

TO MY FAR OFF AND BEST BELOVED FRIEND, BY WHOSE ROYAL BOUNTY
I AM ENABLED TO BRING THIS BOOK BEFORE THE WORLD ; AND TO ALL WHO
FEEL AND LIKEWISE THINK ; AND TO ALL WHO HAVE SUFFERED ON THEIR
WAY THROUGH THIS WORLD AS I HAVE, THIS VOLUME IS DEDICATED BY

THE SON OF FLORA.

# PREFACE.

Some men are daily dying; some die ere they have learned how to live; and some find their truest account in revealing the mysteries of both life and death,—even while they themselves perish in the act of revelation, as is most wonderfully done in the remarkable volume now before the reader,—as, alas! almost seems to be the case with the penman of what herein follows.

The criterion of the value of a man or woman is the kind and amount of good they do or have done. The standard whereby to judge a thinker, consists in the mental treasures which during life they heap up for the use and benefit of the age that is, and those which are to be, when the fitful fever of their own sorrowful lives shall be ended, and they have passed away to begin in stern reality their dealings with the dead. He or she who adds even one new thought to the age becomes that age's great benefactor, to whom in future times grateful men shall erect monuments and statues. Well, here follows the work of a man, for *his* hand penned every line, and the ideas were born of *his* soul, not-withstanding his own disclaimer, for not every one can understand the mystical Blending by means of which he claims to have reached the *ultima thule* of human know-ledge, and most readers, while reveling in the delights whereof so rich a store is laid before them, will insist that these glories were begotten of his own soul. Be that as it may, however, here is one, who, measured by the standard of the world itself, merits a monument stronger than iron, more endurable than granite, the gratitude of every soul that sighs for immortality ; for not a single new thought, but whole platoons of them, grand and magnificent, hath he here presented, a deathless legacy to the world ; and bye-and-bye these thoughts of ' Cynthia,' these ' Dealings with the Dead,' will become a beacon on the Highway of Thought, and be remembered to the everlasting glory of the sufferer who penned them. Rest, Paschal, rest, my brother ; thou brother and lover of thy race, for thy work is well done ; thy thoughts can never die. The bad will hate, but all who love Truth, Goodness, and Beauty, will bless thee, and crown thy name with fadeless laurels.        G. D. S.

# INTRODUCTION.

DEAR READER, your humble servant here presents you with a somewhat curious, novel, yet suggestive and thought-provoking work. So far as mere language is concerned, it might have been sent forth upon its travels up and down the world, clad in better raiment; but as I had nothing better than linsey-woolsey whereof to fashion its apparel, why, it must e'en take its chance in that.

A man's coat amounts to but little at the best, compared to the man inside it,—and so of books. It is not always your gilt-edged annual that either carries the most precious freight, or does the most good in the world; hence so far as the verbal clothing of my precious babe, this child of my soul is concerned, so far as relates to the terms wherein that here offered is couched, nothing need be said apologetically. If the dress suits, well and good; if not, it is even well;—the writer has done the very best that could be done, no one can do more. In making the assertions, the weird and strange revealments contained within the lids of this book, no one can be better aware of the risk encountered of being laughed at by the wise people of this wise age, than I am. Doubtless there are those who will cavil, deride, sneer at and condemn the author and the work: but what of that? My truths, if truths indeed they be, and to me, they are intensely such, will live. Why? Because they were chipped off the Rock of Truth itself, and therefore will unquestionably sur-

vive many a laugh, as have other truths ere now.  They
and their discoverer can well afford being laughed at.
The author feels that when the great Reaper, Death,
shall have done his work, these same truth-seeds will
spring up into Form, Life, and Beauty :—all for the
gladdening of the people :—and this feeling, this inner
prophecy of and to the soul, contents and satisfies the
being.    Friendly reader, when this body shall have
gone back to the dust whence it sprung in the hopeful
years gone by ; when this soul shall be nestling in the
bosom of its Saviour and his God, people who then
shall read these pages will find, if not before, more in
that which the heart-weary one has here written, than
either a psychological romance, or the daring specula-
tions of undisciplined genius.

The foregoing observations have reference more especially to the first part of this work, which is presented in the form of Revelations from the Dead.    It
does not owe its origin to what is ordinarily known
as " Spiritualism" :—it did not come either by the
" Raps," " Tips," " Table-turning," " Speaking mediumship," " Writing," or in any other of the modes so
commonly claimed for the mass of " Spiritual" literature, now so widely circulated and read.    The process by which what follows came, is to me as weirdly
strange and novel, as anything can well be.    I call this
process THE BLENDING.

The people called " Mediums," a singular order among
men, set forth that their bodies are, for the time being,
vacated by their souls, and that during the vacation, the
soul of some one else, one who has died, and yet lives,
takes possession of the physical structure, and then proceeds to give forth his or her wisdom or folly for the
enlightenment or darkening of men's minds.    Another
class tell us that they are " impressed" by a departed
one to give voice to the Spirit's thought ; others declare
that they are " obsessed."    Well, it may all be so, or it
may not.    I do not assume or presume to decide one way

or the other : all that need be said on this point is, that this book does not owe its origin to either or any of these methods.

Machiavelli, the great Italian diplomat, is said to have gained a thorough and complete knowledge and insight of the state, frame of mind, and intentions of other men, through a wonderful power which he, above most, if not all men, possessed, of completely identifying himself by an intense desire and volition, with those with whom he came in contact. To such an extent and degree did he possess this power, that it was an easy task to circumvent and overreach most, if not all his diplomatic opponents. He placed himself by a mental effort, and physical as well, in the exact position occupied for the time being by his antagonists, or the person he designed to read.

No matter what the mood indicated by the physical appearance, or the outward manifestation of what was going on within, away down in the deeps of being, was, he immediately moulded his features by the model thus furnished. "I am now in his place," said he, mentally, "and will see how to act, think and feel from his position ; and, for the time being, I sink my own personality, my opinions, views,—in short all my self-hood, prejudices, likes, dislikes, and all else beside ;—in a word, I transmute Machiavelli into the other man :—which being effected, I shall be, to all intents and purposes, that other man for the time being, and of course will feel as he feels, see as he sees, know as he knows, and be impelled to action by the identical motives whereby he is prompted.

All the world knows that Machiavelli succeeded to a wonderful extent ; and by this power of assumption, this easy, yet mysterious blending, he often, in fact, nearly always, baffled his foes, and the foes of the State, so that now a successful diplomatist is said to be pursuing the Machiavellian policy.

Almost any person can make successful experiments

in this—-Science, shall I call it?—and will be surprised at the results. A man or woman appears before you with features bearing the impress of a certain kind of thought—and you can find out what kind by placing your own features, so far as possible, in the same shape; keep them thus for several minutes, and you will become absorbed in the same that absorbs the individual before you, and in a short time will become an adept in the art of Soul-reading.

Many men, and a still greater number of women, who possessed the power alluded to, have existed in all times past; but, above all others, the age we live in has been prolific of such—so that now it is not at all difficult to find those who will enter at will, almost, the very abysses, labyrinths, and most secret recesses of your being. Indeed, persons abound in nearly all the great cities of the world who attain high honor and re- nown—to say nothing of the benefits of competence, and even wealth—by the exercise of this marvellous faculty.

There are many wise ones who admit the existence of this power, yet deny its attainability by the many, and who stoutly maintain that it is a special gift of the Creator to a favored few. Against such a verdict the writer begs leave most respectfully to protest; and these are the grounds upon which that protest is based :

All human powers and faculties are latent, until time, circumstance, and discipline bring them out. All human beings are created alike in so far forth as the germinal powers are concerned. All men naturally love sweet sounds, and, if this taste be cultivated at an early day, are capable of musical appreciation, if not of vocal or instrumental execution. The seeds of all unfolding lie *perdu*, or latent, in every human being; they are the property of Soul; in Soul-soil they are imbedded, and from that soil they must eventually put forth the shoot, the shrub, the tree, the branch, leaf, blossom, and finally the fruit. Every faculty, strictly human, belongs to, and is a part of, every member of the species ; and that—this fact being admitted, though any given one or more may be manifested most powerfully by some, and not at all by others—all of them are one day to be developed, called out, unfolded, in all, is a plain inference ; nay, an absolute certainty. The power to see without eyes, demonstrated by scores and hundreds of clairvoyants, is *not* a gift peculiar to a certain man or woman, or to a certain order of people. It is a power that can be had for the trying, as any good mesmerist will affirm and prove.

It seems to me that the expression of the Crucified, " I and my Father are one," contains a direct affirmation of the possibility of this blending. God was to Jesus the very essence of goodness ; Jesus strove to be also most thoroughly good, and succeeded in reaching that point where Himself was in perfect blending with the entire universe of Goodness, and therefore with the Fount of all Excellence.

Perfect blending is perfect love ; and whether that love be toward the person, the outer self, the body ; or toward the soul, or the mental treasures, or the secret self of another, the results are in degree, if not in kind, the same.

Mental telegraphy will be a perfect success, whenever two persons can be found in whom the power of entering the region of Sympathia shall normally exist. A few can transmit thought to, and receive thought back from, others, even now ; but presently scores of people will develop the ability.

Now, this blending is not a mere magnetic union of physical spheres, but is a Soul-process nearly altogether.

Love, in its essence, is a thing of the Spiritual part of us, though, alas ! it is often put to base uses.

There was once, not many years ago, a woman to whom I felt such a love as that subsisting between affectionate sisters ; for it was deeper, purer, calmer than that which binds brothers together. In life, her soul drew near, almost fearfully near, to mine ; she thought my thoughts, read my spirit, sympathized with me in all my joys, my sorrows, and my aspirations. Often have we sat beside each other—that poor sick girl and I ; and though no word broke the stillness of the sacred hour, yet not a region of our souls was there but was explored by the other; not a silent thought that was not mutually understood and replied to.  Presently she died—the forms were forever separated, yet not for a day were the mystic soul-links which bound us together severed.  No sister was ever more dearly loved than I loved her ; and that love was fully and as purely returned.  Everybody called her "Sister"— everybody felt that to them she was truly such.

Well, she died ; and after a year or two had passed, I began to understand that at times her soul was near me, and many and oft were the periods in which I did not seem to be myself, but had an invincible conviction that I was Cynthia for the time being, instead of who and what I am.  By-and-by there came a consciousness of this blending, so deep, so clearly defined, so calm, that at last I began to appreciate a mighty, almost resistless Will and Purpose behind it all; for I was myself and Cynthia—never simultaneously, as is asserted to be the case with many of the people called "Mediums"—but in separate instants—now her, then myself ; at first very imperfectly, but gradually approaching an absolute and complete mergement of Soul.

This continued for nearly two years, at intervals, and after about eighteen months had passed, one portion of the process seemed to have reached completeness—for in a degree it changed, and instead of momentary, as before, the transmutations became longer, until at last, as now, the changes last sixty, and in one instance has reached two hundred and forty-five minutes.

It may here be asked : "Where are *you* in the interim ?" and the answer is : " We are two in one, yet the stronger rules the hour."

It will be seen, therefore, that this condition is as widely separated from those incident to the " Mediums," as theirs is supposed to be different from the ordinary wakeful mood. *They* reach their state by a sort of retrocession from themselves ; they fall, or claim to fall, into a peculiar kind of slumber, their own faculties going, as it were, to sleep. On the contrary, *mine* is the direct opposite of this, for, instead of a sleep of any sort, there comes an *intense wakefulness.* Nor is this all in which we differ ; as are the processes and states apart, so also are the results different.

The revelations of Spiritual existences, moods, modes, and conditions of being, as given by nearly every " Spiritual Medium " of whom I have ever heard or read, are, to say the least, totally unsatisfactory to the great majority of those who seek for information on the vital question of Immortality—how, and why, and to what great end we are thus gifted and endowed?

Another, and equally important one, is that concerning the Soul-world, and the inhabitants thereof—how they live, where they live, and to what end and use?

I believe that light is, in this volume, thrown on all these great and vital points ; such light, indeed, as will be hailed and appreciated by all who read and think, as well as by those who read and feel—two widely different classes, but to both of whom these pages are humbly, yet hopefully addressed.

The process, strange, wierd, and altogether unusual, to which allusion has been made, went on for a long time ; and by slow degrees I felt that my own personality was not lost to me, but completely swallowed up, so to speak, in that of a far more potent mentality. A subtlety of thought, perception and understanding became mine at times, altogether greater than I had ever known before ; and occasionally, during these strange blendings of my being with another, I felt that other's feelings, thought that other's thoughts, read that other's past, aspired with that other's aspirations, and talked, spoke, and reasoned with and under that other's inspiration. For a time I attributed these exaltations of Soul to myself alone, and supposed that I was not at all indebted to foreign aid for many of the thoughts to which, at such moments, I frequently gave utterance; but much study of the matter has at length convinced me, not only that the inhabitants of the Soul-worlds have much to do in moulding the great world's future, but that occasionally they so manage things that their thoughts are often spoken, and their behests, ends, and purposes fulfilled by us mortals, when we imagine that we alone are entitled to the sole credit of much that we say, think, and do, when the fact is, we doubtless are oftentimes merely the proxies of others, and act our allotted rôle in a drama whose origin is entirely supernatural, and the whole direction of which is conducted by personages beyond the veil.*

Well, one day, it so happened that I repaired to a beautiful village in one of the New England States, on a visit to some very kind and well-beloved friends—the brother and the sister of the rare maiden whose wondrous thoughts abound in the volume now before the reader; and while there, the conversation ran on topics wide apart from either Mesmerism or its great cognate, "Spiritualism." During the time that had elapsed since my last visit to the beautiful village, some two years, Death had been busily gathering his harvests in all the regions round about; nor had he kept aloof from the house on the hill. No! cruel Death had been over its threshold, and Azrael had carried two precious souls over the Dark River. These were Cynthia and her mother.

After partaking of a sorrow-seasoned meal, mourn-

---

* That many of them are inhabitants of other spheres, beings who never lived on this earth, I am firmly convinced. My reasons will be given in the sequel to this present volume.

fully, and with aching heart and tearful eye, we, the left-behind and myself, took our way toward the ground where lay the sacred form of her we loved so deeply, so fully ; and there I wept, and the great salt tears bedewed the sod—for, indeed, my heart, poor, weary, troubled heart, was almost breaking. Soon we returned to the house upon the hill, and I lay me down upon the sofa, near the window—the very sofa whereon her sainted form was wont to recline in the days now, alas! fled, with her, forever and forevermore— that same little sofa whereon she used to sit and converse with us, with her sister Clarinda, the gentle and the good John Hart, and her well-beloved Jonathan, with my humble self, and a few select and sober-minded lovers of the good and true ; used to sit and converse upon the mysteries of the Great Beyond, and touching the realities of that other world, to which Disease was remorselessly, and with relentless purpose, fast urging her life-car. * * * And I threw myself upon the sofa ; and as I lay there, with closed eyes, I beheld the flitting ghosts of many a dead day, with all its troops of glad and bitter memories, when suddenly it seemed that I was no longer myself—for so deep and perfect was the blending, that I had not merely an insurmountable assurance that my body contained, for the time being, *two* complete souls, but even the very thoughts, modes of expression, and memory of the departed one was mine ; and yet this possession did not, for an instant, subvert my own individuality. I was there, and so was she. For the time being, we two were not merely as, but to all intents and purposes, we actually were, *one*.

Arising from the recumbent position, my body assumed certain singularities of movement peculiar to her before she flew up to her home in the bright empyrean, and these words were spoken : " The experiences and history of a Soul must be written, for the benefit of the people. I, we, intend to write it. A book shall be produced, containing the facts of a living, dying, dead and transfigured human being—containing the reasons why men live after death, and the methods of their after life and being. This book shall contain an account of the experience of two human beings—the one, while temporarily disenthralled ; the other, when permanently so—shall contain the experience of Cynthia during her passage from earth to the grave of earthly hope and being, and a history of what befell thereafter."

These were the spoken words. Once more I resumed my personality, and attended to the affairs of the busy world. In other days the promises were kept, and this first book was written.

Nothing further need be said by way of introduction to what follows, further than to observe that certain Soul-experiences, related in the second part, were mine—the writer's—while the reasonings are not wholly such.

# Cynthia: The Soul-World.

I PURPOSE to say nothing whatever concerning my life as a denizen of the outside world—of my existence or career while clothed with the garments of mortality. It is of my death that first I wish to speak, and of what took place thereafter—of *where* and *how* I found myself as soon as the icy hand of Death had touched my heart, and frozen up my vitals. While with my friends, from whom the change separated me, I was, so far as frail mortals in my condition of bodily health can be, quite happy and contented—contented to endure, with all possible patience, that for which there was no medicament, no remedy ; and, all things considered, satisfied I lived, and in the self-same spirit died. Died? No ; I am not dead!—bodies change ; souls can never die. Why? For the reason that God, who, like human beings, is intelligent and immortal, can Himself be never blotted out of being. He is Mind, Memory, Love, and Will, not one of which can ever perish ; and these being the attributes of man likewise, it follows that, so long as He exists, we must also.

In the year 1854, being ill of consumption, the person, an account of whose experience is given in these pages, although long previously somewhat familiar

with, began to take an especial interest in the great
subject of an hereafter, as revealed by what purported
to be the spirits of departed men and women ; and
then, for the first time, as Death's cold presence
sensibly approached me afar off, and the sense of
GOING began to quicken in my being, I commenced seriously to speculate concerning immortality, and to pay .
greater heed to the alleged revelation's from the mysterious Beyond.

Bye-and-bye, consumption so wasted me, that I grew
tired ; and finally, a mist came before my eyes, and shut
out the fields, the forests, and the faces of my friends,—my
friends—none dearer than whom, were ever clasped to
affection's warm heart. * * * * And so I slept,—but
woke again from out of that strange, deep sleep, called
Death.   The awakening was *very* strange !—was such
as I had never even imagined to be possible.

" Where am I ?" was asked by myself of that very self.
Not mine, but a lower, sweeter, more musical voice, soft
and dulcet as the tinkle of a love bell, answered me
from out a veil of rosy light, that hung between me,
and, whatever was beyond. " In the Divine City of
freed souls,—the land of Immortal, but not Eternal
rest." * * * * I felt, and knew that I was—dead !

As the sense of these words struck upon my soul,
where this voice came from, seemed very strange to me,
for this reason amongst others : I had, to a certain extent, familiarized myself with Physics, and knew that
sounds were supposed to be the result of certain aerial
vibrations.   Now, supposing this theory to be correct,
it struck me, that I, a disembodied soul, ought not to be
competent to discern sounds, for there was neither tym-

panum to *receive*, auditory nerves to *conduct*, nor external ear, to *collect* these waves of sound.

It seemed to me, that one of the two prevalent theories must be false ; either sound is *not* material, or that the Spirit of a human being *is;*—for I had not the shadow of a doubt, but that I was really, and forever, an inhabitant of the soul-world. If sounds are material, how was it possible for me to hear them, being a Spirit ? If a Spirit is but a refined form of matter, then the notion of its eternal durability, is a false one, and there must come a period when it too, like the body, must dissolve away. These things troubled me. I had passed to death, not as a sluggard, and careless of what might await me, but with every faculty keenly awake. Nor do I suppose five minutes elapsed after I emerged from my body, ere I was perfectly alive to all that surrounded me.

I distinctly *saw* certain familiar things, and recognized them; but there was not any difficulty in comprehending the rationale of this; for I perceived that solar light was not the only source of illumination the earth possessed. Indeed, there is no such thing as darkness. The life of all things is light, and although sun, moon, and stars should hide behind an impenetrable veil, yet the things of earth would still be visible to the sight of the soul.

There are two other sources of light; first, the electrical emanations from every material object illumine them, and whatever may be near; and second, the air itself, which fleshly lungs inhale, is but the outer garb of a finer and magnetic sea, which not only encircles the earth, but stretches away in all directions to the outer limits of creation; and in this, all things are radiant, all things visible.

These observations were quickly made; and in an instant thereafter, I turned toward the fleecy veil previously observed, and saw the figure of an old, gray-haired man emerge therefrom, leading by the hand, a sweet and lovely girl apparently about ten years old. The gleesome smile on that angel's face, the look of bland benevolence on the features of the man, surpassed aught of the kind that I had ever seen before. Both of them approached, and greeted me. I could not return the salutation, because the strangeness and utter novelty, not only of my new situation, but of my sensations, were such that it was impossible to act as in other moments, I feel certain I should have been prompted to. The man spoke, and called me "daughter." The tones were precisely those I had formerly heard; and two things surprised me: First, their *serene* and liquid melody,—so very different from those one would naturally expect to hear from one of his appearance; and second, that very appearance itself: for both the man and child were clothed after the manner and fashion of the earth.

This was a matter of astonishment, for I had supposed that the clothing of the Spirit was vastly different from that of the body. Evidently, the old man read my mind, and understood the cause of my perplexity. Drawing near to where I stood, he touched my forehead with his finger, and said, "Be clear, my child, be clear."

As if that touch were magic, there came an instantaneous change over me; it was as if I thought to the point I wished, and that with perfect clarity. Things, which a moment before were wrapped in the folds of mystery, now became transparent as the plainest I could wish.

As a matter of course, I took notice of the friends I had just left behind me—yes, behind me, in what was now in very truth a far-off world:—even though not ten yards intervened between myself and the dear ones, who now mourned me; yet in presence of the fact that I have very momentous revelations to make,—revelations that will startle the world,—I cannot now stop to relate my emotions, my sorrows or my joys, for I felt that at last I was in the realm of pure knowledge ; and now feel that this precious opportunity must be improved, to other ends than a mere recital of my emotions and sympathies however acute and tender they may have been.

The communication between the soul-world and earth is far more difficult and rare than I had believed, or than thousands believe to-day. Much, I learned, that passes among men for spiritual manifestation, really has no such origin, while many things, attributed to an origin purely mundane, are really the work of intelligent beings, beyond the misty veil.

Long previous to my final illness, I had held many interesting conversations with my friends, concerning the higher life and worlds, and particularly with the one by whose aid I am now enabled to make these disclosures ; and I had made a solemn compact, to the effect, that if it were possible to return subsequent to death, I would do so, and, reveal such mysteries as I might be enabled or permitted to. This resolution grew out of the fact, that not one of the theories, regarding the *post mortem* existence of human kind, which I had ever heard or read, gave me the satisfaction that my soul desired. I suspected that many of the current notions regarding the lands beyond the curtain, were, to say the least, largely tinctured with the mind of the individuals through whose lips the oracular utterances came ; consequently I became, to a degree, suspicious of all modern eolism and eolists, because I feared their inspirations had not so high and deep a source as they claimed, and is claimed for them.

My mind, in this respect, is still unchanged. The first lesson that flashed in upon me, after the mysterious clarification of soul to which allusion has been made, was this : People on earth spend a great deal of time in acquiring lessons which have to be unlearned, upon their entrance on the upper life ;—*must* be unlearned, ere they can advance far in the acquisition of the rare treasures of knowledge, to be found *only* by the true seeker, even in that mighty realm which constitutes the soul-world.

God has placed all true human joys, there, as well as on the earth, upon high shelves, whence they cannot be taken by proxy ;—they must be reached for by those who would have them ; and the more precious the joy, the higher the shelf;—the more valuable the volume, the greater effort is required to obtain the perusal thereof. This is the first great law.

Now, in collecting what purported to be scraps of knowledge, from the realm of spiritual existence, I found on my entry there, that I had laid up quite a store of falsities in the magazines of my soul:—laid up great heaps of what I supposed were the gold and diamonds of supernal truth; but which, no sooner had I entered the portals of the vast temple of Eternity, than I found to be the most useless rubbish; and nearly all my treasures proved to be the merest paste and tinsel. The first thing, therefore, which the soul desirous of attaining real proficiency in knowledge, has to do, is to *unlearn* its follies as quick as possible.

This process is called by a term signifying vastation, or throwing off. Some do this at once and with ease ; others linger a long time in error, and only attain the great end through great trial and perseverance, just as persons on earth. My desire was ever to, and for the truth ; hence the process, to me was one of comparative case. The ideas which I had imbibed, and given my heart to, concerning matters spiritual, were the same that are still current amongst those who accept that which is known as modern Spiritualism. Succinctly stated, they were these : first, The spirit of a human being is the product of the physical body ; the human being is a triplicate, composed of soul, or the thinking principle, the body, and an intermediate link, called spirit ; possessing all the organs of, and shaped like the body, and which serves to connect this last with the soul, while on earth, and being its eternal casket after death. The soul, spirit and body are called into being at one time, and that upon the earth.

The spiritual body, like the physical, is subject both to waste and want, for which ample and due provision has by God been made. It has thirst, hunger, and amatory love, all of which have their appropriate gratifications in the Spirit-world. This spiritual world itself is on the surface of a zone surrounding the earth, at a distance of one hundred miles, more or less ; above this zone, is another and another, to the number of twelve ; each zone is a 'Sphere,' and its inhabitants are divided off into classes, degrees, societies and circles. All the zones are diversified with real and absolute rivers, trees, mountains, lakes, landscapes, cities, and so on, just as is the material globe; and all these things are fixtures. Such, in brief, are the general ideas on the subject entertained by the people ; and such as I had believed and conceived to be true. But when I came to pass through the change, and to realize the new condition, I ascertained that so far from being founded in reality, they were simply—nonsense!

According to the foregoing, which is confessedly the most popular conception of the realms beyond, and of its inhabitants, that world is scarcely better than the one that mortals occupy. These notions totally ignore Spirit ; for, according to them, Spirit is nothing more than matter in an exceedingly refined, or rather, sublimated, condition ; whereas Spirit is no such thing. True, it animates material things, but itself is not material. It is above, beyond, and discreted from it. Like the asymptotes of an arc, it forever approaches, but never actually contacts matter. The same general theory accords mankind an origin here in space and time merely, and at best predicates but sempiternity, or a future endless duration for him; whereas, if soul begins to be at all on the plane of earth and matter, it must have but a very ill-grounded assurance of an endless race. No, this is not correct ; for Soul, like God, is from forever in the past, to forever in the distance ; and so far from originating on the earth, it has for myriads of æons sped its career through God's infinite Silence Halls, and now merges, whether for the first time or not, is needless to inquire at this point, into the vocal Harmonead. In the life of earth, the soul awakes from its pre-state into one as different as can well be thought of; and at death, it experiences another waking, quite as startling, but infinitely more grand.

The first lesson, then, that I learned was, that with a great deal of philosophy, I had but very little knowledge; and instead of finding the Soul-world analagous to the earth-world, in fact I found them vastly different, and possessing no one thing in common, so far as the surroundings of the spiritual entrant was concerned.

All that has been said required several minutes to describe, but not ten seconds to experience.

I looked toward the old man and the child, marvelling, as before observed, that they wore clothing after the manner of the earth-kin, and bore the appearance of extreme youth and extreme age. "Is it possible that *years* affect souls? Do we grow old, as well as need garments in the other world?" These queries suggested themselves, and while present in my mind, the old man came to my right side, and took me by my left hand, while the little girl, Nellie,—I subsequently learned she had been called by the dear ones left behind her, took my right hand; and both said, "Come, Cynthia, they await you: let us go to meet them."

I now made three important discoveries: First, that I was yet in the room, where my breath had been resigned: that I was clothed in precisely such a dress as I had usually worn; and third, that so far as I could judge, I actually trod upon, and walked over a stratum of air, just such air as I had been used to breathe, albeit *that* was not possible any longer, for the reason that it was all too heavy for the respiratory apparatus of that which now constituted my body, or at least the vehicle of myself—the thinking, acting, living me. My method of locomotion differed essentially from that of my two companions, who did not walk, but seemed to glide along at will through that same air, which was to me quite palpable, for I distinctly noticed that its touch was of a velvety character, and quite elastic. My feet moved ; theirs did not. And so we passed out of the house through the open door,—for a person had just entered.

From one or two incidental circumstances that took place, not essential to this narrative, and therefore withheld, I became convinced that unless some incarnate man or woman had raised the latch of that door, it must, so far as I was concerned, have remained shut to all eternity, barring wind, decay, accident, or an earthquake ; for in my then state of enlightenment on the subject, I saw no possible means whereby to effect our liberation. It struck me that unless some such agency as has been named, came to our assistance, we must either make our egress by means of the chimney, or stay pent up there until the elements dissolved a portion of the edifice ; or, supposing it to be proof against decay, a dreadful alternative, so it seemed, there we must remain for evermore. Subsequently I learned that even were such a thing possible, and I never got outside of that dwelling, yet it would be far less terrible than fear might lead one to imagine or suspect ; for still there would remain, not only an infinity of duration, but also a universe

to move and be in, quite as infinite in both extent and
variety beside; for the Soul, I soon discovered, was a Vasti-
tude in and of itself; and should it happen that not one
of the moments of its mighty year be spent in the society
of others like unto itself, yet there would be but little occasion for ennui; not one lonely minute need be spent, for all
its days—if for illustration's sake, I may predicate time of
that whereof emotions and states are the minutes and
the hours—might be profitably employed in visiting its
own treasure houses and in counting the rare jewels there
stored away ; besides which, it could perform many a
pleasant voyage, visiting mighty continents, rare islands,
wondrous cities, and marvellous countries of its own
tremendous being ;—aye! it *could* amuse itself for ages
in merely glancing at the hills, valleys, caverns—strange
deep caverns they are too—the oceans, forests, fields
fens, brakes, and marshes of its mighty self ; nor would
its resources be exhausted at the thither end of the
rolling wave of Time ; *because* time is not to the soul : its
duration and successions are of thought, not seconds—
so wonderful, so vast, so illimitable, and, taken as a
unit, so incomprehensible, save by the Over-soul himself,
is the human being.   Soul! thou august thing!   Felt
thou mayest be ; understood by none, save God ; and,
albeit we may explore a little of thy forelands, yet only
He can penetrate thy depths ; only He can trace the
streams that water thee to their source, and that source
can be no other than His divine heart, who, forever unseen, is never unfelt ; an invisible worker afar off, yet
near at hand ; one who spreadeth the banquet, and pre-
pareth the feasters, who worketh ever in secret, yet
who doeth all things well!   Soul!   Mighty potentate!

2

Victim at once, and victor of circumstance and time!
Thou enigma, which millions think they have solved,
even while thou laughest at them; who imagining they
have untied the knot, have not even found the clue!
Strange riddle! Thing of which men think they are
well informed, because they have learned a few of thy
names, and can call thee Psyche, Soul, Spirit, Pneuma
and Breath; word-names, which generally convey about
as much of thee to the common understanding, as the
name-words Algebra, Geometry, Music and Number, do
to the barbarians who hear them pronounced, of the
vast realities that underlie the sounds or the signs.
Soul! Existence, whereof eolists and pedants learnedly
prate and bluster in long phrase and loud tone, as if
thou didst not command silence of him who would
approach thee, and seek to know the awful mysteries
slumbering beneath thy titles. Soul! Whereof everybody talks so much, but of which even the wisest of
either earth or heaven *know* so *very* little.

  Well, in my ignorance, I felt that unless some one,
something material, had opened that door, we must stay
imprisoned there in that house upon the hill, forever and
for evermore.

How little, how very little, I then knew or suspected
concerning the mighty powers latent, and *never* yet fully
unfolded in any human being—no matter whom, no
matter where located, how high in heaven, on earth, or
deep down in the bottomless hell, or the blackest
barathrum of the infinitudes of Possibility. No one
save God can fathom the profounds of Soul. Why?
Because, like Him, it is absolutely Infinite: Him, in
Conscious Power—it, in Capability! Very imperfect

still, and necessarily so, yet my notions of the Soul's powers were then exceedingly vague, crude, and undefined. In other and succeeding states to which I subsequently attained, much of this ignorance was dispelled by new light which constantly broke in upon my being.

And we passed beyond the portal of the house, myself crossing at the same instant its threshold, and that of Time ; nor did I once cast a glance toward the frail and decaying shell from which a joyous thrill of superconsciousness told me that I had forever escaped ; indeed I had no disposition to do so, for the reason that new and strange emotions and sensations crowded so fast upon me, that my whole attention was absorbed thereby ; for they swept like the billows of a wind - troubled lake, across the entire sea of my new-born being. One thought, and one alone, connected with earth, assumed importance, and that was associated with the physical phenomenon of dissolution, and it shaped itself in a hundred ways with the rapidity of lightning—no, not lightning, but quicker, for *that* is very slow compared to the flashings and the rushings forth of thought, even in the earth-made brain ; how much more rapid, then, from a source around which are no cerebral impediments to obstruct. " Death—this it is to be DEAD !" thought I. How blind, how deaf we are, not to see, and know, and hear, that all things tell of life, life, life—being, real and true ; while nothing, nothing in the great domain of our God, speaks one word of absolute death, of a blotting out of Soul—Soul, which, while even cramped in coarse bodies, sometimes mounts the Capitals of existence, and with . far-penetrating vision pierces the profoundest depths of space, gazes eagle-like upon the very sun of Glory, laughs death to scorn, and surveys the fields of two eternities—one behind, and one before it. This thing can never die, nor taste a single drop of bitter death! * * * How strange, how wonderfully strange I feel ; yet these sensations are of excellent health, of exhilarant youth, of concentration and power ; nor hath decrepitude or decay aught therein.

"I am not faint, but strong ; not sad, but joyous." These were my observations on realizing the great change. Many a time had I read and heard of the capacity human beings have of experiencing joys purely nervous. Nearly all present human pleasures are based upon the fineness and susceptibility of the nerves to receive and impart magnetic impressions. My nerves had aforetime been made to tingle with strange, deep bliss when in the presence of those I loved, after their return from long absence ; I had tasted the exquisite nectar from the lips of an innocent prattling babe, and had known the tumultuous thrill of friendship's joyous meetings ; and yet all these were as blasts of frozen air to what now kept running, leaping, flying, dancing through me. It was the supremely delicious sense of being dead—the voluptuous joy consequent upon dying.

At first it seemed to me that keener joy, or deeper bliss would be impossible for man or woman to experience than those that now were mine. After a while I learned better.

Mankind expand from the action of two principles— Intellect and Intuition ; the first being the basis of progression, the latter of development. Some, both in and out of the body, are built up by one, some by the other ;

and many rise from the combined action of both. Many of the dead pursue the triumphs of intellect and investigation, just as when on earth. These are the progressionists—vast in number, great in deed, but constituting an inferior order, as they must ever be secondary to that vaster host and higher order who climb the ladder of intuition. Without egotism, then, but in all humility, I say that great joy was mine on finding myself numbered with the larger army. It was in allusion to the fact that all the learning a man may acquire on earth, really stands him but little on the other side, that one of old declared that in that upper kingdom the first should be last, and the last be first ; for it often happens that one almost ignorant in a worldly sense, may have the highest and the grandest intuitions of truth, divested of the thick coats wherewith learning often clothes it. People in whom intellect predominates over intuition, naturally gravitate to their true position in the realms beyond. Their destiny is to be for a long time (and of such " time" can justly be predicated) pilgrims in the Spirit-world or middle state, whereas all in whom intuition is exalted, can not only be occasional residents, for redemptive purposes, of the outer Spirit-world, but are intromitted to the deeper and sublime realities of the Soul-world—a world as much different from the merely Spiritual kingdom as is the processes of a musician's soul, when at high tide, superior to the mental operations of a midnight burglar. A veil divides those worlds as completely as does a similar one separate earth from Spirit-land. Two beings there may meet, one a resident of the Soul-realm, the other a denizen of Spirit-land ; the former may be in close propinquity with the latter, and yet the spheres of their several existences be as far apart as is North from South. The one sees and knows only from appearances, the other from positive *rapport*. This fact at once explains many of the differences in the accounts which mortals receive, and unmistakably so, from the lands beyond the swelling flood, the kingdoms o'er the sea. My knowledge flowed in upon me through the channels of intuition, and through them I learned that the hyper-sensational joys to which allusion has been made, are ever experienced in exact ratio to the purity of the past record of the life. Those which I felt were only of the fourth degree, there being three beyond, though how mine should have been so intensified and deepened, was, and, for reasons plainly to be seen, must ever remain, a mystery. The amount, degree, and even kind, of joy felt by any soul upon its passage over the Myst, depends upon three things, and these are : First, the nature of the motives which, previous to the mortuary divorce, prompted to all or any action, either toward the self, the neighbor, or society ; Second, the amount of good a person has done on earth ; and Third, the amount of use, in the higher sense, they may have subserved previous to physical dissolution.

Nellie and I, and the old gray-haired man who accompanied her, soon reached the road in front of the house wherein I had lived, and wherein I was born into a newer phase of life. While looking at my companions to find out whither they were going, the child, by the exercise of a power not then fully understood by myself, rose into the air a foot or more, laid her hand gently on my forehead, patted it tenderly, and said : "Come ! We are going to show you your home, and then mine, and then *his!*" She said this with a smile, so pure, so radiant, that I instantly divined that there was truth in the theory that every one has a conjugal mate in the universe somewhere, albeit I shrank from, and dreaded to meet *mine*, if, indeed, I had one, for I had seen somewhat of that which passes for love among men ; and, while hailing and delighting in amicive, I felt a shuddering disgust at anything that assumed the form of amatory love. Love was admired, but its passional phases feared and despised. My tutelage was just begun.

The touch of the child's hand was as plain, palpable and physical as any touch ever felt before,—quite as much so as was that of the dear sister who smoothed my dying brow. 'After all, then, spirits are material. I feel their fingers, see their forms, hear their words, and I am in all respects as nervously sensitive as ever in the by-gone years of sickness ! Oh, this mystery of the double existence, which, after all, seems to be but two phases of a single state ; when, when shall it be solved ?' This thought passed through my mind, nor can there be the least doubt but they both read it quite as well as myself, for the old man smiled gently and benignly, the girl with half-concealed merriment and glee.

I now passed off into a strange and peculiar state, but whether what followed resulted from the touch or not, it is impossible to say. At first I was seized with an intense desire to know more of what must be called my *physique*, and a rapid inspection revealed the fact that I possessed, all and singular, the organs in the new condition, that had been in the old. There were my hands—real, actual hands, evidently,—but they were very thin, pale, emaciated, wrinkled, and of a decidedly blue, consumptive caste,—precisely as they had appeared every day for the past long months of pain and misery. My hair was long, and in all other respects as before ; my feet felt tender ; nor was there any difference between my then, and prior state, except that a nameless, thrilling joy pervaded me, and which left absolutely nothing to be wished for in that respect ; for as the mouth of every nerve drew in the magnetic essence in which I floated, it seemed as if living streams of sense-joy rushed through every channel and avenue of being ; and it struck me that if there were no other reward for having lived and suffered, yet that the sensations consequent upon physical death would fully compensate a life of agony.*

Soon a sense of vacuity stole over me, and brought the realization, that having passed through two worlds, I was rapidly approaching one still more wonderful and strange.

Many a time had I been mesmerized by friends, in my far distant-dwelling, by my well-beloved brother J. in particular, who all sought by that means to alleviate my sufferings; and not seldom had I passed into what is popularly termed the Superior State;† and the feeling

---

\* All the dead people are not thus favored. Up to the present I was an inhabitant merely of the Spiritual world, but had not yet entered upon the vast domains of the realm of Soul. There are two worlds into which it is possible for man to step into from the portals of the grave, as all will be convinced who either study the subject or give this introductory work a careful perusal.

† My researches have proved to me, that in nine cases in every ten, taking an entire average, the sleeping subject never once actually

induced by Nellie's touch was akin to that, but was far more profound. First there came a sort of mental retrocession, consequent upon my previous intellectual activity. The soul-principle seemed to bound back from its investigations of the previous moment, to a pinnacle within itself, from whence it as rapidly sunk down into one of the profoundest labyrinths of its own vast caverns.

Down, down, still lower and deeper into the awful abyss of itself it sank, until at last it stood solitary and alone in one of its own secret halls. The outer realm, with all its pains and joys, cares, sorrows and ambitions, hopes, likes, antipathies and aspirations; all its shadows and fitful gleams of light, were left behind, and naught of the great wide world remained; for its lakes and green trees, its gardens and its tiny brooks, its beetling cliffs and radiant sky grew distant, very distant, until at length a cold and chilling horror crept over me, and suggested that perhaps, after all, the fearful doctrine

enters the domain of Spirit at all, during the trance; but instead thereof, roams and revels in the Fancy Realm of his own, or some one else's soul. A suggestion,—either spontaneous or accepted—serves as the hither end of a clue, the line reaching just where the partially freed mind chooses to direct it. Frequent repetitions of the exercise of this organ of spectral illusion, lead directly to bad results, for the illusions soon impress themselves as realities, and the grossest and most absurd fanaticisms result; as witness the thousand phases of spiritual belief. In addition to this, the habit of mesmerizing, or being mesmerized, is a ruinous one to all concerned, producing pestilence and moral death. True, where both parties are good and pure, no harm may at first ensue, but at last an abnormal susceptibility results by which any man or woman may be led into "the jaws of death, into the mouth of hell." I speak of course concerning indiscriminate magnetizing.

2*

*might* be true, which declares, that some human beings
are God-doomed to annihilation ; and the anguish that
this conceit brought with it, was almost unbearable,
even by a free-born soul. But, thank God! this last
folly of the philosophers,—last and greatest save one—
the doctrine that "whatever is is right," in every and all
senses, is a libel on Himself and His goodness.

Finally it seemed as if my being had been concentered,
or focalized to a single point, and even that soon faded
out, and an utter blankness enveloped my soul. How long
this continued is impossible to be told, but the next experience was that consequent upon a series of sudden
thrills or shocks, like unto those which a person receives
who takes hold of the conducting knobs of a highly
charged galvanic battery,—or rather when touching
the cup of a leyden jar. These instantly aroused me.
I started up as from a death-stupor. But what a change,
if not in myself, at least in my surroundings! I was in
the center of a new, but limited world. Around me
was an atmosphere of mellow rosy light, different from
any ever known to me before,—an atmosphere, radiant,
sweet, soft, and redolent with perfumes of an order and
fineness surpassingly grateful. I was in the Soul-world,
—*my* Soul-world :—a realm whereof God alone was
Lord—and I His tributary Queen. The feelings consequent on this induction were strange, but pleasant.

The thoughts that now arose, were not, as formerly,
mere shadowy forms, inconsistent and impalpable, nor
was the scene of their action within the head; true,
they were born there, but that was all. They were
no longer subjective merely, fleeting and ephemeral,
but were objective, positive and real. I saw, but not

alone with eyes, for the simulacræ of the objects witnessed within that sphere, even the faint outlines of the most far-off memograph, seemed to stream in upon me through a thousand new doors, and I appeared to acquire knowledge by two opposite methods : first by going out involuntarily to whatever was to be known; and second, by absorbing the images of things,—just as the eye absorbs a landscape.

A person beholding me at that moment, would have concluded, and rightly too, that I had just arisen from off a sort of cloud-couch near the center of the sphere, toward which my face was turned. On that couch I beheld the exact image, not of my person, but of the clothes, the resemblance of which to those once worn on earth, it will be remembered, had so greatly surprised me in the earlier part of this experience. While yet I gazed upon that ghost of a dress, it slowly faded into nothingness. Desiring to know the rationale of this occurrence, it came to me that the worlds are not only full of objects, but must necessarily be still more full of the images thereof,—images which fix themselves more or less permanently, on whatever plastic material which they may chance to come in contact with. Sometimes the lightning will pass over a body or object; and in passing will fix and bring out into visibility the images of things already there. Nature is full of mirrors. This is the memory of Matter—the Photography of the substantial universe. Memory is but the photography of soul. Everything that strikes the eye, or the senses in any way, leaves an exact image of itself upon the cylinder of Retention, which cylinder winds and unwinds, according as it takes on or gives off the im-

pression, whatever it may be.   Thus the image of a
tone, a sound, a peculiar trill, as well as of material
things, can be, and are photographed upon the soul.
Nothing is lost,—not even the myriad images floating
off from all things about us, day after day.   The
amazing beauties of a snow storm, a sleet shower, an
autumn forest, a rich garden, the countless flowers on
which man's material eye never rested, are all safely
cared for by Nature's Daguerrian Artist, and they float
about the material worlds until sometimes the frost will
pin a few of them to the window-panes in winter, or
they are breathed through the spiritual atmosphere into
some poetic soul, who incarnates them in canvass, marble,
or deathless verse.   This revelation, of course, proves
that there is a higher world than most men have yet
dreamed of, and that too, right around them.   In fact,
all things and events are but a simple process of what
may be called Deific Photography.   All forms, all
things, all events, are but God's thoughts fixed for a
time.   These mental images go forth in regular order,
and constitute the sublime procession of the ages, and
all human events and destinies are but the externaliza-
tion of Deific fore-had thoughts.   Here is the rationale
of vaticination or prophecy.   Certain persons are so
exalted, that moving in the Spiritual atmosphere, which
contains the pre-images of approaching events, they
read a few of them, and lo! in the coming years the
occurrences are enacted; for the spiritual phasmas
have taken form,—the reflected image of the Deific
thought has at last passed through the dark material
camera, been fixed by a law of celestial chemistry,
brought out to the surface, or 'developed,' by the grand

manipulators of Nature's laboratory, and lo ! anew the world and age rejoices, though individuals and communities may mourn.

There is truth, therefore, in the doctrine of fore-ordination. But this truth is general always, and not particular, for while the current and area of events are pre-established, still every soul, in any and all its states, has an absolute sphere of self-itivity ;—the law of Distinctness permits it to take the utmost advantage of conditions for its own improvement. For instance, take that which constitutes a peach tree, or a rose, give it and its successors the best possible chance to unfold its latent properties, and the rose or peach principle will put forth, in the course of two generations, a forest of beauties, an ocean of perfume, a mine of loveliness, which, judging the plants by what appeared originally, they never contained ; and yet nothing is more certain than that every plant, even the prickly pear, the bristling thorn, and unsightly thistle, contain the germs of a beauty too vast to be comprehended by mortal man. In the succeeding pages there is an account of God and Monads which will add much to the needed light on this subject. I cannot express them now for lack of suitable conditions, which can only be had in the midst of religious calm, holy solitude, and beneath a more sunny sky than bends over us at the present writing.

As the appearance of my dress faded away, and the truth just faintly limned, flashed across me, I began to realize somewhat of the majesty of the thing called soul ; and saw that, while the dress was a mere spectral garb, so also were those of the little girl and the old man—they were illusory—mere will-woven garments,

—nothing but appearances. And yet, had I been questioned in regard to the matter, while in my previous state, I would have freely sworn that all I saw was real,—for in my then unenlightened state, they were so. This suggests the subject of insanity. A man may be in a state wherein he can only behold appearances. To him they are real, to some one else they are false, while to those who can look over the entire ground, both would be deemed right and both wrong. Man is of birthright a creator, and the law of Distinctness forces his creations to resemble himself. If he is poor and lean, so will be the world he fashions around him volitionally, or which shall be his natural and spontaneous out-creation. The highest happiness of man is found in the act of creation, whether it be poem, picture, engine, system of thought, or anything else. Hence the enfranchised soul, dwelling in its real world, on the thither side of time, has the power of assumption to a degree commensurate with its desire for wisdom, its determining motives, the good it has done, and the ends of use it has accomplished. It can, therefore, assume any form it pleases,—but for the purpose of wrong-doing, or concealing its identity, it is utterly powerless in this respect; so that while it may masquerade as much as it chooses to for its amusement, that of others, or to instruct; yet A must be forever known as A, nor can A ever pass for B, save in cases of insanity, wherein A has a firm conviction that he is really B, in which case, and for redemptive ends, he is sometimes recognized as B, till his cure is effected. It is in accordance with this law of distinctness that the righteous dead, who do really sometimes come back on visits to their former homes, always appear to men clad as they used to be when incarnated. They are compelled to this course by an integral law of soul, so long as there are any on earth capable of recognizing them, or so long as a good descriptive portrait may exist. If the likelihood of identification does not exist, then the spirits may assume such instructive or beautiful forms as are either the spontaneous expression of their interior state, or as their goodness may suggest, and unfolded wisdom prompt.

Some of my readers may feel disposed to inquire, " Where was my soul when it made these interesting discoveries?" The response is: NOT in SPACE, not in TIME ; for I was in a CONDITION above and beyond these, just as tune is above tone, or as meaning is above and beyond the mere sound of the words conveying it. I sustained the precise relation to time, and space, and matter, that heat does to cold, light to shadow, shape to essence, phantasmata to reality, bulk to number, number to mass, or any two antithetical things whereof men may have ideas. I had become a resident of a new universe, differing as greatly from that upon which man's vision rests, as that itself is different from dreamland. My glad soul had crossed the shores of time and distance, and the barque of its existence was fairly launched upon the vast ocean of a new eternity.

O, ye babblers of vain philosophy, who nurse folly for aye, and call it wisdom, ye who are so deeply engrossed in nursing your pet theories—theories planted on nothing, and reaching nowhere, what know ye really of the other stages of human existence ? Nothing! Aye, truly, nothing ! and echo, hollow echo, gives back—

nothing! Aye, verily, nearly all your crude specula-
tions, and smooth plausibilities are as void of reality,
are as hollow as is the shell of an echo when all the
sounds have flown! Your fine-spun hypotheses, concerning the origin of the human soul,* its nature and
the mode of its existence subsequent to physical dissolution, are too meager and unsound,—aye! void as is a
vacuum of substance and solidity ; nor with all your
loudly trumpeted knowledge of the state and status
of the soul after its departure from the barbarisms of
earthly life, to the true social state in realms where
civilization is first truly known, have ye much else
than the faintest glimmering of the great reality. Philosophers! Verily, much learning hath made you mad;
else would ye have assigned the human soul a better
than a merely sensual heaven, where lust should be
freely sated, and where appetite and its varied gratifications constitute the sum total of enjoyment. What
splendid conceptions! What a magnificent destiny!
How worthy of the human soul! How great a reward for
years of agony! O, philosophy, how very lame thou art!
Thou tellest man, through thy oracles, that the spirit-
home is situate upon the upper surfaces of sundry zone-
girdles of the planet: and by the same rule we may expect thee to describe God as being so many cubits high,
and so many yards across the hips! Nay, thou mightest as
well describe a thought as containing just so many cubic
inches, and deal out music to us by the quart or gallon!

---

* Which it is firmly believed is herein briefly stated for the first
time since the world began. The meagre outlines hereinafter presented,
will be fully drawn and *demonstrated* in the succeeding volume.—
*Publisher.*

Philosophy, thou'rt sick! else thou wouldest have found a better adapted home for immortal beings, than an electric land formed of the rejected atoms from the various earths. To thee, and in thy light, an oak tree is but an assemblage of material atoms : a rose, its thorns, leaves and moss, are only such : the wild tiger of the jungle, the humped-back camel of Zahara's sands, the sportive lamb, unsightly toad, the serpent in the grass, the dove in its cote ; the flitting bat, and the flap-winged night-owl, the majestic giraffe, and the beauty-plumed warbler of the forest, are to thee but mere forms of exuberant life ; mere natural products, the sponta-neous gifts of an all-bounteous, but unintelligent, non-conscious natural force.   Panthea! Shame on thee, Philosophy, shame, because with the open book be-fore thee, thou hast steadily refused to read, nor ever even dreamed that each one of these things indicates the stage of out-growth to which a monad—constitut-ing its spiritual center, has arrived on its journey from God, through Matter, back to God through Spirit!   It hath never struck thee that each of these things, and all other objects in the vast material realm, constitute single letters in God's alphabet,* and a letter too, hav-ing a fixed and absolute meaning, significance, and un-alterable value.   Weak man! thou dost not even imagine that all these things are of thyself—thy kind—abiding the epoch wherein they *will*, as thou hast already sprung, leap forth to light, and new, and proper human life.

---

* God said, ' I am Alpha and Omega, the Beginning and the End.' How beautiful, how grand is the light thrown on this sentence and its deeper meaning, by the few lines to which this note is appended.— *Publisher*.

Thou dost not realize that they are latent, while thou and thy kind are active, self-moving thoughts of one great eternal thinker! Thou hast not yet learned that every living thing, vegetable or sentient, is a temporary home of a mighty monad. "But do *you* not know that scientific men have created conditions which have produced independent, and therefore unknown, undreamed of forms of animal life, as the *acarus crossi*, and others?" This objection does not invalidate the truth, nor weaken the force of the statement. All things have a use. Nothing has been made in vain. Even the most disgusting traits in animals, are matched in the human; and the poverty and squalor, the obscenity and loathliness of many human beings, rival, nay, surpass their correspondents in the 'lower sentient world. Nature is a system of precise conditions; nor dare you say that there were not conditions that befell a monad or monads, in which the eternal law did not demand and secretly force the effort of the chemist, which resulted in the productions of an acarus, which may have afforded the necessary requirements of various monads, or human germ-souls, in one point of their career.

All matter is alive with imprisoned spirit; every globule of this latter, unique, and existing in innumerable folds, contains a monad, a germ, concealing within itself capacities quite infinite in number and power. During its long probation it ever seeks to escape its outer bonds, just as certain shell-fish and serpents cast their old envelopes. But in every stage of its unfolding, every monad expresses a lesser or higher phase of the one great thought of God--Personality, Coherence, Power Unity. All the characteristics of the floral, vegetable and animal kingdoms, are but elements of something higher, afterwards expressed in the human. Thus a fox means shrewdness—cunning, low cunning; and that some men have not yet outgrown their recollections and applications of fox-craft, is self-evident to the most casual observer. The ass is the natural symbol of patience, the cat of duplicity, the lion of firmness; an elephant stands as generosity, the horse is pride; the peacock, vanity, the dog affection; and so on through an infinite scale of variations. All living things are but developing monads, at whose bottom slumbers what will one day be an imperial human soul! And these monads develope off their surfaces continually; the longer and more varied the process, the more beautiful the grand result at each successive stage. Thus the monad whose highest manifestation ten thousand years ago, may have been a thistle, perchance looks up to heaven this day from the glorious eyes of a rose-bush, or a dove. The great truth seems never to have been apprehended by the great army of those who have made thinking a business; that while beasts, trees and flowers are not, *as* such, endowed with a specific immortality, yet at every stage of their being they constantly give off images of themselves, which are, and ever will be immortal. These images constitute the pictures of the soul-world; but the essence, the innate force that developed that of which they are the representations, returns to God whence it started, a full and regal human soul. Thus it is seen how and why man is the culmination of nature, and is brother to the flower and the worm.

" All are but parts of one stupendous whole,"
All sentient things the body,—man the regal soul !

No telescope has yet enabled man to count the rounds in the ladder of luminous worlds ; no microscope reveals the mysteries imbedded in a grain of wheat. Still he *may* count them, if he will ; may delve into their secrets if he shall so elect; yea, if he will but listen to the fine voice speaking up from his inmost deeps, he may learn somewhat of the

## Story of a Monad.

" Up, up, up, there in the steep and silent heaven there shines a radiant sun, more glorious than even a seraph might tell. Its essence is not matter, but spirit ; and from its surface there go forth three kinds of light; the one in rays, another in waves. Condensed, the former becomes matter, and the latter is the ocean in which it is upborne,—in which the worlds are floating, and in which all things have a being. Aye ! all things ride upon the billows of this infinite sea, even as a shallop or an egg-shell sails upon the tiny wavelets of a lake. The third substance given off from this great sun goes forth in corruscations. The first kind of light proceeds from the surface, the second from the interior, the third from the very heart of this infinite center,—or from God's body, His spirit, and His soul. The first is pure fire, the second pure life, the third is the sea of monads. Every scintilla of that which proceeds from the soul of this sun (like that which proceeds from a human brain in action) is a thought, shot out into the vast expanse, but destined to return by another pathway, not direct, but circuitous and spiral. Well, (says the voice speaking from within to the philosopher who is listening to the revelation) I was one of these monads, and found myself enveloped in a myriad folds and firmly imbedded in a granite rock, where I remained shut up for long ages, pining constantly for deliverance from the thraldom. Even then I found my monad heart pulsing with a divine life, and ardently longed to celebrate the knowledge; for I knew ᵀ. came from Deity, and longed for my return.

My first recollections are of a fiery character, for my dwelling was in the very nucleus of a comet that had just been whirled into being. How? I cannot now stop to explain. Only this will I say: with me there were myriads of others, for in every molecule of spiritual and material substance, was imbedded one of my brethren, all longing to escape and return to the heart of God, whence we had been sent forth to perfect His great design.

The comet cooled : became a world, and finally an earthquake threw the block of granite wherein was I, to the surface; and bye-and-bye, after waiting many ages, I found room to move, and did so. The result was that we—the other monads and myself, changed our outer shells into moss. The moss died, and left us free to try what further we could do; for be it known that our forces had not yet been fairly called into action. The next change was a higher one, and afforded scope for the display of a higher order of power. This time I became a plant; and the next time a plant of a higher character; at each epoch losing one coat;* until at last I could be plant no longer, and so was forced by a law within, as well as laws without myself, to become the center of an animal.    And so I ran the gamut of change through countless ages; every new condition being more and more favorable, brought out new properties from within me, and displayed new beauties to the sun's bright eye.   I was still a monad, and will ever be such in one sense; albeit Time, after reaching my human form, will be of no account,—only states.   Something whispered me that I should ever advance toward, but never reach perfection.   I felt that, monad though I was, yet at my heart, my core, my center, I was the germ of an immortal human soul, and that that soul itself was destined to throw off form after form after its material career was ended, just as I had all along the ages. · And thus I passed through countless changes, exhibited a million characteristics, until at last, I who had at first worn a body of fire, then of granite, then of moss, now put on a higher and nobler dress, and became for the first time, self-conscious, intelligent, and in a degree, intuitive both as to the past, the present, and the future.   And all these infinite changes were effected by throwings off, in regular order, just as material suns throw off ring after ring, which in turn resolve themselves into planet after planet.   During all these transmigrations, my monad body was active, my monad soul quiescent, but ripening all

---

* An onion is a familiar analogue.  As the process went on the monad lost layer after layer, each one developing higher forms of excellence and beauty than the preceding,—yet the same monad still. Each layer demanding and creating, so to speak, its proper requirements and conditions.  Here is the germ of a grand system.—*Publisher.*

the while ; first in plant, then in the lower and higher forms of fish, reptile, bird, beast and mammel,—quadruped and bimanal. Thus I had reached the most distant prophecy of what I was hereafter to become; and as it may interest you to learn the steps by which I ascended, from the pre-human, to the very human, I will recount them in general. The list is therefore as follows: the first approach to the man was, when I found myself successively animating, ·as a central life-point, the forms of Simæ, Satyrii, Troglodyte, the Gibbons, Hylobates, and Cynocephalii, passing through the specific forms of Coluga, Aye-aye, Banca-Tarsier, Maholi, Lemur, Loris, Diadema, Indrus, Marikina, Marmoset, Dourocouli, Saimari, Yarké, Saki, Couzio, Cacajou, Sajou, Sakajou, Araquato, Meriki, Coitii, Marimondi, Charneck, Drill, Mandril, Chucma, (baboon,) Wanderoo, Bhunder, Togue, Mona, Quesega, Colubii, Budong, Entellus, Kahaw, (developing the human nose,) Gibbon, Siamang ; the Hylobates, Orangs, Chimpanzee, Gorrilla, Nschiego, Troglodyte, Kooloo Kamba, Barbeta, Aitcromba, Hamaka, (Troglodyte of Mount de Garrow,) Neg ; Bosjesman, Hottentot,* Negro, Malay, Kanaka, Digger,

---

* This theory *must* be true, for an astonishing confirmation thereof is not only found in the marvelous resemblances between human and animal features, but in the still more wonderful fact, that the human fœtus assumes at various stages of its increment, successively the appearance of moss, lichen, gelatin, reptile, bird, beast and so on, all the way up to its final human form, and if the gestation in even a perfect female be interrupted at a certain stage, the child is born with the characteristics which distinguish the animal whose natural place upon the ascending plane is that at which the gestation was disturbed. The facial angle of some persons is precisely that of the Lemurs ; the human Lusus Naturæ so-called, invariably resemble some beast, bird, reptile or monkey. It is but a few years ago that a negro woman o

Indian, Tartar, Chinese, Hindoos, Persians, Arabian, Greek, Turk, German, Gaul, Briton, American ! There's the list, in general terms ; specific explanations are not needed at this point.  The last eighteen are strictly human, for at the point (Neg) I ceased to develope animal ; and in passing through that highest form of animal existence, I was impelled one step further, and lo ! the first course of transmigrations were ended ; I awoke to a consciousness of self, and man, the immortal stood revealed !

Thus I supply the lost links, O Philosophers, which connect you with the worlds above, around, and below the plane on which you move."

[Note.—The exact order is not stated, for there are many intermediate links connecting the Simiæ, with the Lemurs and Troglodytes,—or with that portion of the genus of the Quadrumana comprising the Gorilla, higher Orangs, Nschiegos and Chimpanzees ; yet the chain itself is generally speaking, quite correct.]

Thus is completed the outlines of the history of a human soul.  Let us return to the awakening. * * * * * * * I now realized that the Soul and Spirit-worlds were far different from each other,

Charleston, South Carolina, was delivered, not only of what looked like a monkey—but which *was* a monkey out and out.  The woman had never seen a monkey in her life, so that this was not a case of mere mother-marking, but gestation was interrupted in some respects in some way, at about the nineteenth day after conception, while it went on normally in other respects.  An additional proof of the truth of this development theory is seen in the fact that ordinary parents often produce extraordinary geniuses ; thus another negro woman of the same city produced a boy by a black and ignorant father who is to-day one of the most extraordinary musical geniuses the world ever saw.

PUB.

for the former is WITHIN, but the latter, like the planetary worlds, is WITHOUT ;—not in the sense of in the house and out of the house, but rather in the sense of in the bed and in a dream,—not exactly, but analogous. The fact is, mankind, albeit many know it not, are living upon the confines, at least, if not occasionally full residents of two or three worlds at the same time—worlds which impinge upon, and interlace each other, just as fine spirit contacts rough matter ; and yet, while this fact is so, it happens likewise that in many respects these worlds are as wide apart, and distant from each other, as is Pleiades from Mazaroth, or distant sun from twinkling planet ; for the reason that states, not miles, separate the denizens of either. Those whose being is in accord with the vast Harmonead, move alike upon the shores of each sphere of being, whence they can catch the echoes and foot-falls of the pilgrims on both banks. Most people are familiar with the stereotyped assertion that ' Man is a microcosm—a universe in miniature,' than which nothing can be more correct and true. The body is not the man ; neither is the nerve-center of his brain that which constitutes his personality, any more than the central spiritual sun around which all material systems revolve, is the supreme God himself ; for even as Deity dwells within the centralia of that august luminary, so also does the very man himself hold his court within the bosom of that magic sphere which exists within his skull. In the subjoined description of the student,—(see part two of this volume) the sentient and conscious point is spoken of under the similitude and figure of a fiery globe. The likeness is imperfect in some respects, for not only

3

is man a world within himself, but he is an entire system of worlds, each one of which is perfect of its order, full and complete. God is at once a center, a Republic and a King. So also is man in a finite degree. His faculties may be said to constitute the distinct members or States or nations of the great confederation, whereof the supreme Ego is sovereign Lord and President,—one, however, who can, if it so elect, assume and wield despotic power over all within the great domain. So far can this power be carried and exerted, that pain may be overcome, and even death itself be kept at bay. The WILL is Lord of man's accidents and incidents, and if his reason guide it well, nothing can withstand its force.

As stated previously, all foregone thoughts and deeds of mine became objectified in my new sphere, or on what I can find no descriptive term, good as that of Memorama, for such it truely was,—and the fact of its existence at all ought to become a significant one to mortals, for even as their deeds and thoughts shall be on earth, even so will be the delights or agonies consequent upon their inspection of these memory tables on the other shore, whither all must go, whether the voyage be agreeable or not. Memory constitutes the basis of man's heaven or his hell. On it is founded the superstructure of his sorrows or his joys, and woe be to whomsoever shall read, and reading, neglect the caution here imparted. I give it in all love, for I know its immense importance.

My thoughts and actions—even the minutest, passed before me, across the polished surface of my enclosing sphere, standing out in bold relief. The pictures in-

cessantly altered their aspect, or gave place to new
ones, but there was something which did not change,
but on the contrary seemed to gather weight and durability all the while. This was the attention point,—
the focalization of all the soul's observant powers, nor
did it undergo any permutation whatever. I stood, as
previously intimated, in the center of a crystaline
sphere. It was translucent, but not transparent. Nothing beyond its glory-tinted walls was discernible, but
all within it stood revealed in grand and cryptic light,
which, as already observed, appeared to proceed from
my own head. The vertical diameter of this sphere
was not more than fifty yards, its horizontal one somewhat more,—for its form was slightly ellipsoidal. Its
floor was as a polished mirror, reflecting not only my
own image, but those of all things else within its beautiful walls. In this mirror-like surface I beheld my
person and features most distinctly ; and it was quite
a matter of surprise to discover that I was, without the
slightest effort on my part, completely and beautifully
clothed in garments of a fashion and style which, of
all others, I should have selected, had opportunity for
so doing been presented. Here is a new mystery of
the Soul-world which may well engage the attention of
Psychologians. Depending from my neck and shoulders
was a long and flowing robe, apparently seamless, and
woven of lightest gossamer. The fore-arms and left
shoulder joint were bare, and I noticed that they, as
well as my hands, had lost the sickly caste, and shrunk-
en, shrivelled appearance formerly characterizing them.
Now, to my great delight, they were fair, plump, and of
the most dazzling and voluptuous mould and propor-

tions.  As I made this happy discovery, there flashed
across me something of the deeper meanings slumbering beneath the phrases " love, loving, and lovely ; "
and I could comprehend why one person should become
so *en rapport*, so obsessed with, and possessed and absorbed by another, as to lose not only all self-control,
but self altogether.  I could now understand why the
most loving must ever remain apart, even in the most
interior communion on earth, until there are no dull
senses to be bridged, and understand the amazing difference between a love that seeks its solace through sense,
and that which brings souls together.  While people
are enwrapped in flesh and blood, love is often obliged
to express itself in modes distasteful to its higher nature,
and unworthy of itself.  Not so in the Soul-world ; for
there the very joy (magnetic, if you please,) which one
lover feels in the mere presence of the other, reaches a
point of fullness, completion and intensity that mere
nervous filaments are incapable of conveying, mere nervous exhalations can never give.  No body is capable
either of giving or receiving, even with the strongest
efforts of will, even a foretaste of the joys which the
soul, freed therefrom, can and does spontaneously.  The
keenest Sybarite,—the finest-nerved voluptuary can
have no adequate conception, either of the nature or
the depth of the joy imparted mutually by two loving
souls in the higher worlds.  Love, I have said, I knew
but little of, and cared less for, previous to my departure ; but now, as I gazed upon myself, and realized
for what I was intended, there arose a something within assuring me of my boundless—limitless capacity to
and for love.  And then the gentle hint of Nellie came

back, and had the mate assigned me then appeared, I do not think he would have met a very cold reception. Thereafter all this ended as God decreed it should—rightly.

Around my waist there was a zone or belt of blue, which kept the fronts of my open robe together, and then fell floorward in two knotted tassels on the left side. The throat and upper portions of my bosom were covered with what bore  the appearance of finest lace, whiter than the driven snow. The hair hung in luxuriant curl-tresses adown my back and cheeks, which latter, as disclosed by the floor-mirror, were no longer sunken, sallow or emaciated in the least degree ; on the contrary they were round, full, white, fair as the cheeks of daylight, and suffused with the softest and most delicate tints of the newly-opened blossom of the peach tree. The teeth!—I had teeth—were ivory-hued, large and even. The eyes were larger than they had ever seemed before ; their lashes were long, dark and drooping ; and they were shaded by a brow far more delicate and finely pencilled than they ever were on earth. My stature was a trifle less, apparently, than when incarnated, and there was a health, vigor, and freshness, which reminded me of the early days, ere woman's estate had come with all its cares and toils, its miseries and deep griefs. About my head there was a shining band, like unto the spirit of a silver coronet, pearl and diamond ′frosted, and flashing back the light from a thousand jeweled points. In the center of this zone was a triangle of ruby hue, surmounted with the cypher " R," and in its center was a crystaline globe, winged, and bearing the motto, " TRY."

Curiosity is the soul of advancement ; it is a female element almost exclusively ; and though all else forsake woman, curiosity never will, either on earth or anywhere else. It prompted me to the investigations above recounted, and to others which followed hard thereon. *I wondered how my feet and ankles looked!* The desire was no sooner formed than gratified. The latter were encased in proper attire, but the former not quite so, for instead of a shoe, as I expected to find, there was only a sort of sandal,—a mere sole, light and graceful, fitting perfectly, and seemingly kept in place by narrow red bands, which were laced to the ankles and over the foot and instep. The bands themselves seemed to be of a material no coarser than cords of braided light. Such, in brief, were the revealments of the mirror. "Mirror!" exclaims the reader, "why mirrors are adapted only to solar light, and that which proceeds from material combustion. They reflect from their polished surfaces, according to the well-known laws of optics, which laws cannot possibly obtain of the strange world of which you were then an occupant, —which realm lies above and beyond the sphere of their action or influence ; how then could you see the image of yourself?" Again : "If the first suit of apparel in which you found yourself after death, were only mere appearances, of what nature or character were these last? If the spirit of a human being is, as we are led to infer from your narrative, in nowise physical, or even hyper-physical, as the Spiritualists assert—and they claim to know all about the matter, —if it is only a phantasmal projection from the VERY SOUL,—an out-attachment of the supreme-self, how do you reconcile your statements concerning 'blue-caste hands, wrinkled epidermis, shrivelled appearance,' and so on, with your subsequent assertions that they afterwards became fair, plump and beautiful ?  Do shadows grow ?  Do phantasms avail themselves of the law of increment ?  Please explain ; clear up, elucidate ! "

REPLY :  These are the very points concerning which the people need light ; for assuredly that which they have heretofore received, instead of illumining the subjects under consideration, have tended directly to increase the already dense obscurity, and only rendered the darkness still more palpable and dense.  In order to a clear conception of what lies before us, it will be well to remind each other that both soul and body act under the impetus of two distinct codes of law : the one volitional, the other mechanical, and therefore involuntary.  An illustration of both is seen in the case of a man who either reading a book or earnestly conversing as he moves along, takes no notice whatever of passing persons or things, and yet pursues the direct path, nor once misses his way.  Both laws are operating simultaneously.  The bodily powers are under the same government ; for the heart beats, digestion proceeds, and all the functions of the physical economy are carried on by a power lying altogether back of will. There is also another law, which from voluntary, at length comes to manifest itself altogether involuntarily. I refer to the law of Habit.  Now that this law governs both soul and body is proved by a simple reference to the swearing man, who also drinks liquor, chews tobacco, falls asleep at a given hour and wakes up at another.  Whosoever hums a tune often, will at length be haunted by it, and cannot rid himself of the tormenting tune-fiend by even the most strenuous resolve and effort to do so.   It, like a fever, must, and will run its course.   We also habituate ourselves to certain forms of expression, and ideal associations.   Thus much by way of preface.

Now it was the involuntary obedience of my soul to the Habit-law, that caused it to array itself in the semblance of the old and well-remembered dress.   The law of the association of ideas gave the 'blue caste,' the wrinkles and the emaciation which so surprised me.

Presently, however, I passed under the operation of higher laws of nature, and more interior ones of my own immortal soul.   One of the first, and most important of these last, is the law of Vastation—whereby the soul throws off the old loves, preparatory to entering upon new ones.   Its first involuntary act, in the second, as in the first case, was to clothe itself; but no longer subject to the old law of association, and coming under a new one, it rejected the things of memory, and assumed the garb corresponding to its new-born loves,—all in conformity to a law within itself.   [In dreams, the garb and surroundings are typical or symbolic of mental, moral and esthetic states : therefore it is possible to construct an exact science of dream-interpretation.]   And the drapery assumed was not merely the result of caprice or an involuntary fantastic taste, pride or vainness, but was the legitimate and orderly result of the triple law, whose elements are fitness, expression, and correspondence.   The white drapery symbolized, if not my absolute purity, at least my aspirations thitherward,—

(and this explains why all men and women array their breasts in white bosoms, frills and laces.) The bandeau, the zone, girdle, jewels, all symbolized an affection, aspiration or quality of the inner being ; and as these latter change, so also do the former. The law is imperative, because it is a thing of the soul itself, whose external manifestations invariably—in the soul-world— represent its inward states : moral, religious and intellectual.

In the light of this explanation, therefore, no one need marvel at the radical changes in my personal appearance. We shall throw much more light on the general subject when next we treat of the mysteries of being. The present undertaking being merely prefatory, as a matter of course, confines us to the mere superficialities of a realm whose vastness exceeds all human conception. In reference to the wrinkles of my hands, and their sudden disappearance, enough has been said ; yet for the information of whoso chooses to profit by it, I will merely add here, that as Time only affects man in his outward relations, it cannot, of course, bring wrinkles on his features, for souls do not grow old by years ; albeit they do grow old by experiences,—without reference to duration, but only as to depth and intensity. A single week of mental agony will ripen a soul far more than would fifty centuries of clock-beats, passed free from the sorrows aforesaid.

Let it not be forgotten that there are two distinct and dissimilar worlds beyond the grave, nor that I had rapidly crossed from the first to the second stage of my transmundane existence. One of these is the mere external world of Spirits, wherein a life, analogous to

3*

that of earth is for a period led by the inhabitants thereof. The other is that, concerning the mysteries whereof, I am now treating.

Millions of beings there are who, although disrobed of fleshly garments, are yet pilgrims in search of the soul-world. The latter is divine and interior, the former natural and merely Spiritual. A man on earth may gaze on the surface of a picture, or mechanically read a book, and yet find nothing therein ; whereas either of these may lead another person not only into their ōwn beauty-depths, and into the soul of the painter or the author ; but they may serve as clues which his soul may seize on and follow into realms never even imagined to exist by the poet-painter, or the painter-poet. So also the mere mortuary fact by no means serves as a free ticket or pass into the grand Temple, at the mere vestibule of which grim Death lands those who take passage in the phantom shallop, whereof himself.is pilot and steersman. The mere post mortem existence does not necessarily entitle one to all the privileges of the Temple, nor make one a resident of, or even spectator of the worlds of Soul. True, there will occur a change in all, whereby they can pass the mystic ferry ; but this change must be worked out from within, and in no wise depend upon outside influences ; it must be volitional, not mechanical. The ferriage must be paid in well-wishing and better doing. The life beyond is a real one, compared to which that of earth is a mere shadow, and the form of Government is an isonomous one ; equal rights, equal laws, impartial justice, administered, not by external agents of an outward power, but by the very constitutional delegates from the secret soul itself ; for no justice is so very just as that which each soul, by virtue of its own nature, administers to itself, and through which its lower becomes subordinated to its higher and nobler faculties, qualities and powers. And this is the law that keeps many a one from entering the sacred penetralia until properly disciplined and prepared for the change.

I wondered at first why these truths were not more generally known and appreciated by the people, who, because they have an intellectual perception of the fact of immortality, call themselves " Spiritualists ; " but as the veil was slowly drawn away, and I saw that much that had to me appeared real, proved now to be but seeming ; there was no more marveling. There was, still is, and for a long time will be, four sorts of Spiritualism in the world : First, a mere bodily sensitiveness, nervous acuteness, and susceptibility to magnetic emanations and impressions,—out of which arises a great deal of the stagnant filth and social corruptions so prevalent,—the debaucheries and license, and great evils which pain so greatly the hearts of true men and women. Second, a Spiritualism of the brain alone ;—a cerebral quickening,—a hot-house ripening of faculty, which gives rise to much talking, and sometimes leads to the discovery of many of the elements of the great principia underlying the Harmonead, and prophecies the good time that is yet to be. Third, " compact " Spiritualism, or that wherein and whereby a certain class of sensitives, be they male or female, become the dupes of their own folly, and the victims of disembodied maniacs, lunatics and self-deluded denizens of the middle state—Spirits who wander on the outskirts of three worlds, without a permanent resting-place in either. These have been useful, however, inasmuch as they have called, and even compelled attention to phenoména which they produce, and which cannot be explained away, nor accounted for, save by admitting two things ; first, that immortality is a fixed fact ; and second, that it is possible to bridge the hitherto impassable chasm which divides earth from regions which lie beyond. The fourth kind, and truest and best, indeed that which only is truely spiritual, is the growing up into a spiritual-ized, out of the merely physical selfhood ; and this growth of soul necessarily admits the subject of it into the mysteries of being, precisely in accordance with the degree of the person's own unfolding. It is the off-spring of good resolutions, well and faithfully carried out ; ignores pride, talk, lust, hatred, envy, malice, slan-der, and all else which characterizes the other three sorts. Immortality is to such, not an acquired, but an intuitive fact. Such Spiritualists are good, moral, hu-mane, charitable, merciful, kind and true ; religious, Christian in deed, as well as name ; and such as these are never pulling down, but ever building up the Good, the Beautiful, and the True ; and when such an one dies, his or her stay in the Middle State is very short, for they have paid their ferriage, and are speedily intro-mitted to the mysteries and grandeurs of the world of Soul.

Such an one is unfolded ; and by this term is not meant that state to which a man arrives after packing the contents of two or three libraries on the shelves of his memory ; by that term is not meant the condition of one who has arrived at honor and distinction by dint of mere acquaintance with learned authorities, and the accumulation and piling up of knowledge of various common and popular sorts ; for it frequently happens that men and women, who are very ignorant of all these things,—and who, so far as they are concerned, are not "progressed" at all, prove on trial to be far more "unfolded" than thousands of those who have grown gray in the service of Letters, and who have, by persistent assiduity succeeded in transforming themselves from human beings into locomotive encyclopedias —splendid to look at, interesting to dine with and talk to—but cold, unheartful encyclopedias after all. Education is often a mere mechanical mastery of useless abstrusities,—coins, which on the social counters jingle well,—but which are not over and above current in the far-off worlds,—where a boor's earnest prayer weighs far more than the ornate, rhapsodical orisons of scores of learned pedants, who, to judge them by their language, take God to be a school committee, rather than a loving, tender Parent.

Thus I found true, what had previously been surmised, that a person may know but little, yet approach much nearer the Divine, than one who has more brain furniture, with a great deal less heart.

It was revealed to my understanding that the great law of Vastation, by whose operation the monad developed moss, threw it off, and brought forth something better and higher, until at last the conscious point—the truly human degree—was, after the lapse of ages, reached, did not cease its functions even after the death of the body, albeit its mode of action was somewhat changed and modified ; for now it was observed by me, that while the soul may, both prior and subsequent to death, draw in knowledge from without—inspiration, progression, procession—it may also expand from within, and enter consecutively domain after domain in the Soul-deeps of its almost infinite being. This is aspiration, unfolding—development; and ever will the immense, the immortal thing, continue to vastate the bad, the ill, imperfect and untrue, so long as any of such remains to be thrown off, as it has been doing ever since the clock of Time struck one upon the bell on Eternity's tower! It will continue the process until that tower itself shall topple and fall with hoary age!

The figure of an onion, though a homely, is nevertheless a good one, inasmuch as it offers a familiar illustration of the monad; for, first, there is the two or three external skins, after which comes layer after layer, until at last we find a center, which center contains an invisible, because a spiritual point, which constitutes the germ or seed-principle, containing, latent in its bosom, countless acres of onions, that are and are not, at the same time—fields of plenty, seeds of mighty harvests, which only need the necessary conditions to prove their power and develop their capacities.

Philosophers have long sought, with their crude plummets, to sound the bottomless abysses of man's immortal soul. Spiritualists, in their turn, have tried to do the same—aye! and loudly boasted of their success. Success, forsooth! Why their lead, even when all the line attached thereto was well run out, rested on one or more of [the very topmost ledges of the unfathomable and vast profound—their weights only lodged on the upper crags of one or more of the tiniest mountains, whose heads are upreared from the floor of the great ocean Soul. Proclaiming man to be a world in miniature, they have, in their treatment of him and his, not only belied and stultified themselves, but have shown that, after all, he was to be classed with "all other worms of the dust"—a semi-voluntary automaton—a skip-jack, to be coaxed, wheedled and driven, just as circumstances might dictate and decree. Theoretically, to them, he is a God; practically, a mere machine, whose office and function it is to eat, drink, be merry, sleep, wake up, labor, and beget his kind—whose destiny, in turn, it is to repeat the same identical round, with perhaps a few trifling and unimportant variations—totally forgetful or unconscious of the fact, that when pronouncing him to be a microcosm, they were uttering a sentence brimfull of God's everlasting truth. Philosophers have a bad habit of saying one thing and meaning another; for while loudly declaring, they never yet have fairly believed, that howsoever vast the universes without may be, yet all and each of them grow diminutive and contracted when compared with those that exist within the Soul. Nay, they have never realized that all that has a being outside of man is met, mastered and overmatched by an infinite universe from *within !*

Crime! folly!—what are they? Philosopher, answer thou me! "They are, they are—they are—well, I can hardly tell *what* they really are." I will tell you : these things frequently mark the career of the 'Progressed' man—*never* that of the developed or unfolded one—and in all cases are either the result of impulse, Spirit-obsession, or of a bad calculation. When

nations merely 'Progress,' every jail-yard has its gibbet ; when the people are ' Unfolded,' temples for God-
worship take their places. Philosophers try to explain
away all crime and evil, knowing it to be real ; yet at
the same time treat the doers of ill-deeds as if they were
not fitter subjects for soul-hospitals than for thumb-
screws and disgrace. They forget that society gains
nothing by making a man think less of himself ! Instead of pursuing really reformatory methods with those
who are vicious or whose souls are sick, they have
favored the policy of revenge and atonement, and
adopted the *lex talionis* instead of the *lex justitiæ*—
as Common Sense, if nothing else, would ever seem to
dictate, counsel, and approve.

The Social Harmonead is yet to be. Discord rules
the age. The human soul is unbalanced. Equilibrium
and Virtue come together. By-and-by, Philosophers
will realize this truth. Men who gaze intently on the
wonderful perfection of the outer Harmonead, and
realize its vast excellence, constantly fail to recognize
the fact that the inner world of man would be the same
were but Charity and kindly dealing, in thought as well
as act, to take precedence of Suspicion and Punishment.
As yet the world is but a baby-realm. There are no
real saints therein at present, for the reason that the
currents of the time are not adapted to the floating of
that species of craft ; nor will the social gardens produce that sort of fruit until it is well subsoiled by charity plows and common sense. At present, probably but
few men or women live on earth, no matter how abste-
mious they may be, nor how correct and staid their deportment, but in whose hearts lurk many a thistle seed,

ready to spring up and pester the world whenever bad conditions shall call them into active life ; nor can there be a pure saint, until every one of these seeds shall be deprived of life. Then, when this is done, no matter what the soil may be, it can produce none but beauty-laden forms of excellence. When the great truth is made apparent to the people, that the greatest sin a person can possibly commit—taking the future as well as the present into the account—is the sin against him or herself, society will rapidly purge itself of wrong, and there will be fewer bad memories to haunt and ter-rify them after life's troublous drama shall end, and far fewer leaden-hued pictures be reflected from the mirror-floors of the world of Soul.

Wealth, the possession of riches, is, on earth and in all human society, the universal passport to honor and distinction. This is one of the fallacies of man, and the greatest ; but the good deeds done to the neighbor and the self are hereafter changed into a kind of coin read-ily current in the lands beyond the tomb.

Now no one thing yet unaccomplished is more certain to come to pass, than that this lesson will yet be learned by the people. When it *is* mastered, there will be far less strife for the honors and emoluments of office, and the universal cry will be, ' Whom *can* we get, who shall we persuade to be our Ruler, President, or King ?' ' Who can we employ to fill those offices ?' instead of ' Vote for me !' as now. Mankind on earth do not, as we of the Soul-world, seek for joys that are pure, and purely human, too ; they do not, as we, drink from cha-lices at whose bottom no dregs are found after the ruby wine has been sipped. Alas, no ! but, instead, they

seek for such joys as are absolutely sure to leave a sting
behind, and Repentance, Agony and Remorse are the
terrible triplet they are obliged to nurse, for O *how*
long ! This is moral and spiritual suicide—so far as
super-mundane joys are concerned—suicide, slow but
sure ; and such souls, on entering the Middle State, are
poor, and thin, and lean, and powerless, for deeds or
thoughts either good or great ; and memory reflects
back but few, if any pleasant images, but, in lieu thereof, presents for inspection and as food for contempla-
tion, an array of barren mountains, fierce whirlpools,
crags toppling over into dreadful darkness, beetling
cliffs, from whose bald summits the vulture and the
night-owl shriek and scream. No pleasant pasture lands
begem the picture—no sweetly-singing rivers of delight—but only things of wierdness, rage and fury, set as
centers into pictures representing boisterous and tempestuous seas, cold and dreary ice-islands, or desert
sands which swallow up the sunshine, the moisture and
the rain, but never smile with a single green or lovely
thing. These are symbols and similes of the Soul's
states, and are the legitimate and inevitable out-creations of itself ; but, thank God ! not of its inner deeps,
else the universe might well run mad, and every living
thing curse its God and—die. True it is that none of
these frightful things are the results of the natural and
unbiassed choice of any human creature, yet they are
none the less real in the second stage of existence, for
the reason that Destiny forever compels a man to be
himself. Sooner or later he will bring himself voluntarily to acknowledge, bow, and bend before it ; and
the instant that he does so, the grand Vastatory law

comes into play, and he slowly emerges from Hell, and takes the road to Heaven!

So far in human history on the earth, the Devil has proved a failure—utter, total and complete. Not so Evil. This latter works out its mission well, even if it does no more than to convince man that his only, best and truest friends are himself and the Infinite God whose child he is.

In the higher realms, to which mankind is destined, his actions are never the result of an applied force from outside himself; but when voluntarily submitting to the pressure from within, he is irresistibly led from bad to better, and from better to BEST. Reaching this point, he no longer rebels—not against God, but against himself—his higher, nobler, better nature—but, giving up all of mere self, begins to desire nothing so much as to love and be loved, to serve God and minister unto others' good—and at last finds himself standing in the Door of the Dawn, having emerged from the Hades of his own and others' making, and stepped into his house not made with hands, eternal in the Heavens—house-spheres such as I have partially described, prepared for, and in, and of him, from the foundations of the Ages—houses which are indeed builded upon very pleasant spots, on sunny glades and love-tinted hillocks on God's Eternal Domain—houses, too, which men often refuse to enter and occupy till after the lapse of years of misery spent in the horrid caves and unsightly huts dug and builded by themselves.

All these things flashed in upon my soul, as I stood gazing into the mirror on the floor, and upon the vivo-graphs of Memory gliding by upon the walls, in which every event of my life, no matter how trivial, was clearly represented.   Not a good thought or deed, no matter how private—not a single sin, no matter how venial—but was there reproduced for my inspection and instruction—moving, with all their foregone accessories, across the walls of that magic globe.   They were living icons, perfect rescripts, of all foredeeds, thoughts, actions—and transcripts, all too faithful, of the volumes of my memory.   Soon all this passed along—the last scene being that of my death within the chamber of the house upon the hill.   Scarcely had it vanished, whither I knew not, than a blank section moved across the line of vision, almost instantly succeeded by a Phantorama still more wondrous and imposing.   Instead of representing myself alone, this second picture revealed the results, both direct and indirect, of my personal influence upon others, whether exerted in a domestic, social, or professional capacity.   I could not help being particularly struck with one tableau, which, as it embodies a moral lesson, I will here stop to briefly describe :

I saw myself in the act of warm disputation with a friend, on a subject well calculated to elicit the best thought of the best thinker.   I had the right of the argument, and this was so apparent that my friend with whom I was arguing lost temper.   At the time of the occurrence, I took but little note of the matter, not deeming it a subject of very great importance.   Now, however, I saw, what surprised me greatly, that this mental excitement had reacted physically, and, in running its course, brought on a slight inflammation of the brain—a sort of slow but positive fever, which, while not confining the patient, yet affected both soul and body to a great extent, and so modified the cerebral constituents, that the immortal soul therein dwelling for a season, could not thereafter manifest itself as formerly. I now realized that chemistry, in the higher sense, was an efficient force in the human mental, as well as in the material economy---that changes in the physical cells of the brain could be made by intellectual excitations, and that these in a great measure affect the mental and psychical operations, even to the extent of a complete *bouleversement*. In consequence of the change effected in the individual alluded to, projects of various kinds, previously determined on, had to be given up---for which reason the entire current of a life was turned completely ; nor is it for me to say whether greater good or ill will be the ultimate or final result--- for the reason that as yet I can neither see the origin nor end. These are only known by the Infinite One above us and beyond. Suffice it, therefore, to observe, that had I known what weight inhered in words, whether lightly, harshly or kindly spoken, especially to the sensitive and susceptible natures of many of earth's pilgrims, never would I have uttered a syllable without well weighing the possible consequences thereof ; especially would I have kept back all which bore the slightest resemblance to heat or anger. O, what a wondrous thing is a human soul ! Until now it was not clear to me that, by virtue of both a static and dynamic law of the universe, human happiness is derivative, and ever depends upon the amount and kind bestowed upon or imparted to another. The law is dual, that is, it works both ways ; for even as a man or woman finds joy in the act of causing or of bringing joy to others, so also the misery and woe which A may cause B, C, D and E to feel or undergo, not only reacts upon A by force and virtue of the great Sympathia, but it is utterly impossible for A to be happy, so long as the least trace of his or her action *mauvaise* remains with B, C, D, E, F and G. Nor is this all; for if these last persons act badly toward H, I, J and K, said actions being the legitimate result of A's, originally, upon B, C, D, E, F and G, then A cannot escape the consequences, no matter how distant or in whatever corner of God's universe he may be, or in whatever crevice of the great creation he may seek to hide. A wave or ray of agony from B, C, and the rest of the alphabet, will finally reach him! A lash from the great whip of conscience or remorse will fall on him, when rocks and mountains, though heart-implored, refuse to. Until the law of compensation is satisfied, he shall never fail to hear, peeling into his soul from the lacerated hearts of others, the terrific sentence : ' Thou art the man! thou hast done it! Pay what thou owest!' If the reflections shall prove to have been good instead of evil, then the words which shall be heard will be : ' Even as thou hast done it unto the least of these, my servants, thou hast done it unto me. Well done, thou good and faithful servant! enter thou into the joy of thy Lord! Take up thine abode in the mansions of bliss, prepared from the foundations of the world!' The coin of heaven is ever stamped with the seal of a person's deeds, be they good or evil.

This soul-law is well illustrated by an anecdote which I remember to have heard related prior to my entrance into the wonderful realm, whereof I now found myself

a denizen. The story was related by a male friend.
Said he :

" Many years ago, when a mere lad of ten or a dozen
years, I lived in the Metropolis of America, where also
I was born. One day several lads of us were playing
at ball in a street then called ' Chapel,' but since known
as West Broadway. In throwing the toy at one of my
playmates, it missed him, and crashed through the window of a shoe-mender's shop, the proprietor of which became greatly enraged, and in a paroxysm of fury not
only cursed and swore most dreadfully at us, but also
seized the offending ball, and threw it on his burning
grate ; we, poor mourners, in the mean while looking
down into the fiery grave of all our sport. Tears, ex-
postulations, and entreaties were all so much wasted
breath, and proved utterly unavailing. The ball, unfortunate ball, was irrevocably doomed to an igneous
tomb; nor could all our prayers, joined as they were,
to abundant offers on our part, and that of several
pitying on-lookers, to doubly pay the cost of the de-
molished glass, soften the obdurate heart of the revengeful cobbler in the least degree. Burn that ball he swore
to ; utterly consume it he vowed to, and most religiously
he kept his promise.

The ball was burned, but as the smoke of its substance,—the remains of two worn-out stockings and
an india-rubber shoe,—and of our torment, went up
towards heaven, there accompanied it a most dire threat
of vengeance from out my boyish heart,—proud, indig-
nant little human heart, which then, for the first time,
swelled almost to bursting with vindictiveness and rage.
In my paroxysm of fury I swore a *vendetta* more fierce

and terrible than that of the Orsini against their mortal
foes, the Borgias of sunny Italia.   I resolved to kill,
slay, totally extinguish the whole race of cobblers,—
but that one in particular.   His doom was, to be killed,
slain, cut to pieces, remorselessly and cruelly murder-
ed, after which his soul was to be eternally damned,
roasted, stewed, broiled and grilled for evermore, upon
the gridirons of the infernal pit—all for burning a sixpenny ball !   For ten long days and nights I pondered
on the subject, and sought to contrive means whereby
to carry out my philanthropic design.   Having heard
and read of battles, bloodshed and gory fields of human
slaughter, wherein he who did the most murder was
the greatest hero ; having heard and read of human
butchers and butchery, my heart had turned from the
one, and I shuddered at the picture of the other.   Now
however, all these images of horror returned.   I still
hated them, but of all others, it seemed to me that that
ball-burning shoe-mender was the most atrocious fiend
that ever trod the earth.   In my boyish frenzy I vowed
he was an ogre, giant, demon, and all else that was
horrible and bad, to rid the earth of whom would be
doing an especial and particular favor to God, nature
and human kind.   Amidst all the scourges and pests
who had ever trod the earth from Ghengis Khan to
Lord Jeffries, not one loomed up who was half so criminal, half so deserving of the intensest scorn and
maledictions of the human race, as was that unfortunate
and guilty cobbler.   We resolved that he must die,
and die by powder and fire ; but in consequence of the
fact, that the explosive grains were rather unpopular
just then, while both guns and pistols, fire-crackers,

double-headers, and torpedoes, being strictly prohibited
by—the constable round the corner,—we concluded to
defer the execution of the malefactor till the ensuing
Fourth of July, then a matter of some eight months distant.  But at last, it came.  Our revenge had slept,
but was by no means extinguished.  The ogre dwelt in
the same place still.  The hour for dire retribution
drew fearfully near—and at length arrived.  The cobbler's doom was sealed.  Our maleficent congress—
boys, all under twelve—had resolved that he must die,
then or never, so far as we were concerned.  Pistols
and powder being still as scarce as ever, we assailed
the enemy with a large string of ignited Chinese crack-
ers, in lieu of guns and bullets—articles *de campaign*—
not procurable, owing to the limited resources of our
combined exchequer.

We suffered a defeat—a rout, total and complete—
nor did one of us escape what the cobbler called a
' welting,' for our shoulders tingled many an hour thereafter from the application of a strip of leather, wielded
by the stalwart right arm of the vindictive man.  Now
it so happened that, nearly opposite the scene of this
farce, there stood a tall flag-staff—' Tom Riley's Fifth
Ward liberty pole' it was called—and with this pole is
associated, not only the moral of my story, but also one
of the most singular experiences ever undergone by a
human soul, while incarnated in a tabernacle of flesh
and blood, nerve and sinew, muscle and matter.  After
mutually smarting from the application of the cobbler's
' welt,' we took counsel and refuge beneath the liberty
pole aforesaid ; and the last I remember of the affair is,
that, while gazing upon his triumphantly retreating

4

figure, it struck me that the very quintessence of my felicity on earth would be achieved could I have the exquisite joy and unsurpassable pleasure of hanging him to the weathercock on the summit of that flag-staff. This would be to me----to us, a very heavenly state indeed.    And so I hung him, in fancy, to the north cor-ner of the vane, enjoyed his imaginary struggles for a while, and then went home.  *  *  *  *  *  *  Years passed.    My childhood's troubles were forgotten, and man's estate had come, with all its griefs, cares and strifes, and, from a student of revenge, I became one of the science of Forgiveness.    During one of these latter years I became interested in the question, ' Has man a death-surviving soul, or not ?' and to the solution of this great problem I bent the entire force and energy of my mind, not hesitating to make all sorts of experiments that held out a hope or possibility of my reaching a defi-nite conclusion in regard to the subject.    In pursuance of this grand object I one day made an experiment which, in some respects, was but too successful ; it was not by means of drugs or potions, magnetism or spiritual circles.  At the end of one of these experiments I became totally lost to the external world, its surroundings and influences, and found myself in the world of Spirit—in the midst of a vast and boundless Chaos, in which no sound struck upon me save the rattling of the bones of a huge and ghastly skeleton which swayed and swung to and fro in the bleak air.from the point of a vane on the top of a vast pole, itself the very spectre of the one on which mentally, I had hung my mortal foe.

Attracted irresistibly by the ominous sounds, I turned my gaze toward it, when instantly the horrible, ghastly

thing became endowed with life and speech—ventri-
loquial power of speech—and it shrieked into my startled
ears these terrible, these ominous words : ' Wretch, look
upon the work of thy hands! Here didst thou place
me in the years now gone, and here have I hung and
swung ; here must I hang and swing during many and
many a coming age! Gaze upon this cord—look on it ;
think of it-—placed around my neck by you—by *you !*
The flesh once with these bones which now rattle in
your ears — *your* ears ! — has, by the elements, been
changed and dissolved into atoms—do you hear ?—into
atoms finer than the flecks of light in a sunbeam—aye,
finer than the scintillations of yonder star, the point of
the buckle of Orion's belt ; and that star is an eye, and
it *watches* you—watches *you ;* and, as you see, is the
only one in your horizon from zenith to nadir. That
star is the sentinel appointed by *Him* to see to it that
you escape not the doom—the doom! Ha! ha! ho!
ho! Yes, it was I—*I* who burnt your ball, in revenge
for which *you* burnt your soul !—you burnt your *soul !*
Ha! ha! ho! ho! And that soul must burn, and keep
on burning, in its own self-kindled flames, until their
fiery tongues shall have licked your joints—your *joints,*
your marrow—your very *marrow,* and keep licking
them until—'

'In God's name, what and when ?' I tremblingly in-
quired. And from between the chattering, clattering,
horrible jaws of that ghastly thing there hissed back
this answer : ' Atom by atom, the elements whereof my
body was formed shall once again cleave to these bare
bones ; and, of their own volition, persuaded thereto by
the spectacle of thy agony, softened by thy prayers,

quit their gambols in space, their festive sport amongst the star-beams, and re-arrange themselves into the original flesh, and blood, and nerve, and cartilage, and lymph, and muscle, wherewith these bones were clothed once upon a time in the dead years of an infinite Past!' 'But,' I cried, as the sweat of agony seemed to ooze even out of my spectral cheeks, 'there must be some mistake. The crime imputed was never committed by me. I never slew you, nor any one else. True, I remember you, but I only'—'Wished and willed to do it!' shrieked my tormentor, from the gibbet; 'and whatever the soul strongly wills is done, so far as human responsibility is concerned. You wished and willed me to be here; and here I am, by virtue of a great and mighty law. Hast thou not heard the law laid down, by the sufferer of Calvary, "Whoso looketh on a woman to lust after her, hath already committed adultery in his heart," and must pay the penalty therefor? And thinkest thou that this is the only application of the great law of justice and compensation? Fool! know that thy crime is just as great as if thou hadst, with thine own fingers, put the cord of murder about my *neck*—about *my* neck! The crime-thought is as great as the crime-act. So it is with thee, thou murderer! Man is judged from the desires and motives of his heart, whether these be for good or ill, and never from or for his act alone; for the reason that actions are often the result of an instantaneous impulse, external pressure and circumstance; but motives are the creatures of will, the perfect offspring of desire!' I groaned in agony, an agony so great that it burst the bonds of sleep, and I awoke from that which was not all a dream. It was an awful lesson, and taught me how to become a wiser and a better man.'*

Such was the terrific experience of my friend, and I feel that I need say no more on a point so well, so very forcibly illustrated.    *    *    *    *    *    *

Still the phantorama glided past upon the wall, revealing many a new mystery, and showing me that every human being is more or less responsible for the result of personal influence exerted upon others.

Much rare and valuable knowledge flowed in while I stood there, in the center of the magic sphere, gazing on the second vivorama, or living picture, delineating the results of my influence on others. Many and many a strange scene passed athwart that globe's interior; and I saw not only what the result of my influence had been, but also what would have resulted had my action, in a given instance, been different from what it really was. Thus, I saw that had a cross word been spoken to a child, whom I had endeavored to soothe by kindness, that child would have been led to restrain himself, instead of, as happened, taking advantage, and attributing my complaisance to fear or something akin thereto. I saw, on that mystic scroll, the simulacræ of every person I had ever known, and found that there, in the Soul-world, people and things passed at their true, and by no means at a fictitious value, like men and money do on the earth. All mankind are divisible into seven

---

* This fearful apocalyptic vision occurred on the night of Feb. 3d, 1861, and was the means of inducing a train of thought and feeling in the mind of the person who experienced it, which resulted in his conversion from all sorts of philosophism to a belief in the pure and sweet religion of Christ the Saviour.—*Pub.*

great Orders, to each of which there are three sub-or-
ders or classes. I shall speak of the Orders, not of the
classes. Many of those who, when living amongst
them, I had ranked with the highest, I now found, in
this place, where the secrets of all hearts are in very
deed laid open, really belonged to a far lower plane,
and, *vice versa ;* for many a civilizee and aristocrat was
now found to belong to the order of barbarians ; whereas
not a few of those usually considered low were seen to
be better unfolded than thousands with loftier preten-
sions. Will it be credited, I even found the purest virtue in one whose occupation was harlotry ! Once upon
a time, long before I passed through death's cold river,
I was walking through a beautiful grove, hard by my
dwelling-place, the house upon the hill. It was a gala
day, and hundreds had gathered there to celebrate the
noon of summer. Mirth, gaiety and sport ruled the
hour, and my soul was very glad.

Amongst the rest who had gathered there, were several females, whose trade was Sin, and who I supposed
came there for their horrid purpose. How mistaken
was I ! At that time it did not strike me that beings so
lost *could* have a pure thought, or in any way be tempted
to quit the hot pavements of the city to spend an hour
in God's great Temple, amidst its living columns—the
stately forest trees—without mischief and wrong-doing
in view. I looked upon them, especially her with the
pale thin lips and large drooping eyelids, with utter
loathing. And thus I passed them by ; years fled ;
never again did I think of them—much less that such
creatures could have aught of goodness in them, or feel
the need of God's sunshine, or of a bath in His pure

ocean of fresh air. In life they were forgotten, bu now, as that mystic diorama moved forward, I saw that very scene in the grove, reproduced in every minute detail. There sat the courtezans—there walked I past them ; and as she of the large blue eye looked up to-ward me, with a mute demand for one sympathetic glance—one kind word—*only* one kind word—I turned heedlessly away ; and in doing so, I now saw that a wrong thing had taken place ; for had I spoken kindly, they might have been saved from ruin, so far as the world is concerned—utter and complete. Then, when it was, alas! too late, I saw how very easily I might have melted and won the heart of the woman with the thin pale cheek, and she would have become a minister-ing spirit for good to many and many a lost and de-graded one. I now saw her antecedents—a young girl, a tender, loving daughter—fair, beautiful and sensitive to the last degree. In her home misery reigned—no work for the father, no bread for her little sisters, a sick mother, and the storms of winter howling in the streets, and the cold wind, sleet-laden, searching for nooks and crannies, that it might freeze the little hands and make the pale lips blue.

And then father took to drinking, and the pampered servants of the rich lordlings of the great city drove her with the large blue eye from their doors ; and she was hungry, *very* hungry ; and then the foul fiend tempted her to accept a handful of silver from—a male ! for MEN never do such things—things so infernal, so hideous, so ineffably mean—in exchange for her body ! * * * * And so she sold it—again, and again, and again ! Great God ! she was obliged to sell it, or starve in the midst of the granaries of Plenty! Starve herself? Yes, but not *only* herself—that were easy—but the mother who bore her, in agony—the father, whose reason had for a time deserted its throne—the little ones, clustering about the scanty fire in the little tin stove ; these, all these, must eat or die ! "The Poorhouse !" A *poor* refuge indeed ! for although *they* may have been better off therein, would *she ?* Doubtful ! for—well, never mind what! She sold herself for bread !

Presently work came, but the stain was on her. She had run down a declivity so steep that she could never clamber up again, unless some friendly hand be stretched forth to help her. And such hands are *very* scarce. And now I saw what good might have been done, in the days gone by, had I " only thought."

This scene passed across the walls of my sphere ; and then there came after it a large blank space, and this taught me that it indicated that some where in my life there had been a corresponding omission. " What can it have been ?" Scarce had this query been framed, than there appeared a picture, which need not be described. but the sum of whose teachings may briefly be stated thus : *I had never married*—had never been hailed by the dear titles " Wife " and " Mother." I had therefore failed in the one supreme womanly duty. Nor can any soul be fully filled with joy who neglects those great commands of God and Nature. Children are the crowns of Heaven ; nor can any one—man or woman—taste the serener and the sweeter joys of Being, who has failed to love and be loved, wed and be wedded ; for this is one and the chiefest of means whereby the soul becomes mellowed, and fit for higher uses in the Soul-home. For these reasons, my joys, though great, were not equal to what they might have been ; and yet, take it all in all, provided the entrance into the upper land is made with a clear and healthy conscience and a fair record be left behind, no sense of clearness, lightness and joy can equal that which is experienced subsequent to the first awakening after Azrael's decree has severed the marriage between matter and soul. The Senses ! Roses emit sweet odors, grateful to the nostrils ; yet not all the perfumes of the Gulistan is worth one inhalation of the celestial aroma in which the spirit of the good man or woman floats when once fairly over the barriers which separate the worlds. Color ! I never knew the *music* of hues before I passed away— never conceived of the sublime mysteries, nor realized the great glory whose temple is the chalice of a flower. Touch ! Ah, what language, what pen, what tongue can describe the deep raptures of a soul, when God's sublime atmosphere first laves the immortal being ! The highest, keenest nerve-joy the body *can* experience must be very, very dull and tame in comparison ; and so on through the Sense-gamuts of Earth and the hyper ones of Spirit. Yet only the good enjoy these pleasures. Sin and pollution, whether of thought or overt act, detract from the senses and susceptibility to pleasure in both worlds alike ; and so absolutely true is this, that sin and folly ought to be shunned by the people, if for no other than the selfish desire of being happy from oneself. It is better to live right, die right, and be right after death, than it is to purchase transient pleasures on earth by drawing too largely on the bank of life,

4 *

to find one's drafts dishonored at the counters of the world above. Suicides and voluptuaries are on an equality up there. Both are only half-men, half-children, half-women; nor can they taste of the higher raptures, unless they grow to holiness.

After a while there ceased to be any more pictures, and I became aware of the fact that an unseen force was at work on the *outside* of the globe, evidently endeavoring to break it down, or in some way force a passage through its walls. What this something could be, was a mystery, just so long as I vehemently desired to know, which of course I, like others under similar circumstances, did. I could not, while thus endeavoring, obtain my desire, and therefore I naturally began to wish that Nellie or the old man would come, because, in spite of my matchless surroundings, I felt quite human in the midst of Spirituality, and the sight even of another than myself would have been a solace and a consolation. No sooner had my mind placed itself upon a new object, than I made two new and important discoveries: First, that loneliness or solitude is one of the most terrible punishments to which either God or man could ever possibly condemn a sinful human being. God pity the lonely man or woman! O, it is very dreadful to be compelled to exist alone!—and there are thousands who walk the great world's streets, who move along in the very midst of a Solitude, as deep, silent and fearful as that which prevails in Zahara's desert wastes, where human footfalls never disturb the awful stillness of the hour. There are those who travel up and down the world's highways, upon whose soul no glad sounds ever fall, and who appear to be condemned to loneliness, as if they were thus expiating some awful penalty as an atonement for great and undreamed-of crimes, committed either by themselves in some pre-existent state, or by their ancestors when the very world was young. There are those who, while all about and around them are merry and jocund as the bees on a May day, are themselves as far removed from the pale of human sympathy, and as utterly ALONE, as if they were shut up in some rock-ribbed cave in the heart of Mont Blanc or the Mountains of the Moon. O, it is a fearful thing to be shut out from the great Sympathia whose function is to blend in one the chords of all human hearts! It is a sad fate indeed to be obliged to live amidst the clamor and the clang of Discord, when all other souls are dancing to the glorious sounds of the great Harmonead; yet many such, aye, far too many such there be, who are thus cut off, shut up, barred out. They *might* have been let in, had the father given the mother a smile, a caress, a blessing, at the proper moment, instead of a frown, a rudeness and a secret curse, as is, alas! too often the case; and yet nothing is more positively certain than that somebody must answer to their own souls, their own consciences, for this most fearful entailment of misery, loneliness and woe. See! yonder is a woman—a wife—big with a man-child, who will ere long see the light; but she is miserable—is lonely, is perchance cursed for becoming—a mother; and so she frets, and mopes, and pines—all the while paining to be delivered of her misery and child. At length it sees the day, the sun's bright laugh meets no responsive smile from its pale, thin, tiny lips. It mopes and grows, but is prematurely old at ten years, a man at fifteen, a mournful pilgrim at twenty-five, and an old veteran at thirty years! Who's to blame? Somebody! else God's justice is, like man's, a mockery!

Brother or sister, who readest these pages, wouldst thou know one of the grand secrets underlying the constitution of the great Brotherhood of Crime? It is because man is a social being, has a mortal and invincible hatred and repugnance to solitude, feels the need of associates and sympathy, and will have both if possible, even though obliged to seek them in the very midst of hell itself. Didst thou ever observe that the majority of spiritual mediums are men and women who are sensitive, lonely, bereft and forsaken? Well, look around, and thou shalt find it so. And these, failing to find sympathy on earth amidst their fellows, search for it in the awful labyrinths that underlie the tomb; and from the Middle States vast hordes of semi-infernals come trooping at the heart-calls of these wretched ones, who are thus preyed on by vampires from both Eternity and Time; for embodied wonder-mongers sap them dry, and wear them out, while disembodied demi-devils delude them, until the fair Soul-garden either becomes an arid waste, or teems with thistles, thorns, and all unsightly and unseemly things. When such victims cry aloud unto God, and keep crying, He will send His good angels to comfort, save, cheer and protect.

Reader, wouldst thou know why millions of women, fair, loveable, and good as ever God's sun shone upon, yearly rush down the mountain's side and plunge neck-deep into the swamps of prostitution and infamy? It is because their human hearts yearn for sympathy, pine for love, long for something good and kind; which fail-

ing to discover and obtain where hope has told them
such things were, they seek for it, at last, in the horrid
belly of social damnation. Their motto, 'A short life
and a merry is better than a long and lonely one!' tells
too truly the story of many a poor girl's heart. My
God, my God, have mercy on the lonely ones! for thou
alone knowest that many and many a sin against society and thee is committed by such and others, not of
settled purpose of ill-doing, but because urged on by
sheer despair. Many a crime has been committed from
a mental aberration caused by the horrors of loneliness.
Human tribunals take but little, if any, account of a
criminal's antecedents and surroundings. He or she is
judged too harshly, in the main; and thus it will be
until mankind learns a deeper lesson of wisdom than
yet presides over its courts and councils. Only God
can truly know a heart; and whilst this fact is so
clear, it is better to err on charity's side, if error must
enter into the account at all.

In prison there is at least a community of punishment, and the sense of this goes far to relieve the tedi-
um of incarceration; for, bad though it be, many a one
has found it preferable to the perpetual and dreadful
solitude to which liberty condemned them.

Why are there such vast numbers of deserted wives
and husbands?—so many ruined and cheerless hearths
and homes? The answer is: because neither of the
heads of the household has even dreamed that the com-
panion had rights which the other was bound to respect; and the greatest of these rights, and the one
most disregarded, is the right of being loved by that
other—loved tenderly, truly, kindly, humanly. The

parties to the domestic compact have severally failed to realize what common sense ought to have suggested from the first—that human happiness is never direct, but is always reflected.  When the married find out this great law, and practically apply it, society will redeem itself from all hatred and harlotry, license and libertinism, free-love and folly, madness, murder and meanness.. Ah! friendly reader, it is a 'fearful state, that wherein a woman's or a man's true and generous love and sympathies are driven down and beaten away by those to whom they naturally cling.  It is hard to have their human kindness misconstrued, and to have his or her affection crushed by the heedlessness or lack of generosity of those who ought to leap, and hail it with all true human thankfulness.  God knows that there is too little real affection in the world, and it is very hard to have that little forced back upon the full, true heart from which it was sent forth on a mission of goodness.  This sort of thing it is that freezes up the spirit, and makes man and woman lonely hermits in the very midst of the teeming hives of human life, society and effort.

It is a terrible thing to be compelled to eat your own heart—to be forced to consume oneself—to hear the harsh, brutal and unfeeling tone, when one should listen to the dulcet notes of generous affections ; for they freeze and chill the spirit, and warp the very ligaments of Soul.  These sad things must be atoned ; the vicarious sacrifice must be self-made by the doer thereof — persons who unthinkingly tear down and wreck their fellows, every soul of whom might be builded up. made strong for the Right, and emulous of

all great and good and noble thoughts and deeds which
God's human children have ever done—and all by kindness, open-hearted conduct and friendly cheer.  Heaven!
how much misery and crime might be stayed by one
kind and loving word!  How many are at this day
wading through Perdition, as they tread the pavements
of the world's broad streets, and all for want of one
kind word !  Wrote Milton :

"———————— Devil with devils damned
Firm concord hold.  Men only disagree."

There is much pith in this couplet, which is far from
being *all* poetry—that is, if a judgment must be predicated upon what the worlds have witnessed of warfare,
robbery, slaughter, and rapine, all along the track of
ages.  Earth is, then, something worse than hell itself !
It ought to be better, for hell cannot be purged nor the
Middle State become pure, until earth is purified, and
the daily delegations sent across the dark River be of a
better, purer and nobler mould than now.

I remember to have dearly loved the Apostles' Creed,
especially my own rendering thereof :

" I believe in the Holy Ghost; the Holy Church; . .
. . . the forgiveness of sins ; the resurrection . . . . . the
communion of saints ; the life everlasting."  Glorious
creed of glorious fishermen—repeated daily by millions!
But do these millions *really* believe the words so freely
spoken ?  Go ask their conduct in the world's busy
market places, where human bodies and human souls
are as so many counters in the scale,—not negro
bodies and souls, but those of lordly bankers, and mo-
nied magnates, who serve as waiters in Moloch's tem-

ples on the four shores of the two great seas.   Pity it is
that people do not believe their own religious creeds,
for if they did there would be fewer lonely ones on
either side of the grave.

Sung a poet, quite as good, if not so great as Milton :

If men cared less for wealth and fame,
 And less for battle-fields of glory ;
If writ in human hearts, a name
 Seemed better than in song or story :
If men, instead of nursing pride,
 Would learn to hate it and abhor it ;
If more relied on Love to guide,
 The world would be the better for it.

If men dealt less in stocks and lands,
 And more in *bonds* and *deeds* fraternal ;
If Love's work had more willing hands
 To link this world to the Supernal ;
If men stored up love's oil and wine,
 And on bruised human hearts would pour it,
If " yours " and " mine " would once combine,
 The world would be the better for it.

If more would ACT the play of Life,
 And fewer spoil it by rehearsal ;
If bigotry would sheathe its knife,
 Till good became more universal :
If Custom gray with ages grown,
 Had fewer blind men to adore it :
If talent shone in truth alone,
 The world would be the better for it.

If men were wise in little things,
 Affecting less in all their dealings ;
If hearts had fewer rusted strings,
 To violate their kindly feelings :
If men, when Wrong beats down the Right,
 Would *strike together* and restore it :
If Right made Right in every fight,
 The world would be the better for it.

Aye! that it would, and *will*, brave lover of thy race, when more shall live the spirit thou hast breathed. But Faith is not yet dead ; Hope still lives in human hearts ; Charity is beginning to be a power in the world, and these three—blessed three—will yet work out the world's salvation. Strong hands, clear intellects, willing minds, are all that is needed to develope true human individuality, a thing of the future ; and then a man and a woman will pass for the self-displayed value, the intrinsic worth manifested by Action. " It is not me they hate and ill-use ; it is the fictitious personality they have given me. They will not take me as I am, but insist that I shall be what themselves desire I should be; and in crushing, slaying, killing this phantom which they choose to attach to my name, they are, alas, crushing, slaying, killing me !" These words were uttered by an almost broken-hearted man ;[*] they were true, and true not only of him, but of many a lonely and sensitive one beside.

In the days when common sense shall reign, the diseases of the social body will be eradicated, and then the loneliness of talent and genius will be exceptional to the rule, instead of the reverse, as in these lonesome latter years. If men could but realize that every human groan echoes up through all the starry vaults, even to the eternal throne itself, they would not cause so many as they do, especially when they discover that every one of these groans must be expiated by the causer thereof. If men knew that every pang endured by a human being on earth, sweeps like a whirlwind of

---

[*] Paschal, R.

agony along the telegraphic lines of infinite space, and that not a soul in God's vast domain but must feel the effects thereof in accordance with the Great Sympathia —itself the nervous system alike of God, Nature, and human kind—they would heartily strive to lessen the amount, and banish all anguish and its producing cause from their midst.

The human race is a mighty harp; touch one string rudely, and all the others vibrate; and the finer the chord, the more it responds to the shock. When Jesus groaned on Calvary, the pain of his body and soul was shared in by every creature beneath God's Infinite heaven; and the agony thrills still go sweeping through the worlds, and will, until all mankind shall go its way and sin no more. No human body is healthy so long as a single atom of disease lurks between the granules of a bone, or between the cells of the most unimportant viscus; neither can society be calm. or the race be happy on either shore of eternity, so long as one unholy man or woman lives to mar the harmony, and be a discordant note in the Great Sympathia. Thus we dwellers of the Soul-worlds are impelled to action in behalf of our brethren below, by the first and greatest law of the universe—self-preservation; for in making man abjure his errors and turn toward the Right, we lay the surest and firmest foundation whereon to erect the great Temple of Purity wherein all alike shall worship God, do well, and think no evil. The discovery of this great principle of unity, the acquisition of the positive knowledge that every sensation, painful or pleasant, experienced by any, even the most distant, low and degraded of the species, was necessarily shared in by all

the rest, surprised me greatly ; and from finding that
the finest nerved and most sensitive were also the most
unhappy, I was led to infer the existence of a great
Vicarious law, whose elements were Sympathy, Compensation, Distribution. True, some may pass through life,
and apparently escape its action—but not forever.
God has said substantially, " Bear ye one another's bur-
dens ;" and borne they must be. Sensitives bear the
greatest portion of misery, and their fate seems at first
sight to be a hard one—a life all full of tears, groans
and sorrows ; yet the law of Compensation is operative
in all stages, phases, and planes of being :

> " And he who the weariest path has trod
> Shall nearest stand to the throne of God."

There are seasons when men and women of a certain
mould, without the least apparent cause, are plunged
into the very midst of the blackest barathrum of misery
and woe, and who ten times a year pass through the
body of a death too fearful in its agonies to be even
faintly imagined by those of a different make-up. They
complain, and are met with the stereotyped : " Fancy !
Hypochondrias ! Delusion !" Delusion, forsooth ! Is
that pale and haggard cheek, that pain-thrilled sea of
nerve, those drops of almost bloody sweat, that utter
prostration of soul, a mere delusion ? Will the hypothesis of diseased nerves, liver, heart or stomach account
for these things ? To the looker-on of surface, Yes ;
to the student of the soul and its mysteries, No ! There
is a deeper cause, a higher power in operation. Will
the theory of physical disease account for the instantaneous plunging of a man or woman into the deepest

anguish who, scarce ten seconds before, were in the enjoyment of perfect health of spirit, soul and body?   Never!
What means the terrible weight of woe which suddenly
leaps upon the soul of the sensitive?   Whence comes
this ocean of mental pain and half-sense of retribution,
knowing themselves innocent and spotless of all wrong?
I will answer.   At that moment some one, somewhere,
is undergoing all these pangs from apparent cause.
The wave of pain has gone out, and, like the needle to
the pole, flies directly to those whose position on the
plane of the great sympathetic nerve of the universe fits
them to receive it.   Some one else receives it in turn ;
but it becomes less intense, degree after degree, until
at last only a faint and tiny wave reaches the foot of
the throne:

"Eloi, Eloi, lamma Sabbacthani!" groaned the dying
Christ; and the throes of his agony went pulsing
through the universal human heart, till the most majestic prince of Seraphim quailed with agony.   Even
so, still, as in the days of yore, is operative the same
great vicarious law.

When the suffering soul turns itself to God, relief
comes, but not an instant before.   This latter law—for
it is one—was well known in ancient times, and amongst
the higher classes of the Orient is so still.   It and its
operation is well set forth by a modern poet of Islam :

"'Allah, Allah!' cried the sick man, racked with pain the long night
        through ;
Till with prayer his heart grew tender, till his lips like honey grew.
But at morning came the Tempter ; said, 'Call louder, child of Pain !
See if Allah ever hears, or answers, 'Here am I,' again.''
Like a stab the cruel cavil through his brain and pulses went ;
To his heart an icy coldness, to his brain a darkness sent.

Then before him stands Elias ; says, ' My child, why thus dismayed ?
Dost repent thy former fervor ?   Is thy soul of prayer afraid ?
' Ah !' he cried, ' I've called so often ; never heard the " Here am I ;"
And I thought God will not pity ; will not turn on me his eye.'
Then the grave Elias answered, ' God said, Rise, Elias ; go
Speak to him, the sorely tempted ; lift him from his gulf of woe.
Tell him that his very longing is itself an answering cry ;
That *his* prayer, " Come, gracious Allah !" is *my* answer, " Here am I."'
Every inmost aspiration is God's angel undefiled :
And in every ' O my Father !' slumbers deep a ' Here, my child.' "

I do not say, nor did I discover that all sensitives, at
all times, are the mystic sympathants of those who suffer ; for such is not the case.   Much suffering comes to
them from other causes and sources ; yet that a great
deal of mental agony *does* come from the source stated,
I became perfectly convinced.

The last twenty years, I also saw—by the action of
a retrospective faculty of my soul, then discovered and
applied for the first time—has been productive of more
misery than any period of equal length since the world
began : for the reason, among others, that the people's
nerves and brains are keener, fuller, quicker in action,
and more alive to sensations than in the years prece-
dent.   The mental and physical culture of the people has
been such, that not one civilizee in five thousand enjoys good health in either department of common human nature.   Much of the misery extant in the world
to-day is solely attributable to the extraordinary sensitiveness now characterizing such vast numbers of people ; and which morbid condition—for there are two
kinds of sensitives, the natural and the hot-house
growths, the last of which I now allude to—owes its
origin to—First, A general overworking of the brain,

to the total neglect of the muscular system. Second, Improper diet, in time, kind and quantity. Third, Heedlessness in clothing, in reference to color, texture and amount; carelessness in regard to heat, light, cold, sleep, and physical magnetico-electrical influences. Fourth, Personal magnetic influences. Fifth, The metaphysical nature of modern thought and study. Sixth, Irregularity and excess, extending to all things connected with human existence, by reason of which the funds in the bank of life are exhausted at the very time they ought to be most plentiful. Seventh, Modern Spiritualism, which, by reason of its intensity, attracts and absorbs nearly all human attention, to the exclusion of every thing else; causes people to exchange common sense for 'philosophies' not half so useful; induces a sort of intellectual fever; lifts a man above the earth; makes him forgetful of his body, by holding up his spirit to his view; promises to set his feet on solid rock, and ends by, as it should, throwing out the factitious props and stilts whereon he has stood to catch glimpses of what lies on the other side, and letting him fall back upon his own resources finally.

All these things, the last included, previous to its ultimate effect, have, by inducing morbidness of thought and sentiment, principle and feeling, unfitted man to either live or die. The result has been, the development of a sensitiveness so acute, that persons are enabled to penetrate the surface of both things and people, and the result of this involuntary inspection is the discovery that there is many a rotten spot in the fairest-looking fruit—many an unworthy motive underlying the fairest pretence—nothing but duplicity where friendship was thought to dwell—lust and passion, under the guise of esteem and love—and many more such unveilings of the seeming, and disclosures of the real. This sensitiveness is morbid, but its revelations are, alas! quite frequently too true; and the effect it produces is an inveterate suspicion of all things and peo ple, and an utter loss of confidence in the entire human race. This is the hidden reason why a certain order of those who call themselves Spiritualists are so unhappy and discontented; and it is this also that has suggested the ten thousand and ten panaceas for all the ills of life now so freely scattered up and down the walks of the social world. To this cause is to be attributed the thousand mad Quixotic schemes for rejuvenating the world—from 'Free-love' to 'Angel-movements,' 'Woman's Rights' to 'Land Reform.' This it is that separates people—engulphs thousands in the sea of idle and useless speculation—entangles thousands more in the meshes of sophistry, under the name of 'Philosophy'— wise and otherwise, "Harmonial' and Harm-only; and this it is that makes people lonely, and throngs the ways of Earth and Spirit-land with pilgrims of Solitude, surrounded by millions.

It is never your boisterous, jolly, rubicund subject who reaches the penetralia of things, and who thenceforth casts off the world in despair, declares the play of life is only a dismal tragedy, and becomes at heart a hermit of the misanthropic order. O no! far from it! Such belong to the first or lower orders of men— *they* can find company anywhere, at any time. Careless they, no matter whether it rains or shines; it's all the same to them, whether school keeps or not. Of those who receive little, but little is expected. It is your fine-nerved people, the really great-hearted man or woman—those who pertain to the second or other and higher orders* of mankind—your natural aristocrats of the Soul-worlds—when they get there—who on earth suffer greatest and undergo the most.

This general information came to me as I flitted on by the home-sides of those whom I loved, and who, in turn, loved *me*. *Loved* me! What a world in a word!

In the preceding pages I stated that there were two draughts of knowledge which came to slake my death-less soul-thirst, while I waited and wished for Nellie and the old man who went with her. The law of soul is this : any question, the answer to which can be comprehended by the asker, may be propounded to itself in the absolute certainty of a correct response, provided the knowledge it conveys be adapted to the ends of good and use, to either the neighbor or the self. This is an integral law of the very being, no matter where that being may be located. On earth men are not pure nor properly situated, hence it is far more difficult for them to elicit the required knowledge, than it is for those who are not embodied ; yet the law is as opera-tive on the lowest earth as in the highest heaven. In accordance with the principle laid down, that which I have faintly set forth came to me ; but the second les-son, which seemed to be a sequential suggestion of what I thought was an attack upon the external wall of my inclosing sphere, conveyed wisdom as well as know-ledge, the good of which will be seen by those who carefully analyze it.

My glance now fell full and direct upon the point

where the disturbance of the crystalline barrier was greatest; and while wondering if it could withstand the effort made by some power on its exterior to breach it, or whether it would remain intact until my wished-for friends arrived, I began to study its composition. It was evidently not material, and yet it was something quite as substantial. Among men the surrounding envelope of the body is called the 'odylic sphere;' yet odyle is material, therefore this could not be formed of. that. It was not soul-substance, because it was far grosser, and served a greatly inferior purpose. It was not spirit, either. Here then was a demand for useful knowledge; nor was it long ere that demand was fully supplied; for it came to me that embodied man represented God in his threefold nature, Body, Spirit, conscious Soul or Thinking Principle: that each of these must essentially differ from the others, and in a scientific sense be high, higher, and most high; and that too, not by reason of continuity or rarefaction, but by disparates, and insulations. Now all three exist in, of, and constitute the same individual; wherefore there must be at least two substances, differing in toto from the three primaries, yet of a nature enabling them to cling to and connect the principals. What were these two substances? At a glance I saw that the materials of a human body gave forth an atmosphere which serves to connect it with the life, or materio-spiritual part of man, and ties each by soluble links to both the material and spiritual worlds. This is the odylic sphere. What connects soul with spirit? The second glance revealed to me the fact that every monad, carnate and conscious alike, embodied or free, mere monad or devel-

5

oped soul, was surrounded by an atmosphere of its own, unique, single, atomless, homogeneous, and elastic. This envelope is very etherial, and is called Ethylle; it connects soul with spirit, and unites all three worlds, body, soul, and spirit together, and constitutes not only the spheres, but the 'Personal Nebulæ,' out of which the immortal spark creates its surrounding sphere or world, when disembodied, and whereof it, while in the flesh, erects its stately *chateaux en espagne*—its castles in the air. Here was a new solution of a mystery that had troubled not only myself, but many a philosopher, and a solution, too, in perfect and strict accordance with the principles of the Great Harmonead; for the Nebulous Ocean enclosing the Spacial Halls of Deity, wherein roll the starry systems, is the ethyllic envelope of the Eternal One, is the material whereof he, through his servants, the FORCES, fashioneth the mighty fabrics now floating in the azure.

Following hard upon the last great discovery, came another, not perhaps so sublime, but quite as useful; it was this: The mental effort whose results have just been recorded, had the effect of uplifting my soul, and firing it with ambition to such an extent or degree, that, seeing how little I knew, and how vast the fields of the unknown were, I regretted my poor weak human nature, and almost hating it, became impatient of restraint, because I could not take wing, and, flying to the Grand Centre, merge my being into that of God Himself, and thus become all-knowing, all-Being, all-Life. I was beset with the same sin that hurled Lucifer down from the empyreal heights of the vast heaven; and like him too, most bitterly did I regret my daring;

for almost on the very instant that this sacrilegious thought took possession of my soul, my mind lost its clarity, my vision became dim and misty, my equanimity was lost, and was succeeded by a state entirely different—a sort of childliness of feeling. Almost instantly my soul lost sight of the magnificent field just opened to its inspection, and was forced by a power not then understood, to turn completely round, and direct its gaze earthward. Resistance being vain, I did so, and observed directly opposite the point of attack upon the sphereal wall, a window-like opening, through which I looked down the vista of a lane of light, bounded on either side by an impenetrable amorphous wall. One end of this lane terminated on earth, the other in the Soul-world; and from the peculiar nature of the lesson shortly conveyed, I became aware of two things: first, that neither knowledge nor joy ever flow into the secret chambers of the soul, unless the receptacle vessels therein are duly prepared to receive them; for although knowledge may become a thing of memory, yet it can only remain stored up like corn in a granary, and never become of positive value, or serve as soul-food, until that soul itself is in a condition to digest and assimilate it. Secondly, there could no longer be a doubt but that I was being practically instructed by an invisible being of masterly wisdom and accomplishments; and from the nature of the emotions within me, to which this thought gave rise, there was but little if any doubt that this invisible teacher was the mysterious ' Him' to whom Nellie had so mischievously alluded, when she invited me to come with her.

If a woman is loved, no matter where she be, no matter by whom, or where the lover may be, she knows it instantly, without being told of it. It comes to her just as naturally as the vapors sail before the summer breeze. I *knew* that somebody loved me; and that although unseen hitherto, that 'some one' was loved by me. The telegraph of Affection is swifter and surer than that of electric batteries, and every true woman knows it, no matter whether she be dead or alive.

As the sense of this flashed over me, my heart went up to God in *such* a prayer of gratitude as only they can feel and know, whose deathless yearnings have been fully satisfied. My soul rejoiced in its new tutelage, and it praised God for this sense of the presence in action, if not in sight, of one who took an interest in clearing my pathway to Wisdom's coast, thus early on my everlasting journey toward the shores of the Infinite Sea.*

The further end of the lane of light terminated at a spot where was being enacted a scene of a drama wherein the actors were denizens of three worlds—Earth, Soul-world, and Middle State. The lesson taught me was, that very often organization, to a great extent, governs and determines human destiny.

Before a vast audience, on a Sabbath night, stood a lonely man—one with massive and active brain, but thin, weak and 'puny body—therefore an unbalanced character. The woman who seven and twenty years before had given him birth, had imparted her own sensitive nature to her child; while the man through

---

* A revelation concerning which will appear in the sequel; and one, too, compared to which, the grandest and most beautiful things contained in the present volume, are comparatively trivial.—Pub.

whose agency God had incarnated the lonely one, was of an ambitious, affectionate, but passionate and passional nature. The son thus congenitally biased and tainted had grown to man's estate, and from various social and other causes, he being a *sang melée*, had suffered to such a degree that his soul was driven in upon itself to a great extent; which, while rendering him still more sensitive and morbid, also caused his soul to expand knowledge-ward, become wonderfully intuitive and aspiring, yet bound up by the affectional nature within his own personal or individual sphere. But such souls resist this damming up; hence occasionally the banks overflowed, and he became passional; forgot his dignity; was led to believe that whoever *said* love, *meant* love; was beset with temptation, and yielded, until at last his heart was torn to pieces, and his enveloping sphere became so tender and weak, that it could not withstand any determined attack thereon; and thus he, like thousands more whose spheres are thus invalidated and relaxed, became very sensitive to influences of all sorts and characters, and a ready tool and subject for the exploitations and experiments of disembodied inhabitants of the Middle State. He became a medium! Of course this circumstance and qualification necessarily threw him into the society of those who accept the modern theurgy.

In proportion to the self-abandonment and personal abnegation, the degree to which the will is vacated, do such persons become good mediums. The more immersed in the theurgic studies and novelties they are, the more they lose themselves, and their value ceases to be individual, but only representative. In the last sense they inspire a liking in the minds of others, but in their former capacity, none so generous as to really love and pity them; for, being perfect automata, subject to any and all sorts of influences, they become all things by turns, and nothing long; hence they are accused of inconsistency and everything else, by the very people, to serve, and amuse, and instruct whom they have vacated themselves, and consented tacitly to be drained of the last drop of man and womanhood by harpies and vampires from both sides of the grave.

The man before me had been guilty of this supreme folly, and, like many a score of others, had failed to realize that no man or woman can ever be loved alone as the representative or official, but only *as* man or woman; nor that the more one merges him or herself in an office, the more one sinks the individual in the representative, the less are their chances of being either loved or respected. This is one of the reasons why mediums are, as a class, unhappy and discontented, always craving love and sympathy for their own sakes, and never getting either. *As* mediums and speakers, they have friends and admirers by the hundred; but let their gift be lost, or themselves be demented or driven into some silly act, and, lo! the 'friends' drop off like rain from a roof. Of course, there are those who will deny this, but it is true, nevertheless, and will remain so, until these sensitives learn the lesson of self-conservation, and exchange the passive for the active mediumship—the BLENDING for their automacy.

Let it be observed, that every human being is surrounded with an atmosphere emanating from themselves, and that these enveloping auras are charged by the man or woman with all the qualities, good or bad, pertaining to the individual. Thus, a person's sphere may be full of snakes, (figuratively speaking), asps, spiders, toads, and all manner of foul, vile, and venom-meaning things ; while, at the same time, the speech and external conduct of these same persons may be of the blandest kind. Now no sensitive can long associate with such without the imminent danger of foul contagion; which, to the extent that it affects them, is INSANITY. Let one of them be in company, pure, good, honest and true, and they will be the same ; let them mingle with Atheists, Harmonialists, Infidels, Free Lovers, Catholics, Protestants, Philosophers, Scientists, Christians, no matter whom, and straightway they become tinctured with corresponding sentiments and opinions. Nor is this all; for people from the transmundane worlds are attracted to persons of corresponding sentiments, as well as to those who, not so, are yet magnetic sensitives, and most gladly avail themselves of the presence of such, to give forth their opinions on everything in general and nothing in particular. This explains why a certain class of mediums blow hot and cold as the days go by ; for scarce an hour in the week are they properly themselves, but nearly all the time are representing somebody else, either in or out of the body, to whose magnetism they have ingloriously succumbed.

I was speaking of spheres which encompass individuals. They, as all other things in the great Harmonead, are rhythmical. Men and their spheres, like musical notes, are of varying quantity and value. Some are whole notes, double notes, halfs, eighths, sixteenths, thirty-seconds, sixty-fourths, and so on. The last four sorts are plentiful; the first three are rather scarce. The last can never approach the value of the first, albeit they will reach to heights and values infinitely beyond where they may chance to be at present; but when they reach the point now occupied by notes one, two, and three, these latter will have attained a vastly higher place on the infinite scale. Nor is this all; for the law of physical gravitation has its correspondent in the·psychical realm. A stone let fall from a height reaches the ground at a constantly accelerating rate of speed, which speed is itself determined by the greater or less amount of density and weight contained within a given bulk. Thus a cubic inch of cork will be longer on the journey than a corresponding cube of solid steel. And so with the human soul. A, B, and C, being more unfolded at the start than E, F, and G, by reason of better antecedents and conditions, will, for all eternity, widen the distance at first separating them. To return. The human notes, (and those of spheres), like their correspondents of the musical staff, and of color, are governed by a law of their own. A perfect human society would be perfectly melodious and harmonic, for the reason that every individual would fill his or her proper sphere, and to which they are constitutionally fitted and adapted. Illustration: The sphere of A is sympathetical, and accordant with and to that of C and E, though not with B and F (the law of thirds and fifths), but these latter will accord with other notes, with which also A can assimilate perfectly, and thus the entire human scale can affinitize, and would, were it not that many uncongenial notes are huddled and jumbled together in that utter distraction and confusion

called Society. The sole cause of all the dissatisfaction
and discord in the world is to be found in the fact, that
human notes, like musical ones, often occupy wrong
places on the leger lines of being ; and all that is needed to set them right is not, as many world-savers imagine, a complete destruction of the existing system, but
merely a little judicious transposition, to be effected by
the great transposer, Common Sense.

As I gazed through the lane of light upon the man
before the audience, I saw that he, like others, was a
good note, capable of filling an important place in the
Harmonead, but he was far from being in the right
spot, and for two reasons ; one of which was a too violent ambition to know mysteries beyond him, and to
change sinners into saints by eloquent speech ; hence
he, like myself a few moments before, became impatient,
the result of which was a self-doom to lower planes of
thought, act and observation. I found that he was un-
successful also from another cause. Believing himself
to be right; that his knowledge was real; that his intuitions were reliable ; and, knowing that many fields
lay open before his soul for exploration which were
sealed to others, his spirit grew restive from neglect,
and the lack of attention he thought his truths demanded ;
and, from the hight of power, he fell to abjectness, because
he could not, would not pander to the popular taste and
fancy. This last was a ' sin' in the right direction truly ;
but one that took many a mouthful of bread from his
wife and little ones, who had been well fed, clothed and
cared for, if the spirit of pride had given way to policy,
imposture and craft; three counterpoints which would
have brought out, set off and relieved certain beauties

5*

whose effect would have been 'Popularity' below, but regrets, deep and bitter, in the Soul-world. Fool was he, or was he not? for refusing to ring the dull changes suited to the edification and advancement of so-called 'Philosophers and Reformers,' people who hold Jesus up to ridicule, and speak of God as "The chap supposed to dwell beyond the stars!" No! His true place was as the center of a few prayerful souls, and the wielder of the pen for God's sake, instead of being the mouth-piece and oracle of and for those, who next day would not only forget, but previously curse him for his pains.

It came to me that such is the fate of nearly all that class of persons who cultivate spiritual acquaintances at the cost of loss of will and complete self-sacrifice. These people, at best, are only the ephemera of the age, and well it is that such is the case. They are sneered at, vilified, scandalized, and traduced—sapped of the last drop of vitality, and then exultingly laughed at for being such fools ; and when the days of hardship come, but very few of those for whom the tremendous sacrifice has been made, will go to their relief. In fact these human-looking and humane-talking people can stand the self-immolated victim's grief and sorrow very well indeed. The rising tide may engulph the lonely ones, and not a hand of them all be stretched out to save. True, such conduct is in strict accordance with the way of the world, but it is a very bad way, and those who follow it will pay for their folly in the coming ages.

Instead of using these unfortunates in this manner, the true motto and resolve of every one should be : 'It may be that God or Destiny is working out some deep and instructive problem through that man or woman, for the world's best good. It is well to be on the safe side, and therefore best to treat them tenderly and kindly ; for it may happen that it shall be said to us hereafter : 'Even as ye have treated the least of these, my servants, ye have also treated me !' It will be pleasant to know, in the upper worlds, that you have dried some tears and bound up some bleeding wounds in the lower ones."

Thus I stood and viewed, at one glance, both cause and result. The man's body was haggard, his spirit very, very weary, and the enveloping sphere was literally torn into shreds. These spheres can only be kept intact and entire by the exercise of an active will ; but this man's will, like that of vast numbers of the mediumistic class—the automata of the dwellers in the Middle State—had slept, and that so soundly that nothing but the echoes of his own misery could break it. Such people let things take their own course, or else rely on Spirits and earthly friends, instead of on themselves and Deity. They pursue the ways of such a false life, heedless of the inevitable consequences of sorrow and disaster that must ensue ; they forget that, to be even a moderately talented man or woman, is infinitely preferable to being the mere machine and mouth-piece of the loftiest seraph in the great Valhalla of the Skies—and that, too, for reasons plainly discernible.

I saw, with grief and consternation, that not one medium in every ten had a perfect envelope—else they would not be so easily influenced by mortals, nor obsessed and possessed by the dead people from the mid-regions beyond the earth.

Through these openings the bodies and souls of mediums may be and are attacked,* the remnant of will destroyed or lulled, the moral sense stupified, and the entire being subjugated by spectral harpies and human ghouls, who wander on either bank of existence.

Many people, when reading the Scriptures, are inclined to explain away many things as 'poetry' which ought not to be so interpreted. Thus the first chapter of the book of Job contains the following assertions, which it would be well to read oftener and more carefully: "Now there was a day when the sons of God came to present themselves before the Lord, and Satan came also among them. And the Lord said unto Satan, Whence comest thou? Then Satan answered the Lord and said, From going to and fro in the earth, and from walking up and down in it."

Satan here undoubtedly means an evil chief of the harpy bands infesting the borders of both worlds, whose sole delight it is to circumvent God and man, and bring all good things to an evil end. Whether this state of things shall continue, depends not upon God or the devils, but upon man, and his actions, influence and aspirations. Those ill-meaning ones who live just beyond the threshold, often attain their ends by subtly infusing a semi-sense of volitional power into the minds of their intended victims; so that at last they come to believe themselves to be self-acting, when

---

* *Good spirits do not break the sphere !* They approach the crown of the head and infuse thoughts, else blend themselves with the subject, but never by destroying either consciousness or will. Evil spirits attack the lower brain, the amative organs, the lower passions, and force the spheres of their victims. In a similar way the bad people destroy and ruin good ones,—PUB,

in fact they are but the merest shuttlecocks, bandied about between the battledoors of knavish devils on one side, and devilish knaves upon the other ; and between the two, the poor wretches are nearly heart-reft and destroyed.

For every ill there is a remedy, God-sanctioned and provided ; and the only one in such cases is the re-integration and rejuvenation of the will, and the repairing therewith of the disrupted sphere. The way that end is accomplished, is through the instrumentality of prayer and a persistent exercise of will. No person, who is at all reasonable, will for one moment believe that any of the profounder mysteries have yet been revealed by the class of spiritual beings who rap, tip, turn tables, and entrance mediums—the effect of all of which should only be to merely call attention, in well-regulated minds, to a new class of demonstrative evidence of the soul's immortality. When the intercourse between the two worlds shall have become normal, healthful and regular, the earth's inhabitants may look for light from beyond, of a nature and character far, very far above aught that yet has come ; and that much of the coming light will reach the earth in the same mode as that which is herein given, must be apparent, because the process is a normal and healthful one, producing satisfaction and content instead of doubt and distrust, as has been the case heretofore.

Mankind, in either world, are as yet only on the borders—the very edges of being and of knowledge—and men must and will come *en rapport* with the higher life only by living correct lives below.

The first step toward this normal inspiration and enlightenment consists in gaining a complete mastery of the self, the purpose, and the will. The man or woman who believes what any spiritual being may rap, tip, talk out, or write about, merely because *it is* a Spirit, has not yet left off childish things. In the coming time, men will derive information directly from the Soul-worlds, and not by the proxy of tables and spirits, as now.

The course here recommended is the true and only one capable of effecting the redemption and liberation of the obsessed from the terrible thraldom to which, by their own unwise action, they have been subjected. The sufferings of the class alluded to ought to be prima facie evidence to themselves that their methods of dealing with the dead are not the proper ones, nor such as should be adopted by any sane or rational being. Their miseries, as a general thing, are severe enough to excite the pity and commiseration of even a fiend ; yet scarce ten in a hundred of these self-immolated victims receive even the poor meed of thanks, much less food and raiment, for their toil and pains. By self-abnegation and resignation of the will, they have brought their misery upon themselves, by opening their spheres for the free entrance of whatever apocryphal philosopher or saint, whose identity they can NEVER prove, may choose to accept their invitation ; and after displacing their own common sense, substitute a very *un*-common kind in lieu thereof. It is only by an assertion of self, of will—a persistent upbuilding and reparation of the shattered fabric of their personal spheres—that the evil can be kept distant and the good be attracted and entertained. The great mass of obsessing and demonstrating spirits are from the Middle Kingdoms ; some of them are very powerful, and are scripturally spoken of as "Princes and Powers of the Kingdoms of the air." The better class are denizens of the pure Soul-worlds, which is as far removed from the Mid-region as light is from shadow. It is only by beating them off, that mediums can ever hope to regain their self-control, establish a communion with the divine City of pure souls, and successfully pass through the body of their double death, into the calm, sweet and holy atmosphere of the blissful regions which exist above.

Millions there are, around whose hearts the tendrils of fondest love do cling—whose happiness is centered in some dear one's heart, and to whom life were a dreary waste and barren, were they deprived of the sweet and cheering presence of their lost ones, at least in memory. The question of questions to these is, 'Shall we meet again ?—shall the broken links be reunited in the lands beyond the River ? When Death shall have sealed us apart, comes there ever a time when that seal shall be melted, and we loving ones clasp each other in a fond embrace ?' Such are vital questions, to which different answers must be given.

One of the secrets which I soon discovered in the Soul-world was that consanguinity, although a very strong bond of union between people, is by no means the strongest. Those souls are nearest who occupy the same position on the plane of development. Thus it often happens that brothers and sisters are really less related than the same persons are to the most distant strangers. Children are often born of the same parents, whose appearance, conversation, deportment, constitution, habits, disposition and proclivities are as different as different can be. Such relations have nothing in common, save that the monad constituting the soul of each becomes incarnate in the same matrix; that is all. All monads vary; some are more unfolded and unfoldable than others, and while the intrinsic quality of each corresponds, yet conditions may cause a higher expression of one than another, or that same one under different circumstances. Thus a monad, be it never so ripe in itself, is *forced* to surround itself with certain spiritual and material envelopes, furnished by the father, on its passage from his soul-cells to the gestative chamber wherein it clothes itself with corporality. Now, whatever clings to the monad on its passage is totally external, and is charged with the man. If he is a sot or libertine, bloodthirsty or ambitious, cheerful or despondent, these states are impressed upon all his juices and fluids, nervous, physical or spiritual; and the envelopes of the *commissioned* monad, partaking of these impressions, subsequently develops in the *same direction*, and, on the principles of attraction and impression, affect the fore-future of the contained monad or germ-soul. That this is true, and that all the ill is impressed externally, is proved by the fact that a couple may have children during one decade, wherein the parents live upon a low external plane, which children will be angular, and manifest any but lovely and genial traits. The same persons, during the second decade, may reform and become deeply moved with religious sentiment, such as expresses itself in prayer-meetings, singing, and violent faith-practice. The children born under this reign will be deeply excitable, fervent, ambitious, sensitive, boisterous at times, and, as a general thing, superficial and changeable. During the third decade, when common sense, practical rationality, and just and noble views of life and its obligations shall have taken the place of their previous state—when cleanliness, light, air, and sunshine, daily-acted prayers instead of loud-mouthed lip-worship, constitute some of the elements of their religion—and when their bodies have become purified by proper living, eating, drinking and labor—their children will be born with larger brains, better bodies, nobler appearances; and their career through life will correspond. All this is as true as the Eternal Gospel, and shows that, although ill and evil are deeply rooted in the human soil, yet they are by no means ineradicable.

All men know that they often feel more love and friendship for strangers than they do for their own blood brothers; and friendship, when real, and not based upon physical properties, or selfish motives, is a thing that unquestionably survives the ordeal of the grave. Persons *thus* bound together will, and do meet, whether of the same lineage or not. But it often happens that the best of earthly friends belong to and represent two distinct orders of soul; and it may be that they pertain to orders so widely separated, that on earth, as in the heavens, they must lose each other, and strike hands and hearts over a gulf impassable by either. Do you not see hundreds of proofs of this all around you on the earth? A tender, gentle, delicate girl often clings, with all the desperate energy of idolization, to some rough, coarse, uncouth, unkempt and brutish fellow. The love of that poor heart will redeem that man from many a horror in the Middle state, and ensure his speedier entrance into the lovely gardens of the Soul-world! The same principle is demonstrated even among the animals, between opposite species of whom the fondest attachments often exist, as is seen in the Happy Families of menageries; the love of a lion for a tigress, a cat for a rat, a horse for a hog, a serpent for a rabbit, and last and greatest, the love of the dog for man—an affection so deep and pure, that it puts that between human beings to the blush of shame by comparison; for the dog—generous, noble dog!—everywhere sacrifices every other love, and devotes his entire being to the services of his human friend.

Dogs and birds abound in both the Spirit and the Soul-worlds. In both they are representatives of states —loves, affections—and are found in the former realm quite as often as in the latter, for the reason that the coarsest, most wicked, and brutal man, he who most violently hates his kind, yet must, and *does*, and will love something, and the dog is almost universally that object, else a bird or fowl; for how often do you see the drunkard followed by his faithful cur, and how frequently the hardest man in a community lavishes the most tender care upon a fowl—a game-cock, a parrot or canary—sweet, beautiful, lovely canary!

The first reply to the question, ' Shall we friends meet again?' must be answered affirmatively. You will *meet*, but whether ye *remain* together is another question, and depends altogether on the rapidity with which the one shall unfold and develope up to the point occupied by the other. But, if the one friend belongs to one order, and the other to a higher, then the electric chain

of unity will connect ye over the vastest ocean of infinite space. Everything moves in elliptical orbits in the
material, spiritual and affectional realms alike. In the
Soul-world the foci of this ellipse are Memory and Hope.
The lines constituting it are also the lines of the great
Harmonead—the vast Sympathia; every human being,
good as well as evil, is located on its plane, and along
its wires forever is flashing love and well-wishing, and
every heart *must* have its pulses quickened by the warm
magnetic outflow. The sun's heat falls at an angle
which enables Nova Zembla's icebergs to laugh at his
efforts to melt them; they have laughed these myriad
centuries; will laugh, perhaps, for hundreds more; yet
the sun is patient, still shines on, and with such a steady
radiance and blandness, that the frozen North begins to
quake with apprehension lest its reign be forever closed;
for somehow it begins to feel that the question of its
regnancy is only one of time, and that heat *is*, after all,
more powerful than cold, love than hatred; wherefore
it must one day yield—resolve its ices into liquid flow;
cause its frozen heaps to ride upon the waves toward
the steaming seas; relieve the poles; let the earth
swing round, and all surface-earth smile with green
gladness. So with the worlds beyond. The rays of
goodness have long shone upon the evil ones of the
Middle State, and have bounded off again. Still around
go the flashes again and again; for neither God nor true
human souls grow tired of loving, even though that love
be repelled seven, seventy, or seven myriads of times!
Around goes the flash, and at every circuit *some* good is
done! Navigators tell you that every year the number
and bulk of icebergs from the Northern oceans increase

in number in the Southern seas. Every one of them is a victory achieved by Persuasion over Force; and even so the population of the realms of the Soul-worlds is constantly increased by the accession of people who, having got tired of Hell, voted it unpleasant, and have deemed it expedient to emigrate to Heaven, a land which, they have learned from missionaries, abounds in milk and honey, and all good things whatsoever. Every one of this host of emigrants is an accession to the Good, and a loss irreparable to the Bad! Every one is a symbol of the victory of Right over Wrong. Bye-and-bye there will be a total depopulation of the Middle kingdoms, and their places will be supplied with something better; and the sooner mankind cease to do evil and learn to do well, the quicker will this much-desired hegira take place.

Pure love changes males into men; and when men become what they are capable of in an upward direction, the Middle State will cease to be replenished by such as love ill.

Of course, in a work professedly dealing with and explaining the principia, like this, it is impossible to enter fully into specialities; that task is deferred till another occasion.

No truer saying ever was uttered than that God helps those who help themselves;—a work which every one, especially the mediumistic class, are especially called on to perform.

There being two sides to everything, there is the same to mediumship. The non-injurious kind is that which I advocate, and it consists in the Blending process already alluded to and explained. No possible

harm can result from it.   On the contrary, the popular
sort, originating in the orient long centuries ago, and
now revived in these latter days, can but be injurious
to the last degree, because it consists in the usurpation
of the living by the UNKNOWN !   There is a better
way—a safer road, a thornless route—by means of
which to reach all the knowledge, and far more besides,
which is sought to be obtained by the other practice.
That surer means does not consist in an abandonment
of self, or stultification of the moral sense and will, nor
in Mesmerism, or the use of hashish—the pestilent
thing—nor in the employment of any unhealthful
means, but in an increase and strengthening of will,
and consciousness, and moral purpose ; not in a *loss*
of consciousness or responsibility, but in an intensification and growth thereof.   This better sort of spiritualism is based upon the heart and soul ; not, like the other
sort, upon the nerves and body.   This better sort protects the sphere from the attacks, amatory and cerebral,
to which the acolytes of the other kind are subjected.
If people went direct to God for enlightenment, instead
of to Spirits, who so frequently deceive, there would be
much less, in fact no evil at all, resulting from the intercourse over the bridges of Time and Eternity ; and,
by firmly relying on Him whose very existence thousands of the inhabitants of the Middle State deny and
scout the bare idea of, people would not only be able to
preserve their odylic spheres intact, but would be pro-
tected from the diabolic influence and machinations of
the harpies who infest the Threshold, and frequently
deliver long and sounding platitudes from the lips of
shut-eyed members of the two sexes ; for they are not

men and women yet, by a great deal.  No one is, who
yields the will and resigns both soul and body to any
spectral experimenter in phreno-mesmerism who may
chance to flit along, in their excursions 'up and down
the world,' and who are continually 'going to and fro
therein.'  Reasonable people, whether of earth or higher
worlds, are beginning to weary of seeing and hearing
sensible-looking men and women, with closed eyes,
pacing up and down a platform, and, with folly-driven
tongue, giving vent to ' philosophy' which neither God,
angels nor men can comprehend a word of !

Before long, something of the realities of the soul and
its hidden history will be known, and then ambitious
mouthers will no longer split the ears of the people
with senseless harangues—*olla-podridas* compounded of
moon-shine and nonsense—pseudo-philosophic hash, con-
cocted of fish, flesh and fowl—most *foul*, gammon of
Bacon and Swedenborg essences—whereof the great
Seer is as innocent as Peter the Hermit was of slaying
Abel.  The time approaches when a better state of
things shall exist, and more rational views of human
immortality be entertained by the masses.  People have
made a great mistake in supposing that all the high-
flown stuff spoken, written or printed, as emanations
from the worlds beyond, were really true ; for much of
it originated in the brains of the deliverers thereof,
whilst more of it is but the result of tricky exploitations of disembodied wags, or downright evil spirits.
Another and very popular error is, that the advent of
Spiritualism constitutes the opening dawn of a New
Dispensation ; that it is to supersede Christianity, or to
become the *nucleoli* of a new order of sects, or even the

nucleus or pivot of a single one. No, no ; Spiritualism has not yet produced fruit in the souls of its believers, at all to be compared to those growing on the tree planted on the stony heights of Calvary nearly two thousand years ago ! It is, in itself, powerless to supersede a system so infinitely grand and sublime as that founded by the twelve fishermen and their illustrious Lord. Nor is such its mission. Supply and demand wait ever upon each other. The sense of human immortality, in community, the wide world over, had grown dull, vagueand indistinct, lulled by the droning music and somnifying humdrum of theology. Churchianity to a great degree had usurped the office and functions of Christianity, and the sense of an hereafter had so nearly died out, that bad advocates of annihilation preached and printed their infernal libels on the corners of the world's highway, and millions began to seriously question wherein man was entitled to what animals were not ; while philosophic hucksters still, with quirk and grimace, howled forth "Books proving God a myth, Christ a bastard, the Bible a lie, immortality a lame delusion, and virtue mere nonsense !" And then these peddlers bawled : " What pre-eminence hath a man above a brute ? Wherein is he better than the dogs which perish ? Who knoweth the Spirit of a man that it goeth upward, or the spirit of a beast that it is blotted out and goeth outward like an extinguished lamp, or downward like a lead to the bottom of—nonentity ? Come, buy my books ! come, buy my books !"

Surely here was a demand for light upon the tremendous question, 'Are we to be, or not to be, when life's fitful fever is o'er ?' Here was a question requir-

ing the lips of the infinite God to answer—and He did !
for with the weakest instruments He confounded earth's
greatest and wisest men.   Through a harlot's daughter
was met and vanquished all opposers of His truth, that
" Death was not the destiny of man ;" through a bar-
ber's clerk was revealed the Hierarchy of the vast
Heaven ;  through a country-school teacher was declared
the Order and the Majesty of Being ;  and through the
agency even of the wicked dead was demonstrated
man's continued life !  Spiritualism came, not as the su-
perseder of the Christ, but as the final demonstrator of
His truth.   It came to transfuse new energy into man
and man's religion ;  it comes to point the better way,
and to foreshadow the radiant glories now beneath the
horizon ;  it comes saying, 'Prepare ye the way of the
Lord—make His paths straight by straightening thine
own !'  It comes to infuse new and glowing hope in
every heart bowed down ;  and from the hill-tops and
the valleys of the world alike, it points man's vision
upward, and bids him, in the midst of all his trouble
and sorrow, to 'Remember, God is there ! up there !
In the steep and radiant sky He paints the picture of
the YET TO BE, and sending spiritual duplicates thereof
to His children in their deep sleep, bids the dreamer
behold them, treasure their memory, and to live—live
highly, purely nobly, manfully !  Live, live, and die no
more forever !'

Spiritualism—true Spiritualism—is one expression
and element of the soul of the age—an age whose body
is exceedingly corrupt ;  and it so quickens the intuitions of some of the watchers on the tower, that they
can already see the glimmer of the rising sun of glad-

ness—a sun too, whose glorious beams will dissipate
all the fogs and mists now bending over human heads,
and shutting out the light of higher heavens than op-
tician's glass can ever reveal.  Aye, truly do some behold the hither end of the bow of promise, and these are
singing the song of approaching joy :

> " The wiser time will surely come
> When this fine overplus of night,
> No longer sullen, slow or dumb,
> Shall leap to music and to light.
> In that new childhood of the world,
> Life of itself shall dance and play,
> *Fresh blood through Time's shrunk veins be hurled,*
> And Labor meet Delight half-way."

There can be no doubt but that the days of Evil by
God are numbered—those arising from obsession included.

Gazing still adown the lane of light, I saw that a
process had been commenced in the soul of the man
upon the stage, who was about to address the assem-
bled crowd—a process, too, which would ultimately set
him free—for already his sphere indicated the beginning of the reparatory action ; and in precisely so far
as he helped himself, and shook off the influence of
others, just so far did one or two attendant and radi-
antly bright beings, of a high and pure order, assist
and protect him ; and, gazing upon the scroll of his destiny, I saw that in five years from that day he would
complete his apprenticeship, and stand before the world
no longer an automaton, but a firm and solid-minded
man ; that, no longer lecturing upon useless metaphysical abstractions, he would, for three years, preach the
gospel of truth and true Christianity, with a power and
effect never to be attained by human machines, but only

6

by good, well-developed, unfolded, and harmonic souls.
*   *   *   *   Slowly the opening through which this
great practical drama was seen, and its beautiful teachings conveyed to me, closed up, and once more I stood
solitary in the midst of my aural sphere.   Looking now
toward the point wherefrom I had turned a little while
before, my eyes observed that the apparent attack upon
its integrity was still going on; but this was mechanical
only, for my mind was dwelling upon things of far more
interest and importance.   Amongst other lessons gained
during the brief time that I had been dead to earth,
alive to a higher existence, was this: The terrestrial
world itself is really spiritual, could mankind but per-
ceive it.   For instance, every tree, shrub, flower, plant
and animal is not only possessed of an ideal and thought-
representative value, but they are themselves essentially spiritual; for the bark, and leaves, and woody
fiber, the flower-petals, and all that physical eyes behold, are not the things they seem, but are merely the
outer-coats and coverings, the cloaks and garments which
the things themselves put on; the nature of the external
form being determined by a law integral to the very thing
itself, just as a picture is merely the physical embodi-
ment of an idea in the artist's mind.   Unfavorable conditions cramp some trees physically; but burn the wood,
and the spirit of the tree is as perfect as the Infinite
One could fashion it.   So also with human trees.   In-
teriorly, many men and women are better than they
seem, and many are worse.   Still, be it remembered,
that beauty and symmetry is natural to trees, even though
storms, and snow, and fierce winds dismember and render them hideous; so also virtue and goodness is natural to the human soul, while vice and deformity are

artificial and conditional acquisitions. A man may lose an eye, leg, arm, be disfigured by accident or disease to an extent that will render him hideous to all embodied beholders; but let him die, or, while living, be gazed at by spiritual beings, and his legs, arms, eyes—the whole man stands revealed in all his true proportions.* This discovery gave me joy, indeed; for I had known some whose disfigurements had pained me exceedingly. No maimed forms ascend from gory fields of battle; no crippled people inhabit the Soul-worlds. Thank God for that! True, in the regions midway, there are many who, being insane, or immersed in phantasies, insist on appearing as they were on earth, or even in worse plight; but this is not necessarily so, any more than the grimaces of a clown or mountebank are the natural expressions of his features. By this time I had also learned that, with the exception stated previously in reference to the essences of things, the two worlds—earthly and spiritual—were in scarce any one thing alike, as had been taught by those whose books upon the subject I had lost so much valuable time in reading—finely written and eloquent books, truly—yet, after all, I found them now to be filled with :

"Rich windows that exclude the light
And passages that lead to—nothing."

My experience demonstrated that the two worlds are not equal, continuous, or even resemblant. In fact, they, being disparates, many failures must necessarily be made in attempting, in the present state of the languages at least, to convey adequate verbal representa-

* A man's spiritual form may be cut, shot, or slashed through ten thousand times, yet never a bullet or knife will injure him; and this for reasons already set forth in earlier pages of this book.

tions of things above to those below—not with the col-
loquial and literary, nor even with the aid of modern
philosophical, scientific, metaphysical nor theological
technics now in use amongst thinkers.   But the people
are longing for information respecting the soul's condition subsequent to its departure from the rudimental
scene ; they want to know what a soul is, where it goes,
how it gets there, and what are its environments thereafter ; consequently the essay to impart the required information must be made, even at the risk of adding to
the hundred failures already made.   The word VAST, for
instance, when I apply it in the description about to be
given, is not to be understood in the sense of enormous-
ness, but in a different one altogether.   Well then, in
a short time, the side of the sphere yielded to the applied force, and broke completely in two from top to bottom, and the two sides instantly thereafter resolved themselves into a vast archway—vast in beauty, grandeur,
color, form and symbolic meaning.   Toward the inviting passage thus presented, as if impelled by an invisible, but powerful force, I slowly moved involuntarily.
Upon reaching it, the entire sphere seemed to draw
into me.   I stepped over the threshold ; turned to look
at it—but, lo ! it had vanished.

This taught me a lesson.   I saw that if one chose to
do so, he might, while on earth, and in the Middle State,
draw his sphere within him, and lie concealed in the
deeps of his own being, unreadable by any, save God
and the dwellers of the Soul-world.   This is effected at
first by strong efforts of the will,—(both Napoleons are
illustrative instances),—which soon becoming a habit,
is effected by the soul mechanically. ' At first, upon finding myself alone, and my sphere absorbed, I could not

comprehend the celestial magic by means of which it was effected. No opportunity, however, was then afforded for investigations of the mystery, for a crowd of new marvels rolled on me, in such quick succession, that all my soul became at once deeply engaged. My vision was clear, distinct and far-reaching, and thousands of objects existed upon all sides to attract it. The scene was the realization of the fairest, brightest Arcadie of which wrapt poet ever dreamed. Hundreds upon hundreds of the most beautiful of human creatures that imagination ever pictured were there, in all the glory of a *fête* in Heaven. Not a line of care or sorrow traced its course upon a single cheek or brow of the vast multitudes who thronged the glades and gardens of that wondrous realm. It was the actuality of the fairest ideal of earth's noblest poet, and something more ; for there was a nameless something about it that earth can never give. Magnificent and lofty trees, the movement of whose very leaves was sweetest music ; streams of living water, whose ripples flashed back ten thousand magic hues of loveliness, to a stately but unmoving Sun in the mid-heaven ; flowers of rare conformation, whose colors and fragrance put earthly roses to the blush, unfolded their glory-cups to God's bright sentinel, and praised His name in incense-offerings ; bowers of shrubs, resplendent meadows, stately groves, adown the sylvan glades of which scores of merry children trooped, and soul-wed lovers wandered, were a few of the things upon which I gazed in a raptness whereof poets may conceive, but which to colder souls will be mysteries for long. Splendid palaces towered in the distance, while near at hand, on the green banks of many a singing brook, numberless cottages gemmed the scene.

Even animals were there—some of familiar and well-known forms, some of new and singular shape and peculiar grace. Birds—rare-birds, of the most brilliant plumage, played amidst the trees, and warbled songs of strange melody and meaning. Such, and a thousand other things beside, not one of which I had ever imagined to exist, were constituents of the scene upon which my eye now rested for the first time. Taken as a whole, the entire vivorama was, in its nature and effect, at that time, incomprehensible, and at first somewhat oppressive; but this latter feeling was very ephemeral, and gave place to a delight, at once pure, deep and unalloyed.

When this scene first burst upon me, my attitude was one of unmingled surprise, and I retained it all the while my soul was drinking in the glory. Casting my eyes groundward, the vision rested upon an opake, cloud-like soil; and while inwardly wondering whether the soil was really what it seemed to be, or not, I heard my name called in well-remembered tones. Turning hastily, I found the sounds came from a grove hard by, whence three persons were seen approaching me. They drew nearer, and I had no difficulty in recognizing one of the comers to be Nellie. I knew her by her general air, not from the appearance of her person; for that was entirely changed, and no longer appearing a mere child, she looked to have reached the happy medium state wherein the girl just begins to be the woman. She was very pretty when she had assumed the status of a child, but *now* she fairly blazed with a beauty most transcendent. By her side moved a young and noble-looking man, yet one around whom there floated an atmosphere of Power, Will, and Intenseness, that inspired me at first with something very akin to awe.

His garb was decidedly oriental, and became his features wonderfully, while at the same time it imparted a freedom and grace, that added to, instead of detracting from his dignity.  Observing that I scrutinized his apparel, he smiled, and  glanced sidewise at my own.  I did the same, and it flashed upon me instantly that myself, instead of being  habited after the fashion of the Occident, I to others must present the appearance of a sultana of the ancient East.  Again my eye met his, and in that meeting there was a mingling too, for I felt and knew that he was mine, and I his own ; that we two were henceforward to be as one—for a period at least, if not forever.  Poor me—I did not then know how long ' forever ' is.  On earth, in love affairs, the term means two months, more or less.  It stands for a longer period here, yet does not include the categories of all the eternities—quite.  I had forgotten that states constitute the marks of duration in the Soul-worlds, and not the tickings of a clock ; but so inveterate is the force of habit and ideal associations, that at first it was almost impossible to predicate sequences upon anything else than lapse of time, or to dissociate the memories of the past, and the menstruum of the events whereof they are the shadowy records, from the realities of the then present, and the action of the New Principia operative in the Soul-world.  Besides this, I had been theretofore deeply tinctured with the folly-essence, so much of which has been distilled by modern eolists, and would-be philosophers, to addle the brains of sensible people, and to dilute what little of common sense themselves—the eolists—might chance to possess.  I had with thousands of others believed that the doctrine of 'eternal affinities' was true; and that every one would somewhere meet with a congenial partner, in whose society all the coming cycles of Time would be joyously passed. I have outgrown that folly long since. The doctrine is a false one for this brief reason. God alone is infinite. No human being is infinite, save in capacity for acquirement; therefore the human soul must be fed by that alone which is superior in its nature, at every stage of its growth, progress or unfoldment; for which reason no one soul can forever supply the demands of another. No two souls develope in equal or parallel lines, or at the same rate, for which reason one *must* outgrow its affinities for another; besides which marriage in the Soul-world is an entirely different institution, as to its nature, condition, purpose, result and effect, to what it is on earth. Lust and passion, selfish interests, and ten thousand other things pertain to marriage on the earth, which enter not at all into that of the loftier stages of human existence. On earth, at best, love and affection are plebeian. In the Soul-worlds they are imperial! In the former these things go begging—in the latter, never. On earth the person loving often embalms the loved one in his or her own sphere, and then clings to the worthless thing thus infiltrated, thus loving the self and not another. Being therefore all on one side, there is no mutuality. Such is not the case in the Sunny Land!

The glowing son of the Orient drew near to me, and I to him. Our spheres touched; they blended—and in an instant I knew more of what love and tenderness really meant, than in all the long years I had lived before.

When first gazing on my reflected image in the floor-mirror, I had suspected the nature and fervor of the regal passion ; but now, as he touched me—as our spheres blended, and strange thrills went bounding and dancing through every avenue of my being, I realized that not one half of the reality had ever been imagined, even in a remote degree.

Among people of the higher orders in human society, the testimony of the 'hear-says' is not regarded as being of the most satisfactory or convincing kind. This book and those which are to follow it, is, and will be, addressed only to those who think and feel for themselves; are intended for those who can pierce through the mere formalism of narrative and statement, to the solid principles underlying them. And for this reason, therefore, have I forborne to repeat many strange and wonderful things told me by him who now stood at my right side notwithstanding that such repetitions would be deeply interesting to those people who believe they have immortal souls, but are not quite certain of that fact. It is better to tell what I saw, felt, learned and experienced, than to relate what others told me.

I may remark, *en passant,* that the sentence 'stood by my side' appeared to be well founded ; for although I knew my comrades to be spirits, yet they were to me quite as really and palpably human, as was the mother at whose dear breast I drew in life many a long year ago.

Mention has been made of the fact that knowledge comes to a person in the higher life, just in proportion to that person's fitness for its reception, the Use in the great economy which it will subserve, and the Good that it will do. I was now in a condition to be taught, and therefore the doors of the soul's knowledge-chambers were swung wide upon their hinges, so to speak, and into them the following answers flowed naturally and sweetly, in response to self-propounded questions concerning all that had transpired since my emergement from the interior of my personal into the general sphere of that portion of the immense Soul-world wherein I now found myself. It has already been stated, and understood by the reader, that the sphere in which the memoramic tableaux moved across its diameter, was the personal out-surrounding of the individual. Precisely the same, with the exception of being on a vastly grander scale, was this new Soul-realm whereof I had become an inhabitant. The fact is, I had been in it from the dawn of the second hour of my disembodiment, only that the opacity of my vision and the walls of my sphere had prevented me from realizing it, just as a person with nebulous eyes is unaware of the glories of a landscape in the midst of which he stands, alongside of a friend whose eyes are clear and good, and whose soul fairly dances with rapture as he scans the sea of loveliness, which is all shut out from the other.

All truths go in couples. I had just discovered one, and its mate very soon thereafter appeared. It was this: What I had thought to be an attempt to break down the walls of my circumvallated sphere, prove now not to have been the work of another, but was the result of the operation of a natural law of the soul—that of In-TROMISSION ; but which law does not act until after certain others have effected peculiar changes in the individual—just as grace and resignation succeed the tumult and agony of repentance and remorse. This law of intromission finds its humble analogy in the grub and subsequent gold-winged butterfly ; and also in the chick, whose tiny bill perforates its hard surrounding stone-and-mortar sphere—for it batters and pecks at the sides of its prison-shell and cell when the process of incubation is nearly finished, whereupon the bird enters upon a new phase of existence ; and so also does the human soul, when *its* period is completed. All Nature is a system of births.

These things are stated and these principles laid down, in order to undeceive those who have accepted as true the many crude and materially defective hypotheses purporting to come from 'Royal Circles' in the Soul-world, through scores of modern eolists. My design is to show the rightly dying what they must expect when rightly dead. True, there is an increasing number of Spiritualists and others who accept the revelations of mediums on the principle *interdum stultus bene loqui-tur ;* yet there are others who accept nine-tenths of what purports to come from the worlds beyond, merely because of its claim. Truth will bear its own weight; if not now, then in the course of coming time ; still it is ever and always best for every one to reason well on every proposition or statement offered as coming from the world of spirits—this book's contents, of course, included. Amongst other notions, which along with my co-believers on earth I had imbibed, was that which declares the Spirit-land to be a fixed revolving zone— a sort of second edition of the earth and its adjuncts. I had expected to find my last home on one of those aerial belts, occupying space just as a town or city does. What an error ! No two antipodal things can be more unlike—for I found that all the untold magnificence that now lay outspread before me was, just as my former

sphere, but the general out-creation, elimination or projection from the countless hosts of beatified and radiant souls who dwell together and create their own
scenery and surrounding, just as a man creates *chateaux
en espagne*, only that in this latter he exists forever on
the *outside*—in the former, dwells *within* them. In
other words, the realm whereof I was an inhabitant
was not physical in any sense, nor were any of its subjects or objects ; neither were they phantasmal, but
were spiritual, in the sublime sense of that much abused
term ; and although not permanant or fixed, as is a
town on earth, yet were none the less true and real.

In order to better comprehend what sort of a place
is that world wherein I met Nellie and *mine*, it will be
well if the reader remember that everything save
thought is perishable. For instance you have a thought
of a pink satin dress, made up in a peculiar style ; your
father has a thought of a new cottage, complete in all
its parts ; your brother invents a new-modelled carriage for your mother's use ; while your farmer invents
a new building, which will serve at once for carriage-
house and barn—and all four of you forthwith proceed
to realize your several ideals ; and in a month the new
barn stands upon the brookside, the new cottage peeps
forth from its bower of elms, the new carriage rolls
along, and in it, clad in your pink satin, you enjoy a
ride with the dear old mother. Three days thereafter
the cottage and barn catch fire, and the dress and carriage become ashes, and so do all your patterns and
models ; yet your thoughts are living, still fresh as
ever, and all that is necessary, is for all four of you to
once more embody them in material garb, and in another month a stranger, having seen the first and not

knowing of the catastrophe, would swear that what now he beheld was the same formerly so much admired—and he would be right. The ideas are the same, albeit the material raiment is not. John Doe is still John Doe, whether in rags or riches ; why not, then, John's thought be the same ?

It will be well to remember that GOD IS A THINKER—that the vast material universe is the visible result of a single effort of a single faculty-organ of the Deific brain, and—tremendous thought !—that faculty-organ will yet make myriads of new movements, each one followed by results still more stupendous and magnificent than the vast array of starry suns which now light up the Halls of Silence and of Space ! Again : the spiritual or rather the thinking part of man is all there is of permanency about the human being. His body is the sport of Death, and his aid-de-camp Disease ! but his soul can never be touched by the former, nor forever be harmed by the latter ! for soul is not to be *permanently* injured by any power subservient to the infinite God. All there is of man is his thought-power ; the THINK is himself. By this we know him ; and he who gives forth most of himself, if he be bad, does the most injury to the species and the world. If he be good, such an one lives longest in men's hearts, on historic page, and in the traditions of the race.

The Spiritual Universe ! What a mighty conception ! And yet, even that, grand as it is—for all the material globes of space, chained together, are, after all, but a mere little island floating, like a bottle, upon the crest of a single wavelet of the Infinite Sea !—yet, even that Spiritual Universe itself, with its amazing SOUL REALMS, made up of countless Soul-systems,

each of which latter is composed of the blended spheres
of innumerable millions of separate dualities—even all
this—all these, I say, are but the result of a single effort
of another distinct faculty-organ of the GREAT BRAIN ;
yet even this grand result will be surpassed by every
one of the myriad efforts that same faculty-organ is destined to put forth.    And when it shall have moved more
times than there are stars in the sky, grains of sand
upon the sea-shores, leaves in the forests, or aspirations
in the human soul—greater than all—the end will not
be even foreshadowed, nor God's laboratory one whit
exhausted !   Man himself, generically speaking, wherever localized beneath the bending dome of the imperial
Heaven, is but the result of another single effort—of
another single organ of faculty.   [For although man is
nidulated in and developed to personal distinctness
through matter, yet the very nature of the thinking
principle at once forbids the assumption that it sprung
from any combination of material essences, howsoever
subtle they may be, and at once explodes the spiritualistic doctrine that matter continues on into spirit.   No ;
soul is discreted from matter by a gulf so wide that an
infinite vaccuum exists between the coarsest soul and
the most sublimated etherial vapor that ever resulted,
or ever will result, from molecular attrition or chemical
resolution.   Individual monads—all men and women—
are scintillas or parts of this third great thought of the
Mighty Thinker, God ; they are corruscations from The
Over-Soul, while Matter is constituted of etherial emanations from God's Infinite Body.*]   Now every exist-

---

* I regret that the limits adjudged to this volume will not permit
an amplification of this part of our subject.  It must abide the next
book.—*Author.*

ence represents a thought of Deity ; so also man thinks himself in his actions, and fills the world with his thoughts, variously clothed ; some in iron, steel, wood, paper, ivory, cloth, palaces, engines, ships, houses, parks, gardens, and so on ; so, also, after his disembodiment, will he surround himself with soul-created forms, whose aspect, shape and texture depends altogether on the cleanliness and purity of the loom wherein these mental fabrics are woven.   The sole difference between the creations of the mortal and *post-mortem* artificer is, that, instead of arraying them in gross or coarse material, as on earth, he in the Soul-worlds, fashions the garments of such stuff as thoughts themselves are made of ; or, to give it still clearer, each thought possesses an inherent vitality of its own, as also form, proportion, and coherence.   Thus, if an engineer thinks a locomotive, all he has to do. in order to impress his thought on others, is to give it a suit of iron, brass and steel to wear, and, lo ! all the world hails, and triumphantly acknowledges the worth of the offspring of his deathless soul.

Just as soon as the man has placed metallic parts where only mental ones were previously, all the people see it, feel it, know it to be an engine—that is to say, an incarnate thought of a certain engineer.

Now, take notice all ye who think, that the combined glories of the separate sections of the great Soul-world are constituted of the *general* projections of the disembodied order, or section of an order, that compose the society around whom the sphere is seen.   There are myriads of these societies ; and no one belonging to society A can enter the sphere of society B, notwithstanding both may belong to the same general order.   True, people can visit each other there as well as anywhere else. But visitors may not be equals for all that. In each society will be found those who love and affect birds; and just as sure as he or she has a bird in the soul, just so sure will that bird be born thereof, and become, to all intents and purposes (except begetting its kind) a veritable bird. Others love trees, rivers, castles, brooks, hills, dales, vales, vineyards, gardens, groves, cottages, palaces, mountains, animals, and so on, through an interminable list, and interminable combinations of what that list may contain.

Whatever be the ideal of a man or community, just so will be the out-sphering thereof. Thus, Mohammed (and the Orientals generally) loved woman, for the sake of the sense-gratifications she was found capable of imparting. Accordingly, when his soul was transfigured, it went directly to that section of the Soul-world where were congregated those like unto himself; and, when he came back, he fired his partizans with the deepest and wildest enthusiasm ever known on earth, by telling them that the women of Paradise were fairer than the full moon, more lovely than the dawn, and that every mother's son of the faithful should be rewarded there, for all their earthly sorrows, by the absolute possession of the moderate number of seventy thousand houris.

Mohammed was not a liar nor an impostor; he told what he believed to be truth. His houris, like the birds and beasts just spoken of, were out-creations of the sensualistic mind of the sphere into which he rode on the saddle of Al Borak. Every man or woman's mind is an empire, and the higher the position each occupies upon the plane of the Harmonead, the more extensive is the domain over which they hold imperial sway. The same laws which govern an individual, also rule a community ; for a man is a man only to such extent as he prophecies and represents something higher and better than the present status. The observance of law, by persons and *en masse*, may be voluntary or habitual, or not. This being understood, it is no marvel that the things resident in the general mind should be objectified therearound as in the case of a single person, nor that in the former, as in the latter case, the things thought of should be present, as well as those which are purely symbolic and representative of the general state, the general love, the general affections and aspirations of the general mind.

As this and similar light flowed into my soul, that soul involuntarily thanked the Giver for such amazing exhibitions of his loving kindness and careful providence. I could now understand many things that were before quite mysterious, and, amongst others, why Nellie and Mine had at first shown themselves to me under the guise of Youth and Age. It was to all the quicker win my esteem and confidence, each of which are prime elements both of friendship and love. Previous to my change, I had often tried to analyze this last-named sentiment or passion (as you will), as it exists amongst the people of the world. The result of that analysis was, ' Love is a mixed passion ; its orbit is elliptical—friendship is at one of the foci, and lust at the other.' Now, however, as my enraptured vision swept the plains of immortality, I found that in the Soul-world it was something more,* but that its essential earthly character re-

* In the succeeding volume, the reader will be carried into a new

mained the same in the Middle States—or merely spiritual kingdom. With penetrating glance I swept the fields
of earth, and the result was a complete conviction that
ninety-five one-hundredths of that which goes by love's
tender, gentle name, was a compound of three constituents—Parentalism, Amative desire, and the softer element, Friendship. Hence sex, and what comes of it on
earth, is at best but the most coarse and external expression of a great soul-law, which can only fully demonstrate itself in those who are in no one respect abnormal or diseased. Sex really means more than people
even remotely suspect. In the Soul-world it does not
serve the same purposes as on earth. *There*, sex is of
mind—on earth it is of the body mainly. I had supposed it to be a fixed physical principle ; and so it is,
but it is also something more—for in the higher realms
of human being, where everything expresses itself as it
really is, and passes at its true value, it is found that
many who, as if by accident, had worn the physical
characteristics of one, were really, at soul, of the opposite sex. For instance, Male means Energy, Wisdom,
Knowledge, Power, Creation, Use—Female is the synonym of Music, Beauty, Love, Purity, Harmony, Good.
Now let two such meet in the Soul-world, and if they
are adapted to each other, their spheres—nay, their
very lives—blend together ; the result of which is mutual improvement, purification, gratification, enjoyment,
and happiness—which state of bliss continues until new
unfoldings from within shall unfit them for the further
continuance of the union ; whereupon there is a mutual

---

Soul-region, of which Love is the key ; and then the world will see
what a vast deal of knowledge exists of which man has never heard.

Pub.

separation—not because they love each other less, but some other one the more; and that other one, be it male or female, is certain to be ready for the reception of the new love. There is no jar, no ill-feeling, no discord about it. Some of these unions may last for what to man may seem to be long ages, but what the final result will be I have not space here to mention.

It often happens that human bodies are so diseased, and by mal-practice so distorted from their true uses, that pure and genuine love cannot express itself—wherefore it soon becomes a sealed mystery, and Passion usurps Love's holy throne. He or she whose nerves have become ruined, either by grief or excess, opium, rum, tobacco, Mesmerism, Oppression, Neglect, and things of that order, can never taste the ineffable joys of love that attend on those who in such regard are healthy.

Love has become either a boyish or girlish sentiment, else a sort of spasmodic fever, which possession speedily and forever chills.

In human society it has become a purchasable commodity. Women sell themselves for gew-gaws—for a home—to escape parental tyranny and unjust espionage. Men buy them, and think they are gaining love—not realizing that joys or pleasures bought at *any* price are not the realities for which the bargain was made, but only counterfeits, which all too soon demonstrate their own worthlessness. Buy a woman! purchase a man! bargain for love! How much is Sunshine worth a quart? How does Goodness sell by the barrel? It is very easy for either man or woman to buy each other's garments, but the souls beneath them must be won by wooing. Physical possession never yet satisfied a soul, and never will.   Soul naturally shrinks from scales, weights, measures, and yard-tapes ; and it quite as intensely despises all protestation.   Why ?   Because pure love is undemonstrative.   Demonstration proceeds from volition, but love flows from a fountain altogether back of will.   People may be proud of their *property*, but the human can have no true deep joys, save such as spring from love, pure, strong, earnest, spontaneous and reciprocal.   Whatever is not thus based is distasteful to the soul in its higher moods.   Joys of a tumultuous character, such as spring from impulsiveness and passion, are both short-lived and exhaustive ; and the pestilent brood of anger, jealousy, hatred, disgust and trouble, ever and always follow in their train—priests of Misery, prime ministers of Evil !   On the other hand, pure manly, womanly, *human* love, is recuperative, re-creative—is a virtue-exhilarant, tonic of good, vice-dispellant, and health-promotive ; while contentment of heart, peace of mind, security, trust, calmness and serenity, are its attendant ministers.   God, who made us, well knows that there is more of good than evil in our hearts, by virtue of our ancestry—Nature and Himself ; yet, for His own grandly-purposed end, He permits us all to wade to Heaven through the malarious swamps of hell !—permits us all to experiment and suffer, in order that we may grow powerful and strong, and thus be fitted for the tremendous destiny that awaits all who wear the human form on the thither side of Time.   People feel before they think, and the act of one single impulsive moment not seldom enshrouds an entire life in gloom.   Have mercy, therefore—always !   Mere thinking without feeling is quite as bad—nay, worse ; for it freezes up the fountains of the soul !   Something will grow and blossom even on an arid desert ; but the iceberg is never gladdened by the presence and growth of one green thing upon its crystal sides—not even moss. So with soul ! It is bad to sin from impulse, but far worse to do wrong from settled purpose. There are two classes of persons who err. Those who do so from no evil intent at heart, soon vastate their load, and become residents of the Soul-world ; those who sin from the head, pass into the Middle State and become the infesting demons of modern spiritual mediums.

The deepest wrongs of human existence are those against the inward soul and sense of right. Illustration : Whatsoever earthly couple shall assume the dreadful responsibility, not only of imbittering each other's lives, but of incarnating a family of souls in discordant bodies, inevitably fashion a hell-sphere for themselves in the Middle State, whence they shall not go forth until the uttermost farthing is paid. The recent partial uplifting of the veil separating earth from regions beyond, has had the effect of removing the sense of accountability from the minds of a great many people, who, having conversed with the dead through raps and tips, and hearing no valid accounts of a burning lake of literal fire and brimstone, straightway fall to laughing at the devil, and snap their fingers at the bare idea of hell. If they could but realize that Devil means Badness, and Hell is the synonym of suffering and self-inflicted torture, the laugh would not be quite so loud and long, nor the finger-snapping near so frequent, as at present.

Such persons reason very superficially—in this respect following the lead of one of their self-elected Prophets, a Regent of Hell itself, and Earthly Prime

Minister to all the chief fiends of the Middle States—
and leap to the conclusion that all a man's sins are
atoned for while embodied—that he is not to be pun-
ished at all after death ; and hence they cut off all re-
straining cords, give a loose rein to boasting and lying,
and solace themselves and blind others with the absurd
sophism that 'Whatever is, is right'—murder, robbery,
concubinage, divorcing two, three, or a dozen, for the
sake of obscene dalliance, and semi-legal infamy—are
just the thing to rid the world of evil and make society
a bond of fraternal fellowship ! And such a system
dares to call itself 'Spiritual,' 'Harmonial, 'Reformatory'! It does. But, thank God ! the days of Pseudo-
Spiritualism, in whose train myriads of insanities,
wrongs, irreligions of all pestilent sorts, non-immortal-
ism, and a host of importations from the pit, follow as
harlots follow an army, scattering death, horror and de-
vastation on every hand ! Yes, thank Heaven ! the
false will soon be succeeded by a true and godly Spiritualism ; and instead of being possessed and obsessed
by the maleficent harpies from the mid-region, as is too
often the case now, people will be enlightened, instructed and saved from ruin, instead of being plunged
therein ; for the noble, the true, the religious and pure
spirits, from realms where God's presence sanctifies all
hearts, will come to aid man in his hour of greatest
need. The true spiritualization will bring peace on
earth and good will among men, instead of hatred between couples, and absurd envyings and jealousies
amongst mediums and believers ; it will effect the destruction of all spiritualistic and philosophic pretence,
the current sophistry of 'All-rightism,' pretentious cant
and mock philanthropy, whereof so much now floats

upon the surface of the singular sea called, falsely, 'Spiritualism.' A man is no more a Spiritualist because he believes in physically demonstrated immortality, than a child is a horse because born in a stable.

If people cannot be Spiritualists without submitting to the pestilent control of wretches from the Middle State, or without losing conscience, virtue, and moral cleanliness, they had better let the whole subject alone, and rest as contented as may be with the faiths and creeds bequeathed by their ancestors. It will not do to meddle with things so mysterious as Spiritualism, in its nature, influence and results, unless perfectly fortified in God, with a strong and holy purpose and a resolute and unbending will.

As I gazed out upon the surrounding glories of my new world, I could not forbear or repress a desire, if possible, to take one glance at those who yet dwelt in infamy, although disembodied. This wish, though a silent one, was perceived by him who stood near me. Sadly, mournfully, he gazed down into my soul, made no reply in words, but slowly placing me between himself and Nellie, who had been joined by one to whom she was very dear indeed, directed our steps towards the pleasant grove before alluded to. Passing swiftly through this, we soon came to its outer verge, from which, to my utter astonishment, we could look down into a very gulf of horrors, as if from the edge of a frightful precipice. I knew that I stood upon the borders of THE MIDDLE STATE. Believing that more is to be gained by descriptions of the good and excellent than by exciting the horror of deformity, I forbear, in this introductory volume, to recount the terrors of the awful Hell of the vicious and the self-damned soul.

Suffice it that I beheld scenes of lust, insanity, debauchery, and all vileness, sufficiently dreadful to appal the stoutest heart of any sane one who dwells in the same awful phantasies, insanities and evils. Around the heads of those who wandered up and down its noisome lanes and alleyways, were wreaths of twining, writhing serpents, instead of crowns and coronets of light. There were many who believed in literal hells of fire, and such were surrounded by spheres of flame, and therein must burn and suffer so long as the fearful phantasy shall last, and till they be redeemed by self-effort. Drunkards, libertines, gamblers—all evil things and persons were there, along with atheists and other intellectual sinners. On an eminence in the midst of the deepest and most fearful hell, I saw the exact image of one of earth's so-called great philosophers; and it was given me to know that the man there represented was doomed, when his life on earth shall be ended, to expiate his terrible offences against God, nature, religion, and his own conscience, and his fellow-men, by sufferings too terrible to be adequately described.

"Men know the right, and well approve it too ;
They know the wrong, and yet the wrong pursue."

So with the philosopher. The man knew better than he taught ; and when he dies, unless he shall repent, his doom is a hell whose terrors are indeed fearful ; nor will he be able to emerge thence, before the cries of his scores of thousands of deluded victims, some of whom have been driven to vice, crime, insanity and suicide by his execrable teachings, shall be changed into appeals to God in his behalf.

One of the punishments after death consists in atoning

for one's bad and baleful influence while on earth; and the more extensive this has been, the more fearful the penalty self-inflicted therefor. The man who has taught millions that God is a revengeful being; that He ever stands ready to hurl ruin and destruction on the world; to rain literal fire and brimstone on the earth, and thus frighten people into woe and insanity, must abide the consequences, and in the world beyond be compelled to face the dreadful music himself may have evoked. And so with others, let their influence be what it may. Eternal justice rules the destiny of mankind; and sooner or later its behests must and will be accomplished.

I turned in affright from the horrible scene, but not without reaping a mental treasure from what I had beheld, both of the Soul-world and the Middle-state. It will be remembered that I had asked certain questions, which were not responded to. These questions, and others had been uppermost in my mind all along, and now as our faces were once again turned toward the bright scenes of the Soul-world, I realized that neither it nor its fearful antipodes were absolute fixtures or fixities. The human soul is kaleidescopic. The scenes it forever conjures up before it from out its mighty deeps, and by which it is surrounded, are constantly and forever changing, no matter whether its locality be on earth, in the mid-region of the great world's atmosphere, on the confines of the two great states, embodied or free; or whether it be a dweller in the city of divine souls, the law is the same and incessantly operative. Change is written on all things; and although in essence soul can never alter, yet its moods and phases constantly do, else Hell would be a permanency, Earth stand still, and Heaven itself grow monotonous. In

7

accordance with this principle, therefore, no scene in the Soul-world is a permanency, but as soon as one has produced all the joy it can to those from whom it is an outgrowth or projection, it changes, but ever toward the higher and more resplendent.

One question there was, of great weight and importance, which I asked of my soul, and to which a response after a time flowed in. It was this : Do spiritual beings live eternally as distinct entities, or are they after a time absorbed into Deity, as the higher Brahmins and other orientalists maintain? The reply to this was : Reasoning from what any human being *knows*, no matter how lofty he may be in intellect, the decision arrived at must be conjectural at best; for whether we are to be forever, can only be known to Him who taketh no one into his counsels. But reasoning from what we already know concerning the nature of soul, mind, thought, and capacity, the inference is plain that no absolute absorption will ever take place, but that the double-unit man will forever preserve his distinct and marked personality.

Are idiots immortal ? *Answer*—All that is born of human parents, all beings who took their external forms through the agency and channels of the male brain, nerves, prostate and testes, and the female matrix, are *necessarily* immortal.

*Question*—But animals have been impregnated by male brutes of the human species, and human females have borne offspring to brutes—if human medical testimony, and the confessions of parties implicated are to be credited ; but whether such cases have or have not occurred, suppose it *were* to take place, would such offspring, whether begotten of, or by an animal, one of the parents being undoubtedly human, be immortal? *Answer*—As monsters, no! Idiots, both of whose parents are human, are essentially immortal. Idiotcy is but another name for weakness; and a monad having once put forth its powers sufficient to build itself a full human body, no matter how imperfect, must necessarily put forth more of its inherent energies, if not in one world or sphere, then in another, in the nurseries of the Soul-world; and as it grows strong it gradually approaches the point of self-ness—the Ego will be attained. It is only a question of time and condition. Not so with semi-brutes.

*Question*—But women have conceived from human union, yet owing to some accident or fright, have brought forth monsters. Are these immortal? *Answer*—Nothing that is not *human* is immortal, in the sense of self-poisedness. and self-presence. If these monsters are cerebrally human, and their malformation be merely limb-distortion, then that thing is destined to supermundane existence.

*Question*—But human bodies, though brainless ones, have been born of women?—Well, they are not immortal. Violent chemical actions *en utero* has destroyed the conditions of successful monad-gestation, while perpetuating the vegetative *fœtal* life. Of course the thing is soulless.

*Question*—But the monad *had* begun to put forth its energies. What then has become of it; is it forever blotted out of being? *Answer*—There stands a human female, but the body you see is not herself. The soul is her, not the flesh it wears. The monsters treated of in medical works are but the product of body—not of soul. In order to an immortality, the germ or monad must pass from the spiritual atmosphere interflowing the material or oxygenic one, into the nostrils and brains and soul of a male, thence through the parts and processes already mentioned. Now the human form born brainless is of the nature of an abortion ; and the question arises, are abortions immortal ? The answer is : A human germ, when first planted at the gestative center, undergoes a variety of rapid and extraordinary changes, assuming successively the typal forms of all the lesser orders of animated nature, from the jelly-fish to the perfectly human. In some women these processes are pushed with extraordinary vigor and speed, so that at the end of a very short period the *fœtus* possesses all the requisites for permanency except physical vigor. If then abortion takes place, the nursling is provided for and grows to comparative perfection, in the Soul-worlds of course. Such beings constitute a distinct and separate order of souls, and are, by the great soul law, condemned to come to earth, and by association and affiliation with embodied persons, through magnetic *rapport*, experience the pleasures and pains of self-development. These spirits will be treated of hereafter, when I come to write concerning "THE REALM OF THE FAY."

But to our subject. If abortion take place before the monad has, in the womb, put forth its powers to a degree wherein the human characteristics rise above *all* the lower forms, before its shape is *perfectly* formed, then immortality does not follow.

But what becomes of the monad, the germ, the human point, the divine spark, the pivot ? *Answer*—It remains with and in the *fœtal* body till dissolution and decay shall set it free. Whereupon it floats again in the spiritual atmosphere, until it is inhaled by a human male again, whereupon it is, perhaps, and perhaps not, sent forth upon its mission once again.

*Question*—We sometimes see double men, as the twins of Siam ; and others still more remarkable, as one body with two heads; are there two souls also ?  *Answer*—Every true human brain contains a true and independent human soul.   All men's brains contain vast numbers of monads; hundreds of these seek incarnation *on every occasion*, but only one or two, very rarely three or more, succeed at *that time !*  The rest, those that fail, float about as before.

*Question*—At what period of life do men begin to attract these monads?  *Answer*—At puberty, owing to peculiar chemical changes in the physical constitution ; and females are capable of receiving and nursing them when a corresponding change has taken place in them.

*Question*—Can impregment occur without physical contact?  *Answer*—Yes; by aid of artificial means, a monad may be successfully introduced, and life ensue ; but a very weak and imperfect life it must be, of necessity.

Having once entered upon this grand subject, I determined to make the series of questions nearly, if not quite, exhaustive ; and, therefore, continued my inquiries, receiving answers as before—for, be it again repeated, no well-meaning human being can possibly ask a question, the answer to which is not recorded somewhere upon the secret tablets of the soul.  In response to further interrogatories, many grand truths came flowing forth into the halls of consciousness ; and, amongst other things, I learned that the purpose of sex on the earths was pure cohabitation, in proper human and God-sanctioned mar-

riage, with prolification, or soul-incarnation, as the result.    But I also saw that this purpose was accomplished on earth, and that *that* use of sex was ended at
death ; that it absolutely does *not* exist in the Soul-
world.    But in the Middle State, as a terrible phantasy, lust and all other abominations abound ; and I
saw that one great cause of the moral looseness of thousands of sensitive-nerved people on earth resulted from
the infernal possessions and obsessions of their persons
by delegations from those realms of darkness and—to
all but themselves—unmitigated horror.    A sensitive
man or woman—no matter how virtuously inclined—
may, unless by prayer and constant watchfulness they
prevent it, and keep the will active and the sphere entire, be led into the most abominable practices and habits.    Many of these denizens of the mid-regions of space
are insane—in the higher sense all are so—and to them
lust and its gratifications, dram-drinking, and mal-practice of all sorts, is a reality, although to others they are
cruel phantasies.    The belief of these unfortunates results from their former habits, voluntary self-illusion,
and their old memories and associations, and they are
devil-kings, gamblers, and keepers of scraglios—something on the same principle that a straw-crowned maniac
is to himself, and other of his ilk, a regal and potent
brow-gemmed monarch—a species of insanity generally
the result of personal excess and congenital disease ;
and one, also, that it is very difficult to cure, either in the
Spirit-world or anywhere else, for the reason that no
man can be healed, morally or physically, from or by
external applications ; the recreative work must be
commenced and carried on from within, or not at all.

    Are the destinies of all human beings parallel ?    *An-*

*swer*—No. On earth there are seven distinct orders of mankind, and so there is beyond it. It is difficult to name these last without resorting to Oriental terms ; but, as these will serve to convey something of the truth, I will attempt to classify them as follows : 1st, Spirits—Angels ; 2nd, Seraphs ; 3rd, Arsaphs ; 4th, Eons ; 5th, Arsasaphs ; 6th, Arch-Eons ; 7th, The Antarphim.

Is this all ? No. For the highest of the last five orders ultimate in a Perfection whereof the human mind cannot conceive. They become Deions, a supreme order of creative intelligences and energies, whose power, in combination, is only second to that of the Infinite God Himself. These constitute the towering hierarchy of the supernal Heaven. Their number is infinite. Nor hath ever a man born on earth reached nearer their glorious state than the second on the list, (Seraphs).

They are creative energies, you say ; if so, where is the field of their activities ? *Answer*—The Amorphous Universe, circumvolving the material creation !

Is space then bounded ? Yes !

By what ? I have just answered.

But what proof is there that this tremendous statement is correct? *Answer*—The nebulous masses revealed by the telescope ; masses constantly being ladled out, so to speak, of the immense sea of nascent matter, by the awful powers to whom that mighty task is assigned, and by those same powers changed or condensed into fire-mist, fire, cometary bodies, suns, planets, life-bearing earths !

Then man is, in very deed, almost a—God ?—You have said !

He creates worlds, and becomes the deity of his creation?—Man is a godling!

These were a few of the answers that came to me, as we turned from the precipice, and moved once more toward the sylvan grove!

Measured by earthly clocks, I had been but two hours in the Soul-world, but felt that I had endured for centuries.

I soon discovered the reason of this. There is, as said before, a great sympathetic chain extending from soul to soul, over and through all past time, and up to God likewise; and on the plane of this great Sympathia, at every point, some one stands; that some one can scan the past, the present, and the future, just in proportion to his or her unfolding; and the true blending of that soul with some other, puts this last in possession of all the other may have attained. I loved and was loved by one who stood high thereon, and the intuitions of my soul were quickened by his presence.

Purity is the price of power. * * *  * Years of earth have passed since that auspicious opening of the inner life. Much greater and higher knowledge has since flowed into my soul, portions of which will, ere long, be given to the world by the same pen which indited every line this book contains—save the preface. At present I am, with *Mine*, endeavoring to gain wisdom, as hand in hand, heart bound up in heart, and soul blended with soul, we together are happily, joyously, climbing up the sky.

C. T.

# PART SECOND.

## Thotmor—The Sphinx.

### THE DISENTHRALMENT.

THE DUKE. Good Palmer, is thy tale so wondrous strange?
PALMER. Else had I not sought auditor so wise.
    'Tis the best legend ever yet was heard,
    Unless I mar it sadly in the telling. .

SOMETHING very unusual has taken place within a little while; what it is can scarcely be told, can only dimly be understood, and still more vaguely conveyed to others. This change, this mysterious something, pertains not to body, but to soul, to the inner person; and while the flesh-form is apparently as ever, the strange inhabitant thereof is conscious that it is not as of yore;—nay, has passed, as it were, within these few latter days, into a new mood or phase of its wonderful being.

But a little while ago, the world—this stony world— was far dearer and more highly prized than it is to-day; and this for the reason that not now, as then, does the airy dweller of the body-house look out upon it as of yore;—no longer glances over its mountains, vales and salt seas from the windows near the ground.

It grew suddenly tired of the weight, and gloom, and lead-heavy air—air so light-distorting, which circulates just above the surface—just high enough to be breathed by those who move along the by-lanes of Vanity Fair : and the Soul took a key from its girdle, and therewith unlocked the door which alone had prevented its ascension to the upper story of the Temple ; and it saw the steps leading toward the Dome—and they were broad, inviting, well carpeted and lighted. Up the steps it went, and presently reached a lofty apartment, within which there fell a flood of glorious effulgence ; and this light was clear, and pure, and pearly white ; and it streamed into the apartment,—this upper chamber of the soul,— through a glorious arched window, toward which it drew near, and lo ! all the world looked different, as did the stars that hung out upon the night, and the beautiful pale moon, and God's rockets—the meteors —*so* beautiful !

There was an occupant of that chamber, one who had been slumbering on a couch therein for many, many years ; but the grating of the door upon its rusted hinges and the rattle of the keys disturbed this sleeper, and woke it up. . The being was a female—so very beautiful that I loved her from the first, for she was *very* beautiful, and came to me, threw her fair white arms about my neck, kissed my forehead tenderly, told me that she had slept too long, pent up in that chamber all alone.

And I loved her dearly, because she was so very pure, so virginal, so fresh and innocent, and withal so *very* beautiful ! I asked her name. " It is Devotion," she replied. Then folding me to her bosom, her tender, loving bosom, she gently drew me nearer to the window, pointed down toward the ground, and said : " The air is thick, and dank, and dark, and dense, and very murky. It is difficult to catch a glimpse of the bright orb of the Heavens, or to feel his genial ray down there, in that thick and heavy air ; but here, up here, the atmosphere is purer, and, if you look well and steadily through that pane, you will see the Spirit of God as He moves across the mighty deep!" And I looked. A great Glory was at that moment marching across the whole bright sky—a mystic but a nameless glory—and the night was very grand ; the emotions it awoke were very soft and tender, so that tears welled up at the sight from the heart of Devotion, and suffused her beautiful features. Oh, magic tears! One pearly drop fell on me, and lo! the icebergs of my soul were melted, and—I wept ;—and the waters, as they flowed, swept away many an obstacle that had thereunto impeded and obstructed my vision, and soon I was able to see the Spirit of God in everything that He had made. Seeing which, the Beautiful Maiden gently chided me for so long delaying the *coming up the stairs* and the entering of that wondrous upper chamber whose windows look out upon the world below and toward the God above. And she told me how happy I might have been in the years agone, had not the lower strata of the atmosphere hurt my vision, and if I had unlocked the great door sooner. I asked the lovely one to reveal the methods by which, when I descended again, the recollection of the present golden hour might never be effaced. Sweetly she answered : "All that is necessary is to look toward the Dawn, and

> " When the dance of the Shadow at daylight is done,
> And the cheeks of the Morning are red with the Sun ;
> When at eve, in his glory, he sinks from the view,
> And calls up his planets to blaze in the blue,
> Then pour out thy spirit in prayer,

" When the beautiful bend of the Bow is above,
   Like a collar of light on the bosom of Love,
   When the moon in her brightness is floating on high,
   Like a Banner of silver hung out in the Sky,
     Then pour out thy spirit in prayer.

" In the depths of the darkness unvaried in hue,
   When shadows are veiling the breast of the blue,
   When the voice of the Tempest at midnight is still,
   And the Spirit of Solitude sobs on the hill,
     Then pour out thy spirit in prayer.

" In the dawn of the morning when Nature's awake,
   And calls up her Chorus to chaunt in the brake,
   'Mid the voice of the echo unbound in the woods,
   'Midst the warbling of streams, and the foaming of floods,
     Then pour out thy spirit in prayer.

" Where by the pure streamlet the pale lily bends,
   Like Hope o'er the grave of affectionate friends,
   When each star in the sky to the bright fancy seems
   Like an island of light, in an ocean of dreams,
     Then pour out thy spirit in prayer.

" When the Tempest is treading the paths of the deep,
   And the Thunder is up from his cloud-cradled sleep,
   When the Hurricane sweeps o'er the earth in his wrath,
   And leaveth the footprints of God in his path,
     Then pour out thy spirit in prayer."

And I prayed.

Since that day* Devotion has been the solace of
many and many a weary hour ; for when grief and
pain and sorrow with their train afflict the soul, it
remembers the key-note and the key, and that glorious
upper chamber, with the great Glory that swept the
Heavens, even from the rising of the sun to the going
down thereof.

These were the circumstances which brought about

* Feb. 4th, 1861,

the change.  It gives a singularly sweet and placid
conviction that my long, long night of pain-life is
nearly past, the agony-hours nearly at their close ; and
so, feeling now emboldened and nerved to the task, the
fulfilling of a design long entertained, I determined to
mould into the following form certain of my

DEALINGS WITH THE DEAD.

In presenting what follows, wisdom dictates the narrative style rather than any other, for the reason that it
is better calculated to entertain, interest, and instruct
the reader.

Not a few people, nor those of the least informed
class either, entertain many serious doubts as to the
nature, perdurability, immortality, and eternality of the
human soul.  Of the last, probably no one in the body
can ever be absolutely certain and assured ; but of the
former, all may be ; not, perhaps, by means of what
herein ensues concerning the points named, but by reason of that greater knowledge whereof what follows is
the key.  I present the subjoined as seriously as could
anything be.  To my soul the truths here revealed,
transcribed from the experimental knowledge-tablets of
that very soul itself, are priceless, and worth as much
more than what people generally receive and accept as
truth, from sources whose external manifestation is
through the 'Spiritualism' of the day, as these last are
more valuable than the mere guesses at the truth of immortality, current previous to the advent of 'The Fox
and Fish Dynasty.'

Some six hundred and fifty years, more or less, before
the birth of Jesus of Nazareth—praises be to his name
forever !—in the thirty-fifth Olympiad, or about two
thousand five hundred years ago, there lived in the East

a famous philosopher, known to us through history as Thales, the Milesian ; and there is no doubt but that he was one of the first, if not the very first man of great mental rank and caliber, who publicly taught the doctrine of human immortality.

Doubtless the same general train of reasoning resorted to by Thales was nearly, if not quite, identical with that which constitutes the basis of nearly all human hope to-day, if we except the modern 'Spiritual' theory, which, while very comforting and satisfactory to great numbers, is far from being so to millions more ; for there are quite a number of questions which a doubting man may ask of those who predicate an hereafter upon the evidence furnished by the 'Spiritualism' of the day, which those who are asked are not able to clearly and satisfactorily answer. To many, the reasoning of the 'Spiritualists,' like that of the ancient, amounts to " It is quite possible that human beings are immortal;" and that is all. Many a man and woman are dying daily deaths from the fearful doubts that constantly arise as to the truth of the Immortality of the Soul ; doubts, too, that will still insist on coming up, in spite of the startling phenomena of the ' manifestations' whose origin is attributed to disembodied men and women ; they still leave an aching void—a void which I am about to attempt to fill ; and, I believe, successfully.

After the great Milesian, came other philosophers— men of genius and intuition—who had dim and indistinct glimmerings of the great truth. Feeling, rather than seeing, that there must be a life beyond the body, they strove to impress their convictions upon others ; yet the sum total still amounted to but a probability, at best. As a result of the great search for light upon

this mighty subject, many glimmerings of the truth were
seen, but they were glimmerings only. By-and-by came
Plato upon the stage of the world's theater. He produced 'Phædo'—a great work, considering the times
in which it first saw the light. It still remains so ; and
yet, so acute is the logical faculty of the people of the
present era, that even that work fails of convincing.
It is, viewed by the modern light, far, very far from being a satisfactory performance, considering the immense
importance and sublimity of the theme it professes to
treat ; yet, nevertheless, Plato did succeed in convincing many of the people of the by-gone ages, as well as
of the present, that he had indeed struck the golden
vein at the bottom of which the wondrous jewel lies,
and in establishing a crude conviction of that great
truth, which the present century will doubtless have the
supreme honor of perfectly demonstrating. In the final
conclusion, to which the world will shortly come, the
author of these pages firmly believes that the elements
herein given will enter as integers—as a portion and
part absolutely essential to the perfect structure.

Plato, not unlike many of our modern savans, seems
to have been sorely troubled—not so much in proving
the immortality of the soul, as in assigning it a proper
habitation after death. But the soul, like the body,
must have a home, he thought, and so he concluded to
locate that home within the boundaries of the 'New
Atlantis Isle,' situated, nobody, not even the great
thinker himself, knew where. The same difficulty presents itself to-day ; a thousand theories, or, more properly speaking, hypotheses, are now afloat on the surface
of the general mind, concerning the locality of the
Divine City of Spirits—the home of departed souls.

The great majority of these suppositions are too material, crude, shallow and baseless, on their very faces, to even challenge the attention of a thinker for a single moment; others are too far-fetched; and not one of them all is there, but presents itself in the face of a dozen objections, from every one of ten thousand objectors.

That this assertion may not appear groundless, and seem to be dictated by improper reasoning, let us merely glance at the three theories held by the people who claim to know most about the matter—'Spiritualists.' One of the lights of that class gravely informs us that the spiritual world is located quite a distance on the other side of 'The Milky Way;' he and his disciples affirm that spirits can and do come back to earth daily; that our desires draw them, and that they, being there and feeling us draw them, instantly quit the land of bliss, and flit toward us, accomplishing the distance in 'no time at all;' which very indefinite period we may safely assume to be three or four hours, more or less. Now, light coming from the nearest fixed star at the rate of two hundred thousand miles a minute, cannot reach us in less than *eighteen years*—while light from any star on the further side of the same great belt of suns, requires a period of time too vast for us to comprehend, ere it can gladden our eyes.

The Spirits' dwelling, according to this school, lies *beyond* even those vastly distant orbs. Supposing, however, that it exists in the neighborhood of the nearest star, any spirit who gets here after a journey of three hours, must travel through space at not less than the rate of *twelve thousand three hundred and eighty-seven* MILLIONS *of miles* DURING EVERY SECOND *of the awful journey !*—a speed that would annihilate any being less than God himself. What an idea!

The next theory, originated and advocated by the *same person*,* is, that the Spirits' home is on a sort of aerial belt circumvolving our globe. Said belt is fifty miles thick; spirits live on its upper surface, which is very like this earth, seeing that it has cities, houses, streets, waters, oceans, rivers, trees, beasts, birds, and reptiles. At the poles of the earth, according to this same self-dubbed philosopher and his 'school,' there are certain openings or large holes, through which the spirits come and go just when it suits them so to do. When they depart hence, they go 'head up,' of course; and when they come to us, they must approach '*head-foremost*,' or with their feet toward their home—a very immodest way for *some* spirits to travel, if the dignity of their sex is still retained—and a very undignified mode of traveling for the philosophers and magnates who so often talk to and *at* us, through the lips of modern eolists.

This, like the former theory, is unsatisfactory—but mainly on the ground of its gross materiality, for it makes the second life but a new edition of the first one. Common sense must reject this last. Of the two, the first theory is incomparably the most magnificent and grand. The fault is, that it is too much so; for it removes us at one leap from the condition of humanity, and at once endows us with the attributes and power of veritable gods.

The next hypothesis concerning the matter is, that this world (our globe) is, and must, and will for all eter-

* A man who knows most when fast asleep, and then *knows* but very little.

nity be, the abiding place and scene of activity of all mankind, who ever have been or will be born on it, through all the past and all the future ages. According to this school (if I may so dignify it), Spirits are here dwelling amongst us, taking note of all things that occur,—are eating, drinking, and doing all that we do.

Now, there is more common sense and reasonableness in these latter notions than in all the rest ; for of the many guesses at the truth, this comes nearest to the mark. The faults which this theory has, are, however, very bad ones ; for, first, it materializes the soul ; second, it confines it here, nor even permits it to leave its prison, to roam the starry fields ; and, third, it does injustice to God and His omnipotence, inasmuch as it practically doubts His providence, limits His power, and assumes that He was incompetent to provide *spiritual* homes for spiritual beings, and was compelled to make this a double world. If a spirit occupies any space at all, then, if this theory be true, not only is the surface above ground one compact mass of Spirits, but they form piles extending far higher than our loftiest mountains ; for, since men have begun to die, they have continued to pass away at the rate of scores of millions every year for at least a hundred centuries.

I could not help disposing of this doctrine by means of the *argumentum ad absurdum*, for it was, and ever will be, totally unworthy of any more respectful treatment ; and yet, as said before, it contains far more truth than either of the others, as will very shortly be, if not already herein seen.

People who lived in the days of Plato, Thales, and the great men of the olden time, could not have the same notions that we have ; could not understand many of the wonders which we, in this age, fully comprehend. They could not conceive of a balloon, railroad, locomotive, steamship, photo-picture, or telegraph, for the very plain and simple reason that the human brain had not, as a general thing, then unfolded many of its wonderful and mighty powers. Its immense capacities were as yet nascent, latent, still. True, the seeds of all that it has since proved were there, but in embryo only. In other words, the soul had not the requisite brain-organs, through which it could familiarize itself with all or any of the marvelous things just enumerated. So now, in these days, men and women worry themselves a great deal concerning the *locus in quo* of their fleshless friends, about the Deity or no-Deity question, and a hundred others of the like, not the least important of which is that concerning the nature, origin, and final destiny of the soul itself. Presently, in the years of the race, if not in those of the individuals on earth to-day, the requisite brain-organs will be developed, the proper function of which shall be the furnishing of the soul with what it wants, in order to take notice of, and comprehend the principles underlying its own existence, here and hereafter. Till then, the facts it sees must be admitted, even while many of the bases of these very facts remain involved in impenetrable mystery. It must take many things for granted—its own immutability included—in many instances, without any very perfect or intimate *knowledge* of the *why?*—on the *cogito, ergo sum* principle.

To return to the ancient philosopher : It may be remarked that, although he had a vague notion of a conscious life of the soul subsequent to the dissolution of its corporeal investiture, yet, unquestionably, the sort of *post mortem* existence, which he conceived, and Immortality—as the brightest intellects of the present age understand it—are two very dissimilar states or modes of being, and widely different in principle, value, nature, and results.

It may be well to present an abstract and brief chronicle of the Platonic idea, in order to clearly indicate the divergences.

To say nothing concerning Plato's doctrine of the Metempsychosis, or the Transmigration of soul from body to body—(which doctrine contains some truth, as doth nearly every notion man entertains, and which took its rise in the plains of Chaldea, was there found and adopted by the great Zerdusht, or Zoroaster, from whom Plato borrowed it)—we will merely glance at certain others of his recorded opinions. According to Plato, the soul is double—that is to say, both material and spiritual; all souls pre-existed; originally, they were inhabitants of Heaven, a place somewhere in the sky, whence they emigrated to the earth; their sole mission is to become " developed," which process is effected in this wise: Each soul must animate successively a prodigious number of bodies, every stage of their career occupying not less than a " period," which may be set down as one hundred years, and must be repeated an incalculable number of times; they then return whence they came—to Heaven; are permitted by the gods to remain there for an allotted term, after the expiration of which, they are again compelled to go forth and occupy successive bodies, as before. Consequently, all human souls are, according to the Platonic theory, destined to nearly an everlasting repetition of the same general processes, are fated to an almost endless round of defilements and purifications ; of returns to Heaven, and dismissals to earth—not to speak of sundry sojourns in very bad localities on the route.

Plato taught that these souls do not entirely forget their experiences, joys, sorrows or ambitions, hopes, cares and anxieties—in short, none of their varied ex- periences during the several incarnations ; and that all, or any portion of human knowledge, at any given point of time, was not the real acquisition of the *present*, as it seemed, but was composed merely of the memories, or reminiscences of innumerable past careers—the pres- sent recognition of facts and incidents which transpired in some pre-existent stage of their tremendous career. That these are truly magnificent notions, scarce any one who can truly grasp them will deny, even though to some persons they may appear to be the very quin- tessence of poetry. Transmigration, in some form, has certainly *been*, if not hereafter to be, the lot of man. I do not believe the Platonic conception of this great truth to be the correct one, nor that man will ever un- dergo the doom again ; yet, that the soul has reached its present through many an inferior state, is a self-evi- dent fact to me. At all events, a formidable array of reasons might be presented to account for the faith that is within me.

This idea of Plato's completely antagonizes two of the most celebrated dogmas that ever held the human reason captive : the first of which is the famous "Monad Theory" of Leibnitz, albeit he came very near the truth, as has been seen ; and the other, the modern doctrine, that souls, like bodies, are formed, made, created here ; and that their origin is a common one—*en utero*.

Before the conclusion of the task assigned me, I shall

have occasion to revert again to both of these latter
doctrines.   At present, let them pass.

Plato maintained that the soul was *Divinæ particu-
lum auræ*, an emanation from God Himself, a portion of
His immaculate Being, detached for a time only, and
that after innumerable transmigrations it is re-absorbed into Himself again, and loses its own distinctive-
ness.   Of course, this notion, if it be true, instead of
proving immortality, as Plato supposed, in fact dis-
proves it altogether; that is, if immortality be conceded
to be a continuance of personal identity, and an individual duration, subsequent to the demise of the physical
body.   Immortality means a continued existence of the
personality, and not a mere survival of the varied *elements* whereof a human being is composed.   The particular Deific emanations which constitute the souls of
A, B, C and D, respectively, as soon as they become
souls, are beings totally distinct from all else that
exists, and must forever remain so ; and " soul" can be
predicated of either, only as beings thus separate, and
therefore immortality can be the prerogative of man only
so long as God and man are not blended into one single
Personality.   So long as each soul shall think, feel, suffer,
enjoy, cogitate and have a continuity of self-knowing,
just so long will it be possessed of an invincible conviction of personal identity, under which circumstance
alone, and only, can its immortality be truly predicated
and affirmed.   But, should any soul ever be re-absorbed
into Deity—again become a portion of Divinity—an
utter, total, and complete annihilation of the *individual*
must ensue ; and that destruction of the human selfhood would be as effective, utter and complete, as if the
varied elements entering into it as constituents were

whirled absolutely out of the universe and into a blank nothingness.

A tree sawed into planks is a tree no longer, although the wood, so far as mere essence is concerned, remains as before. The tree *as* a tree is ruined forever, albeit the *wood* of it may endure for centuries. To sum up : All the theories of the Platonists, the followers of Thales, and the disciples of every one of the ancient philosophers, as well as those of scores of the modern " Spiritualists," especially of that peculiar school who prate of immortality and annihilation in one and the same, the very same breath, are unsatisfactory ; for, after all, their boasted demonstrations of immortality amount, in their final results and effects upon our minds, to but very little more than pleasing hopes, and fond desires, and longings after immortality ! In what follows I have endeavored to solve the problem, in a somewhat novel way, it must be admitted ; yet I am in earnest, and have worked up the materials at my command in the most effective manner that was possible.

## The Disembodying.

The belief in ghosts, spirits, apparitions, wraiths and doubles, is almost universal. Millions of people affect to disbelieve in them ; and yet, deep down in the soul-caverns of these identical millions may be found all that exists in the minds of the most credulous. Disbelief in such things is very near akin to the asserted creeds of atheism. Thousands there be who in *words* deny the existence of a God ; and yet, let any one of these loud-mouthed sceptics become racked with a real, genuine, old-ashioned toothache, and ten to one he cries out " O,

Lord !" fifty times a day, and as often in the night begs God to have mercy upon his rack-tortured jaws. The fact is, there never yet was, there never will be, such a *rara avis* as a genuine atheist; and in spite of all protestations to the contrary, there are but few who do not believe to some extent in the existence of spirits. As with the rest of the world, so with myself; for, notwithstanding the chronic and hereditary scepticism of my nature, a scepticism as unbending as iron, as inflexible as stone, I, from early childhood, entertained a certain vague, indefinite belief in the existence of the spectral gentry of another world; yet with this belief there was not the least realization in my mind that the objects of my belief had the faintest or most distant relationship to the human people in flesh and blood whom I daily saw about me. There was nothing very singular in that, however, for I merely resembled the millions of to-day, who, while entertaining the most undoubted, and, in some respects, salutary belief in ghosts, yet practically seem not to have the most distant idea that in so doing they are fully accepting the mystic's faith,—that these self-same ghosts are but the spirits of mortals who dwell beyond the veil.

Even in my early days I strove, by inquiry and by reading such books upon the subject as fell in my way, to find out whether this earthly life was the only allotment of man,—poor, care-ridden, unhappy man,—or not. Child as I was, I felt the incompleteness of all subsolary things, and longed to know if our experiences here were or were not all we had to hope for, or look forward to. The belief in ghosts did not help me any; for that ghost and spirit were synonyms, never once struck my mind. To the innumerable questions propounded by me to my elders, in the expectation of eliciting satisfactory replies, the old stereotyped response was given,—to wit: Mankind have souls, and these souls live when the body is dead and returned into the dust of the ground; but what the soul was, whence it came, what was its nature, form, shape and size, and whither it went after the loss of its body, I could gain not the slightest information; for every answer given me was as unsatisfactory as would be the Platonic theory to a modern philosopher of the transcendental order.

After a while these repeated failures produced their legitimate fruit; at first, a little doubt crept in, and challenged all I had gathered. It grew apace, and finally settled into a sort of atheism, from which I was happily rescued by my sister Harriet, and the good old Father Verella, a Spanish priest, by whom I was duly baptized and received into the bosom of the Roman Catholic Church, in my native city, New York. How long the connection lasted cannot now be told; but something that occurred disgusted me, and forthwith the Pope had a new foe in my humble person. Years of doubt again succeeded after this relapse, during which the belief in ghosts grew stronger and still more strong. My mind became subject to certain peculiar states,—a sort of *raptness*, so to express it,—a condition precisely identical with that now claimed by thousands in the land, to be spiritually induced. The supposition that it is so, *may* be correct, and it may be that this condition is the result of the development of a new sense or faculty in the mind. It matters not which, albeit I am inclined toward the latter hypothesis. In these states to which I became at times subject,

8

it seemed to me that I held converse with the ghosts, but for a long time was totally unable to realize that they were human spirits.   Much of the history of my psychical life has for years been before the world, and therefore need not be repeated here ; consequently we will pass over several years, to the date of the first occurrence of the " Rochester Knockings." At the first opportunity that offered itself, I went to Litchfield, Michigan, at which place were two females in whose presence the strange noises were said to occur.   I heard them, believed they were produced by a power outside, and independent of the girls, yet could hardly realize that human souls, disembodied, were the makers of the sounds.

The result was an increased and intensified study, not only of the soul itself, so far as was possible by aid of an active intellect and quickened intuition, but also of its modes of action, its phases, and its moods.   And, O, how my spirit loved to dwell upon its possibilities! Was there any person in the country reputed to have a wealth of knowledge on matters pertaining to the spirit, I spared neither trouble nor expense ; but went forthwith to glean what I could from his or her precious stores.   Of the " rappers," " tippers," and " table-turn-ers," I soon became wearied ; for, as a class, they amounted to but little, and, with one or two exceptions, proved unworthy of confidence.

At last, I went to visit a city in New England, where was published a paper devoted to the illustration and diffusion of spiritual light, the editor of which soon became interested in me, (for people said that my ghost-seeing faculty was real, and that I had given incontestible proofs, not merely of the power indicated, but also of what they were pleased to call clairvoyance). While sojourning in this eastern city, I came across a series of crayon sketches, copied from an old English work by their possessor, illustrative of certain portions of the processes of cosmical formation, according to the Ignigenous Theory. One of these drawings represented a vortical sun, discharging from itself countless hosts of lesser suns—a world-rain from the eternal cornucopia. The idea, even if it be *but* an idea, is a magnificent—aye, a tremendous one, and it attracted my soul very strongly. Many and many an hour have I sat gazing raptly upon that bit of pasteboard, which to me told a story too supremely vast and grand to ever find expression in human types or language; and often have I been lost in the lanes of the azure, when striving to reach that almighty center of flaming fire, whence starry systems rain down like snow-flakes in the wintry days.

This particular crayon set me to thinking in right good earnest; as a result of which, it appeared that my psychical vision became intensified. Test after test was given of this power, until the list rolled up from tens to hundreds, and people said, "If these descriptions of dead persons, whom you have never seen when living, and whom you profess to behold now, are not proofs of both the immortality of the soul and the ability to scale the walls which divide this from the upper worlds, what in Heaven's name will prove them? It *must* be true that you, and hundreds of others as well, do really penetrate the heretofore unlifted veil." The display of these powers satisfied others, but to myself they still remained the weary, weary A's and the barren, barren B's; for, notwithstanding all that I had seen, heard and read on the subject of the soul's continuance, it was

utterly impossible to actualize or realize my theoretic belief; and this, too, at the very time that scores of persons, through the practical display of what I can but
regard as a mere phase of psycho-vision, were trium-
phing in a firm, solid, unshaken belief in an hereafter;
singular, was it not?

That the soul can, at times, act independent of the
body, I am firmly convinced. We see daily proofs of
it in the mesmerist's art, in mental telegraphy, and in
various other ways; this has long been an accepted fact.
How often do we suddenly think of a person, who instantly thereafter enters our presence, his spiritual part
having preceded the physical! How often do we visit
places during sleep which, in other days, we recognize
externally! How frequently we dream of persons and
things unknown to us, and subsequently encounter these
very persons and things when wide awake! Many persons possess this power of independent soul-action, and
can exert it at will. The writer has often done so.

The experience about to be related occurred at a
period when the skeptical mood was on my soul; and
it overtook me as I wandered distractedly on the borders of the region of Despair. But this experience,
strange, fearful, and even terrible, as portions of it were,
had a beneficial effect; for it lifted my struggling soul
to hights of grandeur and glory, from whose sublime
summits my vision 'swept the plains of immortality,
and pierced the arcana of death itself!'

Had the wisdom-lessons taught in this immense experience been duly profited by, as they ought, I should
have escaped many and many a bitter hour. But, like
the majority of people, I refused to learn in any but
the severest of all schools.

It so fell out upon a day, that, having taken my usual seat before a copy of the marvelous crayon previously alluded to, and which I had rudely sketched, I became impatient at my continual failures to comprehend the subject it represented. Generally this had not been the case. My mind, on that morning, was unusually clear and vigorous; and yet, despite all efforts, I found it utterly impossible to comprehend the stupendous conception—the Birth of a Universe. At last, heart-faint and sick at my failure, I abruptly rose from the chair, resumed my walking apparel, left the room, and strolled carelessly and mechanically up the street, and continued listlessly onward, until I found myself beyond the outskirts of the city, and entering the open country. It was a bright, sunshiny day; and after wandering about for nearly an hour, and beginning to feel a double oppression—fatigue of body, for it was very weak and slender—and despondency of spirits—it struck me that I would turn short to the right, and lie down for a while beneath the grateful shade of a natural bower, on the borders of a forest clump, hard by. This I did; and having reclined upon the rich, green turf, under the leafy canopy afforded by the trees—rare and stately old elms they were—abandoned myself at once to meditation, speculation and repose. How long I thus lay it is impossible to tell; it may have been one hour—it may have been two or three: all that I remember of the outer world of wakefulness is the framing of a series of questions, and, amongst others wherewith I interrogated my deepest soul for responses, were these: "What is the immortality of man? What is God? Where does He dwell? Is the life hereafter a continuance of this, or is it entirely different? Can it be only a shift-

ing of world-scenes, or is it a change as widely apart
from our earthly state as is this last from the existence
before birth?" These, and many similar questions, my
soul propounded to itself, and sought, by an intense in-
troversion of its faculties, to reach the penetralia of its
being, where it instinctively felt convinced that all the
momentous answers were already registered. Long
and persistently was this endeavor continued, until, for
the first time in my life, I became aware of something
very, very strange, and supremely interesting going on
within me. This sensation was somewhat analagous to
the falling off into a deep sleep, only that it was the body
alone which lost its outward sensibility; it was the
physical senses only that became slowly and gradually
benumbed and sealed, while the mighty senses beneath
them appeared to intensify themselves, draw together,
and coalesce in one grand All-sense; and this continued going on until it reached a strange and awful degree, and a sensation as of approaching death stole over,
and, for a little while, frightened and alarmed me.

With all the clearness of reasoning that I ever possessed, I applied myself to the work of fathoming what all
this meant; but the more strenuous the effort, the more
signal the failure. Finding that the phenomenon taking
place within, was governed by a law which pertained
to soul-life alone, and that my ignorance of that mystic
realm was too great and dense to permit a full comprehension of the enigma, nothing remained but to submit,
and learn, as time wore on; and, accordingly, giving
over all attempts to shake off that which, by this time,
held my entire being within its mighty and resistless
grasp, I abided patiently the result.

Slowly as moves the ice-mounds of Switzerland came

the sense of coldness over my limbs ; inch by inch the crafty hand of Mystery gained firmer hold. The feet, the limbs, the vitals, grew cold and leaden, until at last it seemed as if the ventricles of my heart and the blood within them were freezing, slowly, surely freezing ; and the terrible conviction forced itself upon me that I was gradually, but positively—dying !

Soon all sense of organization below the neck was lost, and the words 'limb, body, chest,' had no meaning. This was also true of the head generally, but not of a something within that head. The bodily eyes and ears were the last to yield themselves up to the influence of the strange, weird spell.

With a last, perishing effort, I strove to look forth upon, and listen to the sounds of the world, now perhaps forever being left behind. What a doleful change in a few brief hours ! Where all had been serenely, calmly beautiful before, nothing was now visible but the huge, gaunt skeletons of forms I had seen glowing with living verdure but a little while ago ; the sunlight was changed from silver sheen to a pale and sickly yellow, tinged with ghastly green. The overhanging branches and profuse foliage of the trees hard by had altered their every aspect, and from stately monuments of God's goodness, had become transformed into spectral obelisks, upreared on the earth to tell the future ages that He had passed that way in savage and vindictive wrath, once upon a time. When I lay me down and gazed up into the beautiful heaven, the fleecy vapors were playing at cloud-gambols on the breast of the vault ; but now they were turned into funereal palls, heavy, black, and gloomy as are the coverlets of Night ; and the busy hum of myriad insects, and the gentle murmur of the zephyr moving through the bushes, no longer pleased the ear by their soft, low buzz, but smote upon my parting soul like a last and dirgeful knell ; while the warblings of the plumed songsters of the wood sounded to my soul like the sepulchral chants of Eastern story. Very soon the deep black pall, hung out upon the face of heaven, began slowly and remorselessly to come down, down, down, until my nostrils snuffed the vapors and sensed the odors of the grave. The far-off horizon began cautiously to approach me, shutting out first one window of the sky and then another, until at last but a little space of light was left ; and still the cloud-walls drew nearer, nearer still ; the darkness and the fetor grew more fearfully dense by degrees ; I gasped for breath ; the effort pained me, and was fruitless ; and the horrible agony consequent thereupon, for one moment re-illumed the brain ; and the dreadful possibility, nay, the probability, that I was to die there alone, with no loved hand to smoothe my brow, no lip to kiss me 'good-bye,' no tearful eye to watch my parting hour, sent a thrill along my brain almost too intense for endurance. The conviction that I must perish, uncared for by kind friends, out there in the wood, beneath the blue sky and the green trees, seized upon my soul, and the cold beads of perspiration that oozed from my brow and trickled down to the ground, attested the degree of mental agony I was undergoing. 'Good-bye, all ye beauties of the sense-world! farewell, all whom I have loved or been loved by !' I mentally said ; and then, by a strong effort of will, nerved my soul for its expected flight. Soon there came a thrill, a shudder, an involuntary 'God, receive me !' and I felt that I was across the

Mysty River, and stood within the awful gates of— ETERNITY !

The majority of people imagine the Soul-world to be *spacially* (to coin a good word) outside of this sphere ; and so it is, in one sense ; but in another, it is not. A notion of what I mean may be had by comparing the other and higher with certain phases of the true dream-life. The scenes of action of either are totally removed from both time and space, and yet the events of each are actual experiences of the soul ; for even in dream-life we suffer and enjoy quite as keenly as in the wake-ful world of grosser sense. A woman who sleeps and dreams, finds herself in two widely-different states within the four-and-twenty hours. Now, the normal spiritual state is very like a prolonged dream-life, to which our world-sense or earthly condition is just the same as is spiritual clairvoyance to an inhabitant of the physical body ; that is to say, it is possible for spiritual beings to become *en rapport* with this earthly world, and the interests, persons and things thereof ; but this is not their normal state or condition, any more than the clairvoyance, induced mesmerically, is the normal state of the subject possessing the faculty.

It requires long and persistent effort to induce a con-dition in a human being, which will for a time intromit him into the greater or lesser Soul-worlds ; and just so it is no easy matter for the inhabitants of those higher and highest worlds to become *en rapport* with this.

These remarks are introductory to what follows.

After the first great thrill of terror had passed over, I became comparatively calm, and soon lost all con-sciousness whatever. Not a sensation ever felt before in all my-life was experienced now, but a new magazine

8*

of emotions seemed to have suddenly been opened in the depths of my being, and began to usurp the places of the old ones.

Some years subsequent to the events now detailed, I read the wonderful experiences of several persons, who had taken the oriental drug known as hasheesh, and a few years thereafter was induced to make an experiment upon myself with a little of the powerful stimulant. I became fully conversant with its influence, but in no instance was there the least similarity between the condition it brought on and the state in which I was when reclining beneath the bower in the wood. I have known the fullest, deepest, most intense effect of that singular drug ;* but nothing I ever experienced from it—nothing I ever read of as having been experienced by others who had foolishly taken it—at all resembled the sensations to which I awoke under the trees near that eastern city. Gradually the sense of *lostness*, which for a time possessed me, passed away, and was succeeded by a consciousness altogether distinct from that of either the dream or the ordinary wakeful condition. Not a sensation ever previously experienced—not even in the very soul-vaults of my being—now swept the nerve-harp within, to solace, actuate or annoy ; but, instead, there came an indefinable PLEASURE-SENSE—a sort of hyper-sensual ecstasy, by no means organic, but diffused over the entire being. I have every reason to believe that this feeling is *always* experienced by the newly dead. Persons who have been resuscitated after drowning, suspension by the neck, and asphyxia, all unite in testifying, that so far as their experience went,

---

* Nothing on earth could ever induce me to take a drachm of this accursed drug again.

death was a pleasant feeling, and its joys supreme, even in what to spectators may have seemed the terrible passing hour. This sensation, like all others, cannot be verbally described ; it was as if the keenest pleasures known to us in the body were infinitely prolonged and *strung out* over the entire nerve-sea, instead of a single organ or two.

I cannot perhaps convey my meaning to some people better than by saying that the sensation was akin to the feeling of an instantaneous relief from the most excruciating pain—the toothache, for instance.  I was not, at first, conscious of possessing a body ; not even the ultra-sublimated material one of which we hear so much said in these latter days; but a higher, nobler consciousness was mine—namely, a supremely radiant soul-majesty.

My ears did not hear ; but Sound—Nature's music—the delicious, but still melodies of earth and space, and all things else, seemed to pour in upon my ravished soul, in rich full streams, through a thousand avenues. The eye did not see, but I was all sight.  There was no organ of locomotion, as on the earth, nor were such needed ; but my spirit seemed to be all motion, and it knew instinctively, that by the power of the thought-wish, it could reach any point within the boundaries of earth where it longed and willed to be ; but not a single yard beyond it.  Let it be here distinctly understood, that the condition in which I now found myself, was precisely the same as that of the higher class of spiritual beings, when they are in the peculiar state wherein they can for a limited period, and to a certain extent, become connected with this world, wherein they have once lived, and from which they have passed over the bridge of Death to the brighter realms beyond ; in other words, I was connected with two worlds, and the states incident to the residents of both, at one and the same time.

Distinctively and most clearly does memory retain all the marvelous changes from the pre-state of that auspicious afternoon.

What is especially remarkable, is, that the condition was so peculiar, that the freed soul could, and did, after a time, take close notice of material things, even while that same soul-gaze penetrated the surface, and beheld their essences. The vision was not bounded by the obstacles which impede ordinary sight. Every object was, more or less, transparent ; and one very singular peculiarity of all bodies, of whatever kind, was this : the trees, stones, hills, mountains, everything, appeared as if composed of absolute *fire.* A certain object I knew, from its shape, to be a large tree, with brown bark, white wood, and green leaves ; yet none of these colors were there now, but instead, the trunk appeared to be a huge cylinder of gray fire, not in one mass, but in interwoven streaks, all actively flaring upward, and bound together by a circle of brighter fire (the inner bark), which in turn was encompassed by a dull brown band of faintly flickering flame. Each leaf was also nothing but a vari-formed disk of purple and orange fire. Thus it was with all that I beheld.

Fire, in some form, constitutes the life of all beings, of whatsoever nature; of this I am firmly convinced. These strange sights caused me to reason in this wise: " If dull matter is so filled with the divine luminescence, what must be the appearance of a human being ? Surely a man must present an astonishing sight! Of a cer-

tainty," said I, " this must be Eternity, and I am now a
free soul! O, that I might behold another soul than
mine, and learn somewhat of its mysteries, and reach
the understanding of a few of the deeper things of its
nature." Scarcely had this desire taken form, than a
sense of involuntary motion took possession, and I felt
myself slowly and positively rising in space, at an angle
of eighty degrees with the horizon. Amazement! The
sensation was not unpleasant; but as the ground receded apparently, the novelty of the situation produced
emotions that most certainly were. It is impossible to
describe one's feelings; nor shall such an attempt be
here essayed. Suffice it therefore, that I rose to such a
height, that, judging by the faint gleams of the earth-
fires in the hills, and the indistinct shimmering of the
city itself, I conjectured, that when at the highest point,
not less than five miles, in a straight line, separated me
from the peak of the tallest mountain within sight.
Having reached this altitude, I began to descend the
opposite arm of the triangle, whose base was on the
earth's surface, and reached the ground in the neighborhood of a city in central New York, distant from
my point of departure not less than two hundred miles.
Of course, it was impossible to even conjecture either
the means by which this journey was accomplished, or
the motives prompting the wierd power which effected
it ; but whatever be the reasons of my coming, one thing
is certain—here I am, and nothing remains but to abide
the issue, whatever it may be, thought I.

Even during the mental perturbation, which was the
natural result of the extraordinary circumstances in
which I was placed, the question-asking faculty and pro-
pensity of my mind—one of its leading traits—found

sufficient time for exercise ; and many were the "whys," "hows," and "what fors" which causality propounded, but to which at first there came no response.  It is almost impossible to convey an idea of the strange processes by which knowledge flowed in upon my soul.  It seemed to be absorbed.  Knowledge, all knowledge may be said to float in the spiritual atmosphere, underlying the coarser air men breathe ; and in certain states, reachable by every human being, this knowledge is drawn in involuntarily, just as salt absorbs moisture.

Near the spot over which I hovered, [for the spirit cannot touch gross substance directly, but moves along on the surface of an aerial stratification near the earth : these strata are about sixty feet apart, and there are transverse, vertical and other lanes leading in all directions through them,] stood a house embowered in trees, and in this house was a "study," and in that study I saw the object, above all others, which had been the theme of my longing, prior to the commencement of my aerial journey, namely, a man ; and that man was apparently educated and refined—for near where he sat stood a library of books, one of which he was at that moment engaged in reading.  The title of the book was "Neander's Life of Christ."

Calmly read the man ; still more calmly I observed him and his surroundings ; and the result of these observations was a firm conviction that the theories propounded by Newton, and generally admitted to be true, concerning light, color, and sound, are not correct, or even approximately so.

No amount of disbelief on the part of others; no amount of cavilling, nor reasoning can ever convince me that the experience now being recorded is anything less than absolute fact—the direct contact of my inner being with the truths here related : hence I hesitate not for an instant in challenging the guesses of even a Newton, and offsetting against them the results of my own personal inspection of the phenomena whereof his Principia treats. In the first place, there are many different kinds of light : in the present instance, there were two sorts in operation ; first, the rays of solar light fell upon the printed page, and with it a still finer, and more subtle, white and velvet light, from the eyes of the man himself ; which proved to me, that men gain a knowledge of external things by means of an absolute and positive irradiation from the soul itself, whose seat is in the central brain ; and this, through the medium of the optic nerves, retina and other delicate organs. In proportion to the central power of the soul, it suffuses and bathes everything in, and with, a subtle aura ; and this aura is that mysterious telegraphic apparatus, by means of which it issues its behests, and receives information.

While gazing upon this beautiful sight I *distinctly heard a bell ring ;* and yet that bell was not sounded within two hundred miles of the spot where at that very moment the body of the writer lay wrapped in a death-like pall of insensibility, as was proved by the actions of the man within the house, near which I stood, investigating the sublimest of all phenomena—namely, the Human Soul, its phases, modes and nature.

The student instantly laid down the book and rose to his feet ; not, however, to respond to the ringing, but to bid his three or four little mischief-loving prattlers be quiet, make less noise, put aside the hand-bell, and not disturb him by its tinkling.

All this was deeply interesting ; but what most at-

tracted my attention was the discovery of the fact that
sound was not, as thousands of scientific men have asserted, a mere vibration of aerial particles, but, on the
contrary, was, and is, a fine, very fine and attenuated
substance, which leaves any and all objects that are
jarred or struck—and leaves in greater or less volume,
in pointed pencil-rays, single rays, broad sheets of
various shapes, and in undulatory waves, according to
the nature of the object whence it flows, the force of the
blow struck, and the character of the object used in
striking. It would be quite worth the while for our
*savants* to make experiments to verify, or, if possible,
refute these statements.

The man resumed his seat ; and I saw that from his
internal brain there proceeded to the outer ears innumerable fibres of pale green light, and that the pencil-
rays and sheets of sound, which were at that moment
floating through all contiguous space, came in direct
contact with the terminals of what,—for want of a better
name,—I will call fibres, or, more properly, fibrils ; the
contact took place within the rim of the external ear,
and the sound was instantaneously transmitted, or tele-
graphed, along the auditory nerve to the *sanctum
sanctorum* of his very soul.

The question naturally arises in the reader's mind at
this point : " How was it possible for *you* to become
cognizant of *sound* under the very peculiar circumstances and conditions by which you were surrounded
for the time being ? *You* could not hear by means of
the outer ear and auditory nerves, for it is plain, if your
story be indeed a recital of actual events, and not merely
a splendid philosophical fiction, that your material hearing apparatus had been left behind you, in the body,

beneath the trees on the outskirts of the New England city?" A very fair question this, and one demanding a fair answer. To it I reply thus: The human being, externally, is a multiple thing, at the bottom of which lies the invisible soul: Soul is the thinking, feeling, knowing essence; spirit is its casket; the body but its nursery-garments, the clothing of its juvenility. By means of the body, the soul, in which alone all power and faculty inheres, is enabled to come in contact with the material world. By means of its inner or spirit-body, which is but an out-creation, it holds converse with the worlds of Knowledge, Spirit and Principle. The fibrils alluded to are not mere emanations from the physical brain, or its ganglia, but they are wires, one end of which is eternally anchored in the very soul itself, which latter is, of course, *the* man *per se*. The wires, though passing through, are by no means rooted in the corporeal structure; hence, the man or woman, without a flesh-and-blood body, experiences but little, if any, difficulty in hearing sounds made in this material world. As it is with regard to hearing, so also it is, to the same degree, with reference to the power of seeing the corporeal forms of earthly things. The perfection and ease, however, with which this is done, depends upon the normal condition of the disembodied man himself. If he or she, as the case may be, is sound, sane, clear and morally healthy, its powers, as with one yet in the flesh, are augmented and positive; therefore it can, by processes already sufficiently explained, see, hear, feel, and even read, not only books, but the unexpressed thought of a person still embodied with whom he or she may for the time being be in sympathetic contact. Very seldom, however, can the recently dead do these things with the same ease and facility that others can who have been over the river a longer time. This I have abundantly proved ; and this, too, explains a point which, as certain believers in the Spiritology of the day inform me, has puzzled thousands of investigators, *i. e.:* why some of the dead people, with whom they claim to hold very frequent converse, can only be communicated with by means of hard labor on their part, while others readily understand and respond. Some can faintly, others clearly see and hear ; some can correctly read people's thoughts ; others cannot, and must be addressed vocally ; others still require all questions to be written, in order that they may *see* and understand. The faculties and powers of dead people are doubtless as varied, dissimilar and unevenly developed as are those of persons on the hither side of Time.

The study of the human soul is a great one, and entirely worthy of a life's devotion. It has been mine to seek the solution of many of its mysteries, and in a few instances success has crowned the effort and rewarded the laborer. The final answer to the question is this : the sounds were conveyed to my inner being directly, and without the need of any flesh-and-blood organ of sense. Let us now turn toward a far more sublime mystery, namely : THE VERY SOUL ITSELF.

---

## The Winged Globe—Soul.

WITH unmingled astonishment I gazed upon the man as he sat there in his quiet study. I had often been told that man was a microcosm, or a world in miniature ; but closer observation proved to me that he was more than that—for, instead of a world, he was a universe of worlds and mysteries, a few of the latter of which were comprehended by me for the first time.

Standing thus, I reasoned after this wise : 'Unquestionably all the faculties and qualities pertaining to man, as we find him upon the earth, are the results of a design on the part of the august Mind which placed him here. The purpose and function of these faculties and qualities, are to subserve man's best interests, his proper unfolding, and the divine purpose—here ; and, doubtless, when by death he shall be transported elsewhere, to meet a new destiny and act in a new drama, other qualities and faculties, adapted to his changed position, will be given him ; or, if already latent, will be duly brought into action. Perhaps their seeds are already planted in him ; if so, they will assuredly spring up at death, blossom in the Soul-world, and bear golden fruit in that place, and at that period of the infinite year, when God shall so ordain it. We none of us know what we fairly are ; and no one, not even the loftiest seraphs, can tell positively what we shall be ; yet, that man is *re*-served, and will through all his trials be *pre*-served, for some great, some yet undreamed-of destiny or end, there cannot be the shadow of a doubt. Nor will this final end be the mere eternal dwelling in the Valhallas, of which we sometimes dream ; nor in the 'spheres,' about which 'spiritual mediums' so glibly talk, nor in the gold-paved cities whereof we so often sing. Our final destiny is none of these. Beyond all question, much of the knowledge acquired in the earth-life will be found at death to have served its purpose here, and will never again come into play.

Not a single one of the grander, more noble longings and ambitions of the soul can find their field of action here ; but they are deathless ; and as God has provided a supply for every proper demand in all things else, so He has in this instance ; and therefore, though the aspiring soul may pass away with its strong wings drooping, and weak for want of exercise, yet, up there—in its grand heaven—the air is pure and the field immense, the mountains tall, and the oceans wide ; and the eagle soul shall essay its loftiest flight, and grow stronger from the trial.   What a person acquires here is but a prophecy of harvests to be reaped in the great hereafter.

Man is really a unitary being, but seemingly is duplex, and even multiple ; but this is seeming only, for in fact there is but one real sense in man—which truth I learned as I gazed upon the student in the chamber ; and that sense is intuition—the human sprout of an infinite and God-like faculty, dormant in most people, yet incontestibly destined to an immense unfolding in all ; albeit, it is so deeply buried in some that it can only express itself through organs.   " And God said, Let us make man in our own image ;" and so He made him ; but God is ubiquitous, omnipresent, omniscient—man is not ; and yet, if Scripture be worthy of our regard, and Progress be not a sham and delusive dream, the tremendous prophecy implied in the line from Genesis just quoted is certainly to be realized ; and man is destined to move, through thorny fields—and slowly, it may be— yet *still* to move, towards UBIQUITY and OMNISCIENCE ! Intuition is the sprout of which they are the full tree. True, man shall never reach absolute godhood, yet ever will he move toward it.

"If this be so," says the caviler, " and God be stationary, and not an advancing Being, there must come a time—even though when many a yet unborn eternity shall have grown hoary with age—still there *must* come a time when man *will* overtake Deity ; and then there can no longer be a God !" Specious this, very ! Why ? Because God, though not a progressive Being, as we understand it, yet is infinite ; and man must ever be finite. God's omniscience is what the word proclaims it—all-knowing ; but man shall be much-knowing. He is forced to approach Perfection in straight lines, and when he shall have attained immense power in any given direction, there will still be forever germinating new faculties, before the untold millions of which there shall ever be an infinite stretch, a limitless field, an endless road. God also is kaleidescopic ; and, supposing it were possible for man to reach the point of greatness at which Deity is .to-day, yet one exertion of His volition—and, lo ! He presents a new aspect to the wondering souls of infinitude, more marvelous than before, and reveals points which will place a new infinity between man and their attainability ; and so on for all the epochs yet to be—epochs whereof eternities, as we understand them, shall only count as moments in the everlasting year. Death is but an awakening, and there are to be myriads of these.

All this I knew and felt ; all these mighty foreshadowings flowed into my soul, as, with clarified intellect, and spirit bowed down with awe, I stood gazing at the man within the chamber. More : Reason, the king-faculty given us here, was only intended to act as our pilot through life, and will have fulfilled its main office when we step into the grave ; but very soon after we step out of it, on the other side, the UNION OF THE SENSES begins to take place, and the SENSE—whose elements are the senses—comes into play—the all-absorbing Intuition. This uni-faculty is not a thing of earthly origin, though it here deepens and grows strong ; it was an integer of the original being—became a part of the soul at the very instant wherein it fell from God ; it is a triple faculty, and its *rôle* is Prevision, Present-knowing, and Reminiscence.

The skin of a man is not himself, although whoever sees one, recognizes *something* human. Beneath this skin is the muscular system, interlaced with a magnificent net-work of nerves, all in the form of, yet by no means the man himself. Next we come to the osseous system—the skeleton—the God-fashioned framework of the house he lives in—and a house only—one, too, that is often let to bad tenants, seeing how zealously they abuse it and batter down its walls. Now, when we see a skeleton, we know it is something that points towards the human, yet do not for that reason, even momentarily, confound the bones with the individual ; for we instinctively know that the wonderful occupant of this bony edifice is, and to bodily eyes will forever remain invisible. Whoever looks for a man, must go below and above skin, flesh, muscles, and bones, to find him. Well, let the searcher enter the domain of the senses— a country that lies a long distance beyond the nervo-osseous land. Ah! here is the man, somewhere in this region of sense. Let's see! one, two, three, five, or a dozen—no matter about counting them—yet nowhere in all this region have we found or can find the man. We are certainly nearer to him than we were awhile ago ; yet, not finding him, we conclude to go a little further in the search. ' He dwells in the Faculties.' Not so ; try again. 'In the passions.' Further still ; not home yet. 'In God-like reason, and the quality-parlors of vir-

tue, aspiration, expression—each one step nearer the
goal.' Go a little deeper, and in the centre of the brain
you will find a WINGED GLOBE OF CELESTIAL FIRE, IN
WHICH DWELLS THE MAN !—his part of God crowded
into less than three square inches of surface.   Here is
the seat of the soul ; here is the Grand Dépôt, at which
all the Nerve, and Thought, and Knowing, Thinking
and Feeling trains, and telegraphic lines converge and
meet !   This Winged Globe is a House of Many Mansions, eternal in itself ; and the principal parlor, in the
grandest palace of them all, is devoted to the Peerless
Power—INTUITION !   Born in man, it often lies *perdu*,
or latent, till the final passage, and never bursts into
full activity at once, save in very rare instances, as in
the case of those wonderful genii, Newton, La Place,
and men of that order ; and even in these, it is only
partially active.   It requires peculiar *conditions* for its
expansion, just as the reasoning and other faculties require time and exercise.   The soul is really a divine
monad,* a particle, so to speak, of the Divine brain—a
celestial corruscation from the Eternal heart ; and, for
that reason, an eternal existence—immortality being its
very essence, and expansion constituting its majestic nature ; and the Soul, this monad, was once an integer of
God himself—was sent forth by His fiat—became incarnated and an individual, separate and distinct from,
yet having strong affinities for all things material—
stronger for all things spiritual, and for its brethren—

---

* Monad—first definition, an ultimate atom ; a simple substance
without parts, indivisible, a primary constituent of matter.  Second
definition—a monad is not a material, but a formal atom, it being im
possible for a thing to be at once material and possessed of a real unity and indivisibility.

and an attraction toward its ultimate Source stronger than all else beside. Here, then, I lay bare the very corner-stone of the splendid Temple of Progress, whose foundations are laid in Time, but whose turrets catch the gleams from the Eternal Sun of suns, whose warming rays diffuse themselves over every starry island in the tremendous Ocean of Being !

Intuition is but an *awakening* of the inmost soul to an active personal consciousness of what it *knew* by virtue of its Divine genesis.

Suffering appears to be one means toward this awakening, and the consequent intensification of the individuality ; and the passions of man, labor, and evil, are also agents to this end.

Man is beset by evil on all sides, doubtless to the end that, in shunning it, and conserving the selfhood, he may effect the earliest possible completion and rounding out of his entire being, and, consequently, be all the better prepared to encounter the immense destiny that lies before him in the Hereafter. * * * * * * And I gazed upon the man within the chamber ; the weather to him—but not to me, for I was totally unaffected—seemed to be oppressively warm ; and it was exceedingly difficult for him, after a while, to overcome the somnolent or drowsy influence thus induced, and prevent himself from falling asleep. However, he made strenuous efforts to conquer the tendency, and for a time it was mastered ; but, in the struggle between himself and the slumber-fay, a secret was disclosed to me, and another beautiful arcanum of the human economy revealed.

The student of these pages will remember that erewhile I mentioned the astonishing fact—one of great

value to all who think—that I was as a perfectly disembodied soul during the experience now recounted,
and could and did behold, at one and the same time,
both the external and the essential part of whatever my
glance fell upon. The reader will perhaps arrive at a
clearer understanding of what is here meant to be
conveyed if this double power be thus illustrated : A
person may look through one glass vase at several
others, many colored, within it, the last of which contains the image of a man, in still finer glass,—his eye
resting upon the surface of each particular vase, yet at
the same time penetrating and grasping the whole.
Thus it was in the present case : I saw,—and what
obtained of that student in the room obtains of all immortal beings,—the clothes ; beneath the clothing his
body ; and interfilling that, as water does a sponge, I
beheld the spiritual man.

Here let me define a few terms : Body is that which
is purely material, corporeal, dense, weighable, atomical
or particled ; spirit is a thing of triplicity : in the most
external sense, that which interpenetrates, flows
through, from, and constitutes the life of material existences is spirit ; second, the great menstruum in which
the universe floats and has its being is spirit, but vastly
different from the foregoing ; and third, the mental
operations, as well as their results, are spiritual—a
man's thought, for instance. Great care must be taken
to distinguish these last two from the first, which is the
effluvium from, or surrounding aura of all material
forms and things. Soul is that more stately principle
*and* thing which thinks, feels, tastes, sees, knows, as-
pires, suffers, hates, loves, fears, calculates and enjoys.

Hoping that these definitions will be retained, and

that my meaning only will be given to the terms used,
we will now proceed. I became a rapt observer, not of
the man in the study, as a person, but as a rare mechan-
ism. The clothes he wore, emitted a dull, faint, leaden-
hued cloud, perfectly transparent, and extending about
three inches from their surface in all directions. His
body was apparently composed of orange-colored flame,
and its emanations reached to the distance of fifteen
feet on all sides ; it penetrated the wood-work, walls,
chairs, tables,—all with which it came in contact ; and
I noticed two facts : first, that its form was an oblate
spheroid, and second, that a portion of it adhered to
whatever he touched.

Thus it is true that a man leaves a portion of himself
wherever he may chance to go : this explains why a dog
is enabled to trace his master through the streets of a
crowded city. * * * * * When the man rose to silence
the noise of his children, I discerned the form of this
sphere, in the centre of a similar one of which every
created being stands. Its poles were the head and feet,
and its equator, whose *bulge* exceeded the polar dimen-
sions about one-fortieth, was directly on the plane of the
abdominal centre. This sphere penetrated that of the
clothes ; and, although it was so marvelously fine, still
it, like its exemplar—a large soap-bubble—appeared to
be particled, or heterogeneous. Within the physical
body of the man there was a second,—itself constituting
another human form, like the vase within a vase. The
substance of this last was beautiful and pearly ; its mass
was apparently in perfect coalescence,—indivisible,
atomless and unparticled. This was the man's true
shell—his house, his home,—the outbirth of, but not
the man himself.

And now the question is asked me : " What constitutes the *ego :* what, is the man ?" The answer' is :
Soul is a thing *sui generis,* and unique. Sight, taste,
and the senses generally, are some of its properties ;—
reflection, reason, and fancy are a few of its qualities ;
—judgment its prerogative ;—physical scenes its thea-
tre ;—earthly experience its school ;—and the second
life its university, whence it will graduate to—what ?
This shall bye-and-bye be answered. Time is but one
of a vast multitude of other phases of existence, through
which it yet must pass. We know something about
its propensities, powers, methods and qualities ; but
only a very little about the soul itself. We realize
somewhat of its accidents and incidents, and not much
else beside. Most assuredly, modern "Spiritualism"
has not added much to our knowledge ; it may do so
in the future, but some of us do not like to wait.

The human being may be likened unto a circular
avenue, divided by a central wall, which separates the
known from the unknown. We begin at the centre of
this wall, our conscious point, and look toward the
outer edge of the circle ; we see one hemisphere, and
one only. What pertains to the other hemisphere,—
the one *behind* this conscious point ? Make the trial to
ascertain what lies on the thither side ; seek to fathom
the soul within you, and what results ? Why the wall
is reached, nothing more ; you strike it, think it, feel
of it, but cannot recede from nor look behind yourself.
But that there is a greater mystery behind than the one
before you is proved by the fact that your entire being
is but the result of an infinite, propulsive power, which
whirled you into being, but will never hurl you out.

There *is* a point reachable, quite beyond that of outer consciousness.

Well, the man strove to baffle the tendency to somnolence. His brain was one living mass of phosphor-like luminescence; there was a large and brilliant globe, apparently of white fire-mist, encompassing the head. Its center rested exactly on what anatomists call the *corpus callosum;* and this body—this central cerebral viscus—I affirm to be the seat of consciousness,—the blazing throne of the Immortal Soul!

On other occasions I have beheld similar bright globes of what can only be compared to pure fire. Others claim to have witnessed the same; they have described it, and uniformly, nay, invariably locate this ball on the precise spot indicated. The volume of this singular *something*, varies in different people, from the bulk of a large pea to some three or four inches in mean diameter, in which latter case it, of course, has only its axis in the place indicated, while its body penetrates the circumjacent brain. The effulgence, as the volume, also varies in different persons. In some it is, comparatively speaking, no brighter than the flame of a good candle, while in others it is an infinite intensification of the dazzling radiance of the Drummond or the calcium light. In the man before me this globe was nearly a perfect sphere; in other instances I have observed its shape to be somewhat angular. The better the person, the greater the intelligence (intuitive, not mere memory-learning), the larger, smoother, and rounder is this wondrous Soul-Sun.*

---

* This central globe is the sun of the microcosm; a duller globe of fire, situated behind the stomach, in the Solar Plexus, is its moon, and the phreno-organs are the stars; the Passional organs are the planets;

In the student I beheld the operations of this great mystery ; whenever the drowsiness came over him—and he exerted his will to keep it off—I noticed that one side of this winged globe (for there were two wing-like appendages attached thereto, something like the connections of the *uterus*) would collapse, and straightway a perfect stream of radiant fire-flecks went forth in the opposite direction, like spark-rays from the sun. These corruscations sped through all parts of the brain, causing it to sparkle more brightly ; they ran along the nerves, leaped to the muscles, and diffused new life and animation throughout the body,—which being accomplished, the globe resumed its former shape again. This struck me as being at once both sublime and curious ; but something still more so now took place.

As I observed above, when he strove to keep awake, the globe became indented, *from the outside*, which was generally smooth,—albeit a countless multitude of filmy rays of light streamed forth in all directions—the surface meanwhile retaining its polished, burnished, and ineffably dazzling general appearance.

The man laid down his book, lifted a pen, dipped it in the inkstand, held it over the table for a while, and appeared to be concentrating his thoughts ; and while he did so the winged globe within his head began to enlarge until it occupied not less than four times its original space within the brain. This it did gradually, and as gradually resumed its former bulk ; but, in the mean time, his hand had flown over the paper, and the man had indited A THOUGHT ! Anxious to know what

the Sensations are the meteors, &c., &c., there being not merely a perfect correspondence, but a wonderful similarity, complete and full, between the universe without and the universe within.

this thought was, I looked upon the paper, and was
surprised by observing a very curious phenomenon.
The words written upon the paper were : " The an-
cients were far behind the moderns in general intelligence, but far, very far beyond them in isolated instances
of mental power.   Probably the simplicity of the lives
of devout men of yore had a powerful influence in
bringing out the concealed treasures, and in developing
the extraordinary conceptive power which not a few of
them undoubtedly possessed.   Isaiah, Jeremiah, Job and
the great Cathayan have never been equaled, in their
several specialties, by men of later times ; it is ex-
tremely doubtful if they ever will be.   Really great
men are few and scarce in any age, but popular men
are plentiful in all eras.   It is only the sad-hearted
man,—he who stands and walks alone in the crowded
cities of the world, shunned, laughed at, derided,
scorned and unsupported,—who succeeds in engraving
a name upon the walls of Time ; and of all that ever
lived, Jesus, the Nazarene, looms up in such magnificent
proportions, over the edges of the dead years, that we
instinctively know that he was a real personage,—one
who lived and loved, suffered and died with, for, and
among men ; and we reject the absurdities of Strauss
and the Cavilers, and triumphantly proclaim that Jesus
was not a myth.   He sought to do good, and not to merit
the plaudits of the mob, or of those who rule.   A popular man is one who keeps just within the front ranks of
the human army, leading it whither its fancy and whim
may at the moment prompt ; but a great man is one
who volunteers to become the pioneer of the race, and
is, at the same time, the Herald of the coming age of
Goodness.   He feels the pulse of God in his heart,—

and he KNOWS to live and lives to KNOW. We are approaching an era when human genius shall be the rule,
and not the exception, as now. When that day shall
dawn, the earth will fully blossom. It has painfully
labored heretofore, and brought forth abortions—perfect, seemingly, to their contemporaries, but, in view of
her yet untested energies, abortions still."

Now, the ink had scarcely dried upon the paper, and
yet the dark violet of the aura, emitted by it when in
the inkstand, and which rose from the paper wherever
the pen touched it, was almost immediately obscured
by a far brighter one, which proceeded from the general writing ; by which I discovered that THOUGHTS
WERE LIVING THINGS, ENDOWED WITH A BEING IN THEM-
SELVES ! This thought was really a part of the man
himself. I beheld a small cell within the winged globe
open and emit a line of fire, which leaped to one of the
cerebral organs, passing up one of the fibrils and down
the other—thence to a nerve along it to the arm, the
pen, and to the paper, where it became diffused and
sealed in the inky letters. And at that moment it came
to me, from the far-off regions of positive Knowledge,
that, should the paper containing the ideas be burnt, yet
the THOUGHT itself could never perish, because it was
part and parcel of a Soul ; but it would float about
in the human world—at some time be absorbed into a
human soul, undergo a new gestation, and in due time
be born again into the conscious realm around us.

Much more the man wrote ; but at length his weary
task and the sultry weather overpowered him, and,
rising from his seat, he closed the blinds, threw himself
upon the lounge, and in a few minutes was fast asleep.
While watching the process, I became aware, for the

first time, that I was being practically educated by a glorious being—an inhabitant of the Soul-world—whose presence was now made clear, direct and palpable. This bright one conversed with me by a process not easily explained, but an idea of which may be gained if we call it *infusion of thought.* . His lips moved not, and yet the full meaning he intended, was transmitted, even more perfectly than if by the use of words. Such beings *can* speak, but not so effectively as by the silent language.

The object of his visit, he said, was to instruct me in certain essentials with reference to future usefulness on my part, but principally that the world might gain certain needed light upon the soul, and its career, through a book or books thereafter to be written. His name, he said, was RAMUS—that, in history, he was best known as Thothmes, or Thotmor, and that he was an Egyptian, of the second dynasty—a king, and the eleventh of the line.

This was all I learned of him at that time ; for after the brief introduction, he pointed toward the man upon the sofa, and bade me " Look !" The man was wrapt in deep sleep, and the winged globe within his head was rapidly altering its shape. First, it flattened out to a disk ; this disc concaved toward the skull ; then it put forth a point in the direction of the *medulla oblongata*, into which it rapidly passed, entered the spinal-marrow, and ran along the vertebræ until it reached the vicinity of the stomach. Here it left, and instantly immerged itself within the solar plexus. The man was in a death-like, dreamless slumber. " The soul," said Thotmor, " has gone to infuse new life throughout the physical body, in doing which it also recuperates its own energics. Souls can grow tired, but they find rest—not in inactivity, as doth the body, but by a change of action. The mathematician, weary of figures, finds repose by performing chemical experiments or in studying music. That man's soul is now supplying fuel to the body, by converting the essences of his system into the pabulum of life. Presently its task will be finished, whereupon it will again resume its seat upon the regal throne of its own mighty world."     *     *     *     *     *

Thotmor ceased to speak. I turned from the sleeper in wondering awe, and, guided by the rare being at my side, felt that I was once more rising through the air.

## Transmigrating—The Soul.

TURN where we will, ask whom we may, for information, we are sure to be met with the stereotyped "Know thyself." As well tell me to leap over the salt sea! I ask all mankind, the ocean, land, air, sun, moon, stars, history—everything else, both material and mental, sacred and profane—to point me out a single human being who really knows himself, or even approximately so. Where, I ask, is the wonderful mortal—tell, O tell me where?—and from hollow space the echoes mock me—where?

To know oneself! The words are easily spoken or penned ; but to *do it*, is, of all things, the hardest and most difficult ; for this very selfhood's personality is, beyond all others, the special acquaintance of whom we know the least.

The sentence "Know thyself" was written over the porch of an ancient temple. The man who placed it there must have been deeply spiced with satire and cyni-

9*

cism, else he certainly would have assigned mankind a task less arduous—a task compared to which the twelve labors of Hercules were mere child's play. Now, although this feat may never have been accomplished, still it lies within the range of the possibilities ; and in declaring that a man may, by study, find out both himself and God, I fly in the face of current philosophy, and deny the truth of the noted dogma of modern sophists, that "It is impossible for a man to explore the labyrinths of his own nature :—a principle cannot comprehend itself." Why is the logic of this doctrine faulty ? Because, first, God can certainly comprehend man. All there is of man is mind ; all there is of Deity is the same. A principle thus comprehends itself.

Man is God's image, and can do on a small what He does on an infinite scale ; and the only difference between Deity and a full man simply is, that the former can comprehend the parts of the Realm separately and together, while the latter can only grasp each truth as it swims to him on the rolling waves of Time's great sea ; yet, so far as he goes, he comprehends himself. The day will dawn when, looking back at what he was, he shall fully understand the mystery ; and as he advances, he will continually read the foregone scrolls, while new accrements of being will ever be his—each one in turn to undergo the scrutiny, each one to be fully understood, and so on forever and for aye. Were it not so, Being would be worthless and our existence a dreadful farce. Secondly : Intuition has already been proved to be the shoot, of which Omniscience is the tree—which fact disposes of the absurd dogma just quoted, and forever.

There are two mighty problems up for solution.

These are : " What and where is God ?" on which I
intend to write some day ; and the other is, " What is
the Soul ?" which I am now partially solving. This
last has proved itself to be the profoundest of all questions, and very difficult of solution ; but only so because
investigators have mistaken their vocation, and analyzed a few of the faculties, qualities, and affections of
the mind—all the while imagining the soul itself to be
under their microscopes—whereas the soul was calmly,
placidly looking on, and wondering why they were so
busily intent upon examining the furze and bushes, instead of the deep, rich soil whence they sprung.

Faculty, Fancy and Dream-life are but three of the
Soul's most common moods; and yet metaphysicians
have confined themselves to but little else than their
analysis. These are but three little rays from amidst
a multitude of others, proceeding from one common
source; yet, if even these were all analyzed, understood,
and known, the great center whence they emanate
would still remain as great a mystery as ever. Nearly
all that we know of soul is really not of it, but of its
methods of display.

There is something more of man than life, limb, sense-
faculty, affections, feeling and sex. There's a depth
beneath them all, and into these deeps I believe it possible to dive, and to bring up many a pearl, and crystal, and grains of golden sand from the floor of his
being—from out the silver sea of life, whose waters
flow soul-ward, and have their rise beneath the throne,
whereon sitteth for evermore the Infinite Eternal—the
great I AM: Aye, it *is* possible to know oneself, notwithstanding that, to ninety-nine persons in a hundred,
there seems to be an impenetrable cloud, circumvolving

them—an obscurity, thick as darkest night, hemming
them in on all sides.  Yes, thank Heaven! man *can*
untie the gordian knot, and triumphantly pass the Ru-
bicon, but not over the bridge of Mesmerism, obsession,
drugs, or any of the ordinary means usually resorted
to ; but through the continued exertion of STEADFAST-
NESS, ATTENTION, PURPOSE, and WILL—the four golden
posts to which are hung the double gates, which open
in both worlds.

Souls are, of course, the subjects of number, and in
this sense are "particles,"—souls of course being plural;
yet soul is not, for although you may subtract forty-
eight from forty-nine, and leave a remaining unit, yet
that unit is absolutely *one;* and you could no more dismember it, than you could find the lost particles of dust
upon a midge's wing.  Spirit is substance in absolute
coalescence ; matter is substance, whose particles never
touch each other ; and soul is a developed monad.  A
thought of a house is, until that thought be actualized—
surrounded with matter conforming to its shape—a
monad.  There was a period when God was alone ; he
thought, and the product of that thought is the material
universe, as we see it; he thought again—and lo! those
thoughts, each one complete in itself, took outer garments, and became human beings.  Far off, in the past
eternities, God's thoughts went forth; these were the
monads.  First, they entered into lower forms, then
higher and higher, till at last they reached organizations adapted to the perfect ripening of that which had
all along been growing.  The ripening produced Intelligence : that intelligence is the soil, out of which
Intuition grows ; and what this last advances to, we
already know.  How long, and through what countless

numbers of diverse forms, these transmigrations lasted, and passed, it were impossible to tell. We all have indistinct retrovisions, flashes of back-thought, dim and vague reminiscences of a pre-state of existence ; and we also know, that there are marvelous resemblances between men and the animal creation, just as if the soul, on quitting an inferior for a superior form, retained something of its former surroundings and characteristics. Some men physically resemble the ox, lion, tiger, dog, owl, bat, deer ; and we know that myriads resemble in their mentality the traits of character, habits and dispositions pertaining to all these animals, and others, as the fox, snake, eagle, peacock, swine, and so on to the end of a long chapter. "When I was a flower," said a little child. That child had an intuition of a mighty fact!

Now all these astonishing likenesses are not accidental, but exist in accordance with the great law of Transmigration. Mind me : I do not say, or believe, that any man or woman was ever a dog, viper, vampire-bat or tiger ; but I do affirm that the monads, which now constitute their souls, once sustained a very close relationship to the beasts of the field, and have not yet got rid of the effects of the alliance. This is a matter too clear to be disputed : else, why these very remarkable resemblances? I know, that some people will "pooh! pooh!" at this idea ; but that wont account for the *likeness !* A man never was a dog, or an owl; yet, that both dogs and owls were originally made, in order that the human monad, in passing a sort of gestation period in them, might be ripened slowly, and prepared for what he is now, I have at present no manner of doubt. Indeed, human bodies, both physical and spiritual, are but

other and higher forms, to which the Winged Globe,
Man, has transmigrated in its passage from minus to
plus—from bad to better, and from better to best. A
dog, owl, bat or human body is only so much matter ;
and the sole business of 'matter' is to furnish so many
different sorts of huts, houses, and palaces for spiritual tenants, wherein the primary schools may be attended
by the regal student-soul. I *know* that even the disenthralled spiritual body is itself but a mere vehicle of
Soul, on its next upward transmigration—is still but
an adjunct, an out-projection of, and scarcely second
cousin to, the tremendous mystery—Soul—the Winged
Globe within it. We know that man can live without his
carbonaceous body, which is but an incidental assumption in his career, a sort of garb, worn at the longest
less than a century ; that this period is scarce one second in its immense year ; and that he can see without
eyes, and know without cerebral organs.*

It is an axiom that whatever has one end, must also

---

* Many persons desire to know how to produce and cultivate clairvoyance. To such I present the following rules, knowing them to .be
efficient, and only requiring patience for success. 1st, Set apart the
first hour after retiring to bed nightly. Eat a light supper ; bind a
light silk bandage over the entire forehead and eyes, turn the face toward the darkest corner of the room, and endeavor to see. 2d, Never
call on a spirit to assist you. 3d, Keep the skin pure by daily ablu-
tions. 4th, Learn to concentrate the mind on a single object, and
keep it there. 5th, Fix it on something good, useful and true. 6th,
Pray fervently to God. 7th, Ask a mental question, and desire that
the symbolic answer may be given. 8th, Wish well to everything and
everybody.

The results will be—1st, You will see a dim haze. 2d, A spark of
light. 3d, A greater light. 4th, Misty forms will float before you.
5th, They will grow distinct. 6th, Answers will flow into your mind.
7th, You will gradually merge into a radiant light ; behold the actual
dead, converse with them, and realize your soul's desire.

have another : now, if a human soul has its first beginning here, nothing is more certain than that it will have an end somewhere. But the soul is mind—mind is God : and God is eternal. He ever existed, and ever will ; and the monads, the germ-souls here developed, and hereafter perfected, are also eternal ; they existed in all times past, and can never cease to be, for their very nature is Permanency. All bodies here, or elsewhere, are but accompaniments—instruments, tools of the royal spirit in one or more of its multitudinous phases of existence—that is to say, it creates, uses, and puts them on to serve its purposes, till it can afford to dispense with them : for human existence is a synonym of Eternal Duration—is an'immense circle : a circle is but an infinite polygon : and bodily vehicles serve the soul's purposes during its passage over a very few of the straight lines whereof this polygon is composed. And, beyond all doubt, the period will arrive—it may be away in the far-off eternities—but nevertheless *will* arrive, wherein the soul will dispense with all these characteristics of its juvenility. No one associates legs, arms, eyes, stomach, or sexual organs, with the idea of God : why then should such things be eternally predicated of man, who is fashioned after the model of the Infinite God Himself?

The body of a man is a greater thing than any object on earth beside ; is far greater than even the physical world in which he lives, because it is the master production of all the elements and forces in that world. The spiritual form that man assumes, and to which he may be said to transmigrate after the physical decease, is of far more importance, and altogether greater than is his previous physical and material structure.   A

single faculty of his measureless soul is infinitely greater
than the spirit, nor may even an archangel comprehend
fully one of these faculties, at a glance, in view of its
limitless and expansive power.   From one point he may
comprehend what the faculty was and is, but not what
it can be: yet the soul itself has untold myriads of
these ; and only God himself can embrace all at one
mental grasp—He alone can fully and perfectly know
a soul as it was, is, and is to be.   This does not con-
flict with previous assertions that a soul *can* comprehend itself ; for God's omniscience embraces the past,
the present, and the future : man only seizes upon the
first two.   Virtue and Vice, and the organs it now
uses, are but incidents in the career of this UNDER-GOD.
These things are of time—are transitory and fleeting ;
but the man is *forever !*   In view of this, what is a vice,
what is accident to this majestic being—the perfected
work of the viewless Lord of Infinite Glory?

They are but flecks upon the rose-leaf—atoms on a
moon-beam !   The immortal man is not fashioned of
such material as can be forever marred by vice, forever
happy in what now constitutes the virtues.   Its destiny
is ACTION, and in the perpetual transmigrations, con-
trasts and changes of the hereafter, it will find its truest
account, and the proper subservence of the purposes of
the awful WILL which spake it into being.   " Rest for
the weary," is there ?   There is no rest !   MAN CAN
NEVER REST !   God does not ; why then should he ?

The immortal spark within is a thing of ceaseless
activities ; not in sins and repentances, but in noble
aspirations and high and lofty doing.   Great God !   I
cower in the presence of the tiniest soul ever spoken
into being ; for I feel, by reason of the great UNVEILING

that occurred upon that wonder-filled afternoon, that, insignificant as it may seem, yet within it there are energies that now lie sleeping which shall one day awaken into Power, Beauty and most surpassing Glory. Hell is its experience of the unfit, improper and untrue ; but its wings are too powerful not to lift it, in triumph, above the flames and the deepest pit of all.   Earthly virtues are the offspring of contrast ; vice consists in bad calculation, and both will prove in the great Far-off to have been but the disciplines ordained to fit it for the business of Good and Use on the other side the curtain ;—and I clap my poor weak hands in gladness !   Who with true heart can help it ?

Man is supremely greater than, not only law, that he has found it convenient to violate or conform to, but to any and all that it is possible for him now to conceive of or imagine ; because, in the order of the great Unveiling, he will discover and come under the action of new ones, as the Night of Time moves toward the Dawn.

Those who go about in the exercise of benevolent offices are not always the most virtuous ; nor are they who heal the sick and give of their abundance to the needy ; for all these things are often done for fashion's sake.   But the man or woman who ever acts up to the highest conviction of Right and Duty, even though rack-threatened, is the most virtuous ; because in so doing the great design of God, which is individualization, and of intensification of character, is all the sooner carried out.

Human beings, male and female, talk much of virtue, which means strength, and loudly boast its possession ; yet how very few there are who will stand up and face the music which their very talk may have evoked? How they shrink when the storm comes down; how they cower when bitter denunciation and abuse pours in upon them from the ramparts of the world! All hail the glad and coming day, when we shall be what we ought! When he who wears the garb shall in very deed prove himself A MAN, the most glorious title on earth save one, and that one is—woman!

Once in a while we are greeted by the magnificent spectacle of a female who dares to stand up and practically vindicate her escutcheon, not in loud talk and "strong-minded" diatribes against what exists, but in her daily-lived truth, and the practical knowledge of those tender virtues which so endear all true women to all true men. And whenever such a woman crosses my path, I rejoice; I rejoice in the presence of such a fact, and fold her as a sister folds another to her soul. People are false to the light within them. It is a great thing to be true to self—to stand forth the champion of your noblest thought, when all fingers point at you with scorn, all heels are upraised to crush the sweet life out of you, and when only God and your own stout heart are on your side. To do this,—and, thank Heaven! some there be who dare it,—is to be more than human: is to be divine; and this heart-wrought divinity allies us to the immortal gods. This it is that I call virtue.

## The Ascent.—Marvel : The Woman.

As previously stated, it was not possible for me to understand the nature of the mysterious power by which, in company of the peerless being, Thotmor, I volitionless clove the ambient air. "O, it was a projection of your soul," says the modern novitiate of the mystic school. Not so, friend ; for the Ego then and there ascending, under the influence of a power similar in kind, but immensely superior in volume and display to itself, was not a mere psychical phasma—a thing of *appearance* only, and possessing no substantiality of its own ; it was no flimsy projection from the fancy-faculty ; was not a meaningless substance-void image of myself. It was no mere subjective state objectified, but was indeed my very self, wearing the body of immortality for a time, during which certain lessons must be and were learned, fully and practically, demonstratively and perfectly, so far as the lessons went. The man himself, and not his mere shadow or ghost was there, in proper form and essence, to the end, no doubt, that the mysteries there learned might be given, as they now practically are, to the world of thinkers.

As I, or rather we, ascended toward the zenith, it began to rain ; but this did not incommode us, nor in any way hinder the ascent, which was continued until it became necessary to penetrate a dense region of thick, black convolving cloud that was now rolling up in vast and heavy masses from the northern verge of the immense horizon, driven by the fierce breath of a mighty blast. Looking earthward, it seemed as if the deep black night was suddenly going down ; the wind howled through the buildings, and the trees shook, as if with mortal fright and terror ; the sorrowing clouds shed great drops of tears, as if mourning in comfortless grief over poor human frailty, while the soughing and the sighing of the sea was a fitting sympathium to their forlornness and despair.

Thicker rolled the dense black pall over the face of the vaulted heaven, hiding all its glories, and shrouding it in the very folds of gloom, whose density was only relieved when the broad glare of the lightnings rushed out upon the sky.  The sheets of flame were of various colors—violet, green, white, red and purple.  The three former appeared to issue from the earth's surface ; the others, from the space above and immediately around us.  There were occasionally lines of purely white fire, and these took the form of chains, every link of which carried ten thousand deaths along with it.  These came singly ; and sometimes two separate lines of fire would leap out from the bosom of the clouds simultaneously, but from opposite quarters of the gloom—in which case they appeared to meet in anger, like as if two angry gods were warring with each other, and their junction was instantaneously followed by the most terrific bursts of thunder that ever fell on human hearing since the mighty worlds were made.

I shook with mortal terror ; and this terror increased and intensified into positive, almost unendurable agony, as crash after crash of horrible roaring, rolling, bursting god-cannonry swept down the vast concave, drowning the clangor of the mad winds, which were rushing and rumbling through the spaces, striving desperately to rival and surpass the awful voice of the electric god himself.  I felt that I was lost ; and in that moment of anguish, from the deeps of my soul there went forth a prayer to Him whose presence and majesty was then recognized, with heart bowed down, and with a fervency never realized before. I feared to be swept into nothingness by the tempestuous breath of heaven ; I feared to be hurled into destruction by the driving blast! But no ; for *seemingly the wind passed through me, just as the electric current passes through human or any other material bodies, and touched me not destroyingly.* The fiercest wind that ever raged can never blow a shadow from its place, neither can it in any way blow away a spirit! for the reason, amongst others, that spirit is not matter, any more than is a shadow or a sound substantial, as this last word is generally defined ; hence wind, which is a material substance, can in no wise touch it. And so I was not blown away before the driving gale.

"But suppose a column of wind, just three yards square, and moving at the rate of two hundred miles an hour, sweeps toward the very spot on which a human spirit stands, or is ; it cannot turn this wind aside : How, then, could anything remain unmoved?" This is the question ; now the answer comes. A bar or column of sunshine streams through the air, and its volume is just three yards square. It will require something far different, and much more powerful than a column of air, moving at the rate of two hundred miles an hour, to blow away that sunshine, or to drive a hole through it ; yet the sunshine would still be there, and so would the wind! This is my answer to *that* objection. I lifted up my soul in unspeakable thankfulness and adoration, as I realized that spirit was superior to matter, even in its most subtle and rarified forms—superior even to the glaring, seething, melting, white fire of the clouds, when the lightning furnaces overflow with fervent heat!

Safely, slowly, majestically and holily we passed through this terrible battle-ground of the elements ; and to a question internally framed and put, this answer was given by the illustrious being at my side :

"That you might practically realize the indestructible nature of the human being ; that something of human majesty might appear to your understanding ; that you might be shown somewhat of the dignity of being, and the royalty of things, elements, laws and principles, hast thou been by me brought hither. This is merely a first lesson—the mere Alpha of knowledge ; but others far more important are yet to follow. Fear not!"

But this last injunction it was utterly impossible for me—and would have been for any human being under similar or analogous circumstances—to obey or do ; for what with the dizzy sense of height, the sensations attendant upon the movement through space, the glare of the lightning, the elemental strife, the perfect obscuration of my dwelling place (the earth), together with an indefinable dread of a something impending, and which I might never be able to comprehend ; this, all this, had the effect of almost palsying every faculty of being, and blanched my very soul with fear ; for the rush and crush, the horrible din of the tempest, and the thunder, made terror my constant associate. It was as if the trial hour had come ; it was like the breaking up of mighty mountains ; it was as if a hungry earthquake were feeding on a world! Instinctively I looked to Thotmor for protection. He smiled at my weakness, and bade me remember that a greater than himself was present. Yes, I realized then that God was there, and I was safe ; for He smiled between His frowns, and whispered "I AM HERE!"    *    *    *    *    In other days, when I gave my soul and body up to the guidance and control of invisible beings, whom I did not know, whom I did not stop to prove and identify—apocryphal persons, at the best—persons disembodied, if indeed they ever wore clay upon this footstool—beings who seek their own amusement at the expense of human dupes—beings who take supreme pleasure and delight in the exhibition of human weakness—beings who silently, but surely, infuse the most deadly and destructive venom, in the shape of philosophic assurances—beings who mock at our calamity and laugh when our troubles come, both of which they themselves bring to pass—beings who persuade people to believe in all sorts of inanities, dictate senseless platitudes, and encourage persons to believe themselves philosophers when they are only—fools! I repeat, when in other days I yielded to this evil influence—in other days, when both God and Thotmor were practically ignored and forgotten—in other days, when the pride and power of Eloquence turned me from the USEFUL—an eloquence weird and almost magic, that welled up through my soul and went forth from eye, and tongue, and pen, and drew my soul from God,—there came occasional twinges of regret, and an assurance that, in forgetting to profit by the teachings of that afternoon, I had bartered off priceless joys for the empty bauble 'worldly fame and ephemeral glory'—that for the hollow music of man's praises and a few claps of the hand, I had given up the Key to the magnificent Temple, one of whose apartments I that afternoon entered for the first time. Great God! how I *have* suffered for that foolish estrayal—that fearful *lege majesté*—that silly vanity and supreme folly!

We rose above the fierce turmoil, and for the first time a fair opportunity was presented for a closer scrutiny of my guide. As I drew nearer to him, he said— not in words, but in the silent language used by the higher citizens of the Republic of Souls—" All thoughts have shape : some are sharp, acute and angular, many-pointed, and exceedingly rough. These cut and bore their way through the worlds ; others are flat and disk-like : these are thoughts that must be incarnated in matter ere they become useful ; their mission is to be SEEN ; others to be *felt.* Some thoughts are light and fantastic, like bubbles on the sea ; they are beautiful while the sun shines, but the very ray that reveals their beauty also seals their doom—for the heat kills them ; they burst, and forever disappear, being hollow and of but little substance : other thoughts are round, heavy, and solid as a cannon-ball, and like them, too, their mission is to batter down the mounds erected by un-wise men. Words are but the garments of thought. Geometry is the Soul of all Sciences—order, symmetry, and form ! Everything, line, point, shape, angle and figure, corresponds to something in both the Spirit and the Soul-world (the outward and inward Soul-life), and are, independent of magnitude, absolute and arbitrary symbols, embodying an absolute and fixed principle : and every line, dot, point, shape or angle has a fixed definition in the lexicon of the Starry Heavens.* All pure and good thoughts, being themselves full of sym-

---

* What a stupendous revelation is here! What an astounding idea! For, if this statement be founded in truth, of which there can be but little if any doubt, what ages must elapse ere we be fully able to read the myriad volumes of God's great library—the boundless Universe of form, color, and sound.—PUB.

metry and beauty, can only be outwardly conveyed or
expressed ; if by the voice, by harmony, music and ryth-
mical speech and sound ; if by the pen or type, only in
characters themselves geometrically perfect, and harmo-
niously so.

" Now," said Thotmor, " you have seen much—heard
much. I have just given you a key, and to prove your
proficiency in learning, I propound a question. It is
this : What thinkest thou of Nature ?"

Now I, to whom this was addressed, could not precisely comprehend what he meant by ' Nature ;' but
naturally supposed that reference was had to the elemental disturbances and the fearful exhibition of material energy we were witnessing, and which was at that
moment unabated in the least ; for the storm still raged
with as much fury as ever—not over the same portion
of the earth, it is true, but in its own track, as it moved
on its southward march. I, therefore, answered in the
same silent language, " that, in view of all that had just
been witnessed, it was evident that an overruling power
existed, ever wakeful, ever on the watch ; that His
power was exercised for the greatest good of all the
creatures of his love ; and that God worked mysteri-
ously through nature, expressly to effect the good of
human kind." To this general answer he responded :
" Right : but what think you of Nature ?"

Here was a repetition of the identical question already propounded. It caused me to ponder a little
more deeply, and after a while, thinking that this time
he was perfectly understood, I replied : " It seems to
me that what we call ' Nature' is simply God in action ;
and that God in the sublimer sense is Deity in repose."

" Apt learner," said he, " right again. But what
10

thinkest thou of Nature?" Now here was the same interrogation a third time repeated. I now determined to study well ere venturing to reply. This I did, all the while upborne on the air by a force whose nature was not easily understood, but which I inwardly resolved to investigate and explore. The resolution was, as will be hereafter seen, most faithfully kept, with results highly gratifying and satisfactory, which will be presented in the sequel to this volume.

While delving in the mines of my soul for a proper answer, I took notice that we gently floated off and upward, at an angle of fifty-one degrees with the horizon. The storm was going in one direction, and we in the other; so that in a little time we were entirely beyond its influence, as was also that portion of the earth over which it first began to rage. There was no standard by which the rate of our velocity could be measured; but it must have been prodigious, judging by the rapidity with which the mountains, rivers and cities of the earth seemingly swept by us—for indeed there was at this point of the experience but very little, if any, sense of motion,—no cutting of the air,—no hissing as we passed through it; but it seemed as if we were in the center of a large transparent globe or sphere, which itself moved on as if impelled by a force entirely superior to that which governs rude matter. The earth itself, from the elevation we were at, seemed to have lost its general convex shape, and now looked as if it were a huge basin, so singularly did it appear to concave itself. Instinctively I realized that this was the appearance it would naturally assume to a person who looked upon it through bodily eyes from the great height at which we now were; but it was not so easy to understand why a spirit whose sense of sight was unimpeded by physiological organs or conditions—a spirit to whom the electric atmosphere, which lies embosomed in the outer air—served as the vehicle of ocular knowledge, should behold it in the same way.

But while studying the answer to the first problem, the solution of the second came to me, and I saw that the similarity of phenomena, viewed from opposite states, was attributable solely to the former habitudes of my mind, and to the association of ideas.

Thotmor saw my embarrassment, and the conclusions on the subject to which I had arrived. "Right!" said he. "But,"—ere another moment elapsed I replied: "I think that Nature is a system of active forces, ever radiating from God as beams from a star—that they go out, and as constantly return to the point whence they emanated." "Paradox! Explain!" "I mean that"—here a sudden thought struck me, and I said to the guide, "You have not dealt fairly by me; you are not Thotmor, an Egyptian of the early centuries; on the contrary, I am convinced that you have disguised yourself, and for certain reasons and purposes of your own assumed another name. You are—I feel perfectly convinced that you *must be* Socrates, the philosopher, come back for a time to pursue the old and honorable avocation,—the teaching and enlightment of the ignorant; for Socrates alone, of all earth's great children of yore, was the one who taught by asking questions of such as sought knowledge and wisdom, where he sat to dispense them. Am I not right?"

The rare being gazed tenderly down into my eyes, and his countenance glowed with a radiance quite glorious and divine, as he replied: "Yes.—No. I am Socrates

and not Thotmor ; and still am Thotmor and not Socrates. Here is another enigma. Do you comprehend ?
TRY ; for remember the human soul is infinite in its
nature ! Its capacities are boundless. You aspire to
comprehend the mighty secret of the TRINE. You
seek to become an acolyte of the imperial order of the
Rosy Cross, and to re-establish it upon the earth ; and
no TRUE ROSICRUCIAN dares shrink from attempting
the solution of the mysteries and problems that human
minds in heaven or on earth may conceive or propound.
Our motto—the motto of the great order of which I
was a brother on the earth,—an order which has, under
a variety of names, existed since the very dawn of civilization on the earth—is 'TRY.'"

Again the same method ; again this strange weird
being not only provokes to mental exertion, but reveals
a clue to millions of profound and priceless secrets !

He is then the great Ramus, the imperial lord of an
imperial order,—that great and mystic brotherhood at
whose power kings and potentates have trembled most
abjectly. And this lordly being condescends to teach
a few of the mysteries of Being to my humble self, and
through me to the world. How wonderful ! How my
soul rejoices ! Verily, from this day forth I will endeavor to prove worthy of the kingly favor.

This was my resolve ; how it was afterward forgotten
has already been stated. Men ever neglect and forget
their best friends ! But even this forgetfulness, so I have
been told, was foreseen ; it was known long years ago
that the painful career since accomplished, was the
decree of a power above my feebleness, and it was
known that all the terrible sufferings, trials, tempta-
tions and repentances were to be instruments toward

high and noble ends, not yet wholly, but to be wrought out in His own good time, who doeth all things well.

And now, on this tenth day of February, eighteen hundred and sixty-one, as I look back over the ruins of the dead months, I resolve in my soul to TRY—and, as near as may be, to approach the standard of goodness and use : for these are the ends sought to be attained by the Order.

To resume : In reply, I said : " Yes, you are, this time, fully understood ; you are Thotmor, but adopt the methods of Socrates, because they are best calculated for the purposes of teaching ; and these methods are"—" Wisdom's,—and were applied practically by the great teacher," said he, interrupting the sentence, and completing it for me, but not quite as I had intended.

" Now, scholar, answer the first question, and tell me what you think of Nature ?"

" I think that Nature is an emanation from the Glorified Person of Deity ! Tell me, truly, *is* God a person ?"

" As certainly and truly as that you are an individual, just so certain and truly is God an absolute Being— not a mere king—who, seated on the Throne of thrones, watches the procession of the worlds ; but the INEFFABLE ONE is a *working God*, who pursues His march across the vast Eternities, reducing Chaos as He goes, and leaving a train of luminous worlds behind him. You shall know more of this hereafter. Go on : tell me what you think of Nature !"

" The principles, I think, are radiations from Jehovah ; the purpose and design of this irradiation must be to perfect the universal organism ; by a commingling of forces and elements, by mutual and diverse action and counter action, the end sought is doubtless attained ; and it is through the same agencies that He reduces to Order, Law, and Symmetry the————"

I could go no further, for the reason that my conception and descriptive power had run against the wall. He saw and pitied, while he completed the sentence for me :

———— " *Nebulous Systems, which lie beyond the pale of the inhabited and waking Universe of Forms.*"

Whoever reads these pages, and clearly comprehends the meaning of his last fifteen words, can but agree that here was a stretch of thought amazing, and absolutely awful to even contemplate. They distinctly imply that God is still making worlds—worlds hereafter to be peopled with glowing forms of a life, intellect, and beauty, that shall put to the blush the highest ideal of the loftiest Seraph, now in being, when the present Universe shall have died of hoary age.

Yes ; Thotmor's thought is a vast and mighty one. Do you not think so, my reader ? Try to compass and master this idea, so terrifically great and sublime, and you will forthwith coincide with me.

What becomes of many of the ordinary conceptions of God's character now extant among even the philosophers—conceptions so unjust, puerile, and even contemptible, as many of them are ; what becomes of them all, in the presence of the estimate of the great Creative Energy just conveyed to your brain ? They fall and sink into utter nothingness, while this one looms up before our mind's eye in proportions majestic and grand. We catch an intuitive glimpse of its outlines— its edges ; but the whole thought is too great for our puny brains to contain. Try to master it, and ere

long your soul, like mine, will fold its wings in presence of its majesty.

——" The Principles and First Elements, after performing one round of duty, return to the Fountain
Head, become newly charged with portions of His
essence, refilled with the Deific energy, and then go
forth again to complete and finish what, under a less
perfect form, they have before commenced ; for all principles and elements are at bottom only one—but one
which acts under a thousand different forms :—all science is based on Music, or Harmony ; Harmony is but
Geometry and Algebra—these are but Mathematics ;
this is but one branch of Celestial Mechanics, which
in turn is only Number—but number in action ;" said
the august presence at my side, as he completed the
magnificent lesson—a lesson so full, so pregnant with
meaning, that my reader will not soon exhaust its treasures, even though he most persistently may ' TRY.'

Still benignly gazing on me, Thotmor said : " What
thinkest thou of Nature ?"

Great God ! that identical question a fourth time !
How is it possible to answer it ? I felt that, clear as my
intellect now was, it would be sheerly impossible to
proceed one single step further in definition, and was
about to abandon the attempt, when a voice, sweeter
than the dulcet melody of love, softer than the sounds
to which dreaming infants listen, more persuasive than
the lip of beauty, whispered : " *Try ! the Soul groweth
tall and comely, and waxeth powerful and strong only
as it putteth forth its Will ! Mankind are of seven great
orders : the last and greatest are the Genii of the Earth,
the Children of the Star-beam, the Inheritors of the Temple. Weak ones can never enter its vestibules ; but only*

*those who Try, and trying for a time, at length become
victors and enter in.   Man fails because of feeble, sleeping, idle Will—succeeds, because he wakes it up and ever
keeps it wakeful!"*

In an instant I turned to find whence these *spoken*
words proceeded ; and a sight of rare, surpassing
beauty, such as ravished every sense of my inner being,
fell upon my gaze.   A female of regal aspect floated on
beside the form of Thotmor ; her radiant mien, beauty
of form, loveliness of expression, and the grace of her
every movement, were such that the language we apply
to embodied woman can never convey an adequate idea
of the peerless Queen before me.   It was from her lips
that the spoken words had come.

As I gazed in utter bewilderment upon the houri,
Thotmor smiled, and said :

" This is Cynthia, whose sun I am ; my moon she is :
she is mine—I am hers—WE ARE ONE !   On earth her
body sleeps ; here her soul is awake, and tuned to the
melodies of Heaven.   We are working for the World,
and in that work find pleasure and excellent joy ; but
we only reached the bliss by Trying.   Do thou the
same, and tell thy earthly brothers to do likewise !"

Thus recalled to mental effort, I strove to conquer
my admiration for the woman, and address myself to
thought ; albeit the task was *very* difficult.

We are human beings still, whether in or out of the
body ; and the same surmises, guesses and wonderments
possess us, wheresoever we are.   Thus, I could hardly
help envying the Egyptian his glorious prize, nor wondering if he did not see much trouble and come to deep
grief on her account.   Certain it is, that no man on
earth could rest quiet with *such* a treasure of beauty

under his care ; and it struck me that, even in the Soul-world, all people could not be free from *all* the human passions, as we know them here below ; and that jealousy *might* disturb the Oriental's peace of mind, I could scarcely doubt.

He saw my mind ; and, turning to the full moon of beauty who clung to his side, said to her, " Answer for me !" She did so, and said : " Purity is the soul of Beauty, Symmetry is its spirit, and Justice is its body. Every human being, in the Soul-worlds or elsewhere, loves nothing so well as to be well thought of by all other human beings. Ambition, Emulation, and Personal Joy are the three bars, which constitute the pivot of all human character. The bad passions, as envy, strife, anger, lust, and revenge, on earth, not only destroy the body, but also mar the spirit. Every one of these, and all other evil things, thoughts or deeds, inevitably leave their marks upon the soul, and deep, sad marks they are.

"The law of *Truth*, the law of *Individuality*, and the law of *Distinctness*, (by means of which the man is rounded out into a perfect character, and is afterwards kept for all eternity totally distinct from any other being in all the universe), reign in the Soul-world ; nor can they ever be broken or evaded ;—consequently, there can be no mistakes in regard to *Identity*. Cynthia is Cynthia, Thotmor is Thotmor, Clarinda is Clarinda, and John is John—and all must remain so till the end of the Ages. It is so now, whatever it may have been in the ages wherein the angels fell.

" On earth, the real thoughts and sentiments of a soul are hidden beneath the garniture of language and assumption ;—not so here in the Soul-world, where every

10*

one must appear to be what he really is at the moment. There are no disguises; and while any one can do wrongly, if they so elect, yet they cannot *intend* wrong and *pretend* right, for the presence of an evil thought *in* the soul, is immediately marked upon its surface— upon its features, by a law of that very soul itself; and these marks and distortions are so very plain and un-. mistakable, that all Heaven can read them at a glance; and such instantly gravitate to the Middle State.

" Self-preservation, therefore, and self-respect keep Heaven clear of sin !

" In the second place, it is well known here, as it ought to be on earth, that the deceiver is, in all cases, the deceived ; the wrong-doer wrongs himself more than any one else ; and the unhappiness a person may cause another to feel, must be expiated by the causer, not by the victim ! This is a safeguard against jealousy here. No one will do an ill deed if he is aware that it cannot be kept secret, even for a moment.

" In the next place, I chose Thotmor, and he me, be- cause of all the inhabitants of this starry land, he suited me the best, and I him ; wherefore, there is a stronger attachment between us than there possibly could be be- tween either and any other individual in the great Do- main. All Heaven knows *this* fact also : hence, no one in Heaven would attempt to sunder a natural tie, be- cause they are well aware, that, even if that were pos- sible, misery, and not contentment, must be the inevita- ble result. Wherefore none in Heaven *would* attempt such a thing, and no one from other regions *could* essay it."

Like drops of water on the sands of Sahara, her blessed words sunk into my soul : the Wisdom-chambers received a new family of ideas; and my soul felt exceeding glad of this instalment of the treasures of the upper worlds.

For a moment, I remained pensive and silent; and then, inspired by the ineffable presence of Thotmor and his Cynthia, who floated on beside him—his pearly arm engirdling her glorious form in an embrace, which spoke of something higher and holier than we mortals call love—I answered: "It now seems to me that Nature is the birth-place of Affection, the tomb of all evil, the primary school of human souls, the alembic of the Virtues, the gymnasia of Thought, the"—

I was forced to stop again; nor could I go on. Thotmor came to my relief, and added:

"A plane inclined, beginning at Instinct, and ending in Omniscience; the telegraphic system of all Being, connecting its remotest points; the workshop of the Infinite and Eternal God; the grand orchestra of all the Symphonies, and the ladder reaching from Nonentity to the great Dome, beneath which sits in awful majesty the Lawmaker of the Universe, the Great I Am."

## Curves.

THIS book, which after all is but prefatory to a volume on the general subject of the life beyond, which we are, ere long, to give to the world, would be incomplete were we to neglect or omit to answer certain very pregnant questions, that must arise in the mind of the reader, as he or she proceeds in its perusal: accordingly, this section, a short one, shall be devoted to that end.

As I rose in the air, and passed over a sunny region,

which had not felt the effects of the terrific storm of thunder and rain, there came a feeling, that there was a vast difference between my then present state, and that in which the aerial journey from the city in the East was accomplished. In both cases, the altitude reached was probably the same, or approximately so ; but in the first flight I was not one-fiftieth part as conscious, or awake, as during the second : there was also a difference in the rapidity of motion.

The individual calling himself Thotmor, and concerning whose reality I am perfectly convinced, now moved through the air at but a slight elevation above me ; while formerly, I had not seen him at all, previous to making his acquaintance near the house of the sleepy student.

At one time, among my other miseries, there possessed me a very uncomfortable apprehension, lest, by some mishap, my guide should be unable to sustain me, and that I should fall. Now the reader will say, " That was impossible ; for a spirit, being lighter than air, must necessarily *ascend*." Another one will say, " True, so it must; but being so very much lighter than air, what is to hinder it from going up with a rush—what prevents it from going up vertically with the speed of a rifle ball, seeing that the pressure of air *must* force it upward with a power almost inconceivable ? *How is it that a spirit gets to earth at all, seeing that light bodies cannot displace heavy ones;* and how could a spirit move off at an angle at all ?"

These, and a multitude of other questions were present in my mind, along with many novel suggestions, provoked by the peculiar circumstances in which the narrator of these experiences was placed.

Let us try to make the matter clear, by remarking, in the first place, that the prevailing sensation was such as is experienced by those who go up into the great deep in balloons, during their novitiate in the business of cloud-climbing.

Among other questions that arose, and which I put to myself, was this: " Do I as a spirit, for the time being, actually ascend? Am I really here, on the breast of earth's great cushion—the atmosphere? or is all this an experience of the soul—an episode of dream-life? Am I really here, or is this, that so resembles me, only an *alter ego*—a second self—the result of a pushing forth of faculty? Is it a mere phantom, which my soul has shaped, and sent forth, and then lodged its intelligence in, for a time, by way of experiment and freak? If so, how is it done?

" In either case, the question is a grave one; for if it be not myself, here in the air, but only a soul-created phasma, of what sort of materials is this appearance made, and whence comes the wierd and mighty power that can call these images into being, and endow them with all the resemblance of reality?"

These and similar queries suggested themselves to me; and while the last one was still fresh in my mind, I noticed that the earth beneath me was smiling in glad freshness ;—for the storm had not passed over that part of the land, although even then and there it was raining—a soft, gentle, sweet and sunshiny summer rain, such as happens when the " Devil whips his wife " —I beg pardon—*used* to whip her ; for, according to modern philosophers, of the " Harmonial " order, he has deceased these eleven years, and, of course, cannot thus chastise her any more. Be that as it may, however, it was raining; and here was an opportunity to solve a much mooted point, namely : " Do spiritual beings get wet in a rain storm ? Do the rain-drops and hail-stones pass through them, or do they bound off as from a solid body ?" Most attentively did I make the closest observations, in order to be able to solve the question. *I decided that the rain passed through us, yet touched us not at all, as apparently did the wind.* Preferring to make every point as clear as possible, I shall attempt to illustrate this one, even at the risk of a little prolixity and repetition. The subject is an interesting one, and demands it.

Now, everybody knows that nothing less dense than water, save air, in violent motion, will turn aside or shed it ; and that which constitutes the spiritual body is, of course, infinitely finer and more subtle than even the rarest gas, much less the thick and heavy atmosphere surrounding this and all other globes.

This fact being conceded, it follows that all such bodies must be pervious ; and they are so, and *not so* at the same time. Remember that spirit is not soul ; forget not that the latter is the Winged Globe, of which I have spoken, and the former is a projection, an out-creation from it. This out-projection or spirit is, of course, perfectly atomless and unparticled. We gaze into a mirror, and behold a semblance of ourselves ; and the same figure may be gazed at by a hundred thousand eyes ; everybody will at once acknowledge that the likeness is perfect and real, yet every one knows that not one single atom of any sort of matter enters into its composition.

It cannot be handled, but everybody can see it ; nor would a pistol ball, shot through the head of that figure, harm it in the least degree, because it is not substance, although it is *substantial*. It is not a shadow, for it is real,—which latter fact is proved daily by those who first coax this image to enter a camera, and no sooner does it get fairly in than the clever artist impales it against a tablet of glass, or ivory, and lo! everybody carries the chained image to his home for everybody else to look at, who chooses so to do. This is Photography.

Now, the wind and rain, cold and heat, are as powerless and inefficient to act upon a spirit as they are upon the image in the camera, or a mirror. In other words, the spiritual body is a projected image of the soul,—is a sort of objectified subjective state ; or is a fixed idea —an out-creation.*

The image in the glass is not made up of parts,—it is a unit,—an entity,—is homogeneous. "If so, how can it be scientifically true that the rain passes through it? If it does so pass, it *must* make holes through it ; and if holes *are* made through it, then its homogeneity is at an end for evermore."

This is a fair, as it certainly is the strongest objection that can be urged against the position assumed. But the answer, which forever sets it at rest, is this : "Spirit is not matter."

The subject may be further illustrated, thus : Suppose a large sheet of flame issuing, not from a jet, but from the edge of a hollow disk, and that the rush of gas is great enough to impel the sheet of flame six feet into the air. Now, try to *wet* this flame ; it will take some time before you succeed in the enterprise. Take a watering

* This sublime truth will be elaborated at length in the second volume, of which this is the first.—*Pub.*

pot and sprinkle it to your heart's content; but, although the drops of water will reach the ground through the disk, and displace portions thereof, for an infinitesimal space of time, yet they will neither wet nor touch it.

Every drop of water has an envelope of an electric nature, doubtless ; and that each particle of flame has a corresponding one is self-evident. The respective envelopes may come in contact with each other, but their respective principles—never.

Now, the spirit is far more difficult to reach than would be this flame. As stated before, every perfect thing is globular : the sun, within the brain, I have called by its true name—a winged globe ; the electric moon, whose seat is in, on and about the solar plexus, is literally *an electric moon*, perfectly globular. The human being, body, soul, spirit, is surrounded by an at-mosphere of the same form, or nearly so ; and this enveloping aura, this spirit-garb, protects its centre— the man—from injury or contact with other things (unless, indeed, it be voluntarily broken down, or yields to assaults from without by the abjectivity of the will). True, a person may be injured magnetically through this sphere, by pressure or malaria, although itself remains unruptured and intact ; just as a pistol ball will kill a man, without actually touching his flesh. If he chance to be dressed in silk, it may drive its bulk into his flesh, yet not a particle of lead shall touch it.

I observed the aura or sphere which surrounded myself and my two glorified companions. The rain-drops passed through it, as also through portions of our respective persons, just as they would through a sheet of flame-lightning, but without actual contact or wet-ting either. We have every reason to believe that, as we ascend, the air grows colder, until at the height of forty-five miles the cold must be in the neighborhood of three thousand degrees below zero. Now, spirits frequently pass through this—they *must pass through it* to reach us, yet they are unaffected thereby, for the reason that they are superior to all material influences.

Moses, Elias, the spiritual visitants of the Patriarchs, of the man of Uz, he whom John saw,—and others, had to come through this intense cold; and the fact that they did so proves that material forces have but little, if any effect upon spirit. It therefore defies one extreme, and consequently ought the other. It does so. For the spirits seen walking about in the fiery furnace, which was heated seven times hotter than its wont, for the especial grilling of Messieurs Shadrach, Meshach and Abednego, bade defiance to fire ;—a fatal fact against the theory of a physical hell—the spirits proving not only water, ice, and wind, but *fire*-proof also !

Continuing my scrutiny, I observed that never a drop of rain fell upon the centre of the heads of either of the aerial party : for just over the crown of every human being *in* the body is a thick bone; *out* of the body, a magnetic shield, impenetrable by anything whatever ; for every drop of rain slides off it, as from an iron roof. Place a spirit under a stream of falling water, and the central globe would instantly condense to infinitesimal proportions, so firmly embraced by its. shield as to resemble the original monad ; nor could water ever come in contact with it, any more than the same water could come in contact with a plate of iron at a white heat, which every one knows is a physical impossibility. I humbly trust that I have been understood.

In reply to " How can a spirit reach earth at all, or

move through air at any angle up or down?" I reply: Electrically. It projects an image of itself to where it would be;—every man who thinks of a distant point does the same, only that the thing cannot be seen with · earthly eyes. There is a magnetic railway between the projection and the projector, along which this latter moves.

Throw forth an image by glasses across the street. It will find no difficulty in reaching the spot whither you send it. Analogous to this is the power of soul to go whither it listeth, unimpeded, and of its own free will.

The ultimatum of all philosophy is, to teach men how to live; to instruct them how to die; establish a conviction of immortality; and explain how this latter is, and why, and to whither it shall lead. The sole business of this book, and that which is to follow in due season, is not to controvert any current system of philosophy—Harmonial, Spiritualistic, or otherwise—but to present, not a mere theory or hypothesis on the subject of an hereafter and its sequences, but to give forth what I know to be the truth, so far as that truth extends; nor do I fail to be impressed with a deep assurance that, although much herein given necessarily antagonizes a few of the popular Spiritual theories, yet I believe that that which I have now given concerning the soul and its destiny, is perfectly true and correct. I care not how much soever the reader may doubt the aerial experiences herein narrated—for these are but illustrative, at best, and in other respects are of little account—yet the *Theory I know to be the only true one yet advanced;* and it is to the *principles* wherein this theory is founded, that I call the attention of the Thinking World, and challenge its respect.

Not a human being, whom I ever saw, was fully satisfied with either Modern Spiritualism, or what is called Harmonial Philosophy ; for the more a man bases his hopes of a life hereafter upon either of them, the more he stands on slippery ground.  Doubt after doubt seizes on the mind, until at last people turn away, sad-hearted and desperate, from so-called systems of Immortalism, to take refuge in the church, which erewhile they so loudly berated and condemned—resort once again to the Blessed Book, or else unhappily drift out upon the shoreless, hopeless sea of atheism.  There are untold multitudes who will gladly hail anything that promises to remove the dreadful doubts concerning, not only their continued existence, but their chances of bliss beyond the veil.  To such this book and its fellow comes ; for the benefit of such they both are, and are to be sent forth upon the world's great tide.

Thoroughly imbued with the *spirit* of the truths here written—with the principles set forth and running like a gold-vein through that portion which is descriptive mainly—no one can help feeling strong in the certitude of an hereafter—this being the only attempt ever yet made in this country to treat of the soul *per se*, and in its higher and deeper relations, so far as the writer is aware.

Concerning the absolute origin and final destiny of the soul itself, the answer to the question, What is God, and a few others of equal import, the reader must wait for the second volume ; for, in the present, we have only entered the outskirts of the illimitable course—have scarcely touched the preface of the mighty volume,

SOUL. Herein we are only at the top of one of the lesser hills, from which we catch a faint, very faint view, and hear but the distant throbbing pulses of the vast ocean, on whose swelling bosom, and upborne by whose wisdom-crested waves all men shall ere long sail.

As true lovers of our race, we ask all good people to embark with us anon upon an intellectual voyage across the Deep, in search of facts and truths far more stately and sublime than those usually purporting to come from super-mundane sources.

All truths are necessarily dogmatic; nor has any attempt herein been made to hinder their expression from being the same. Our great Master and Exemplar in virtue was dogmatic—why not his followers be the same?

It seems essential, at this point, that the writer should say something, not concerning the spiritual realms, but of the man-spirit—the self—the developed and developing monad. Now, what is a monad? The reply is: Something quite analogous to, but not exactly, the Leibnitzian 'Particle,' but that which is to universal spirit precisely what an atom is to universal substance or matter—with this difference: you cannot cut an *idea* into halves or pieces, for it is, was, and ever will be, a unit; so is a monad.

An atom of matter is divisible to infinity—a single grain of sand being, by a mental process, capable of disintegration so great, that were each portion to be separated from its fellow by only the millionth of an inch, yet the vast concave of the dome, the walls of the sidereal heaven, the awful height and depths of space, the dizzy steeps of the great Profound, would not afford room to hold them all, even though the worlds were rushed out of being for accommodation's sake. Yet not one of these portions would be spirit, because *that* is indivisible ; *they* can never be. It is a philosophic truth, as well as a scientific axiom, that "Matter is divisible forever ; spirit is not."

Beasts have spirits, but not immortal ones ; for the reason that they are the result of mere physical energy, and natural elements acted on by natural forces. Their mission is to serve certain uses, the greatest of which is that of affording, in some mysterious way, temporary homes for higher beings, or rather for what is thereafter to become such—as already alluded to in the article on Transmigration.

Nothing material is endowed with perpetuity ; for nothing particled can ever be so. True it is, that the spirit of a beast is many degrees finer in texture, and more sublimated than the luminiferous ether by which we come in contact with colors ; but the soul of a man is myriads of degrees more subtile in constitution than even this essential part of animals. The last is particled, the former homogeneous, *sui generis*, Deific in origin, peculiar in nature, expansive in power, infinite in capacity of acquirement, and probably eternal in duration.

Comparisons are useful : Suppose, then, that the sacred rite is to be celebrated that shall call a new soul into outer being. Well, at the moment of orgasm, there leaps forth from the very heart of the winged globe a monad ; with the speed of light, it rushes down the spinal column, supplied in its route with a nervo-magnetic garment—a voluntary contribution from every particle of his physical being. It reaches the neighborhood of the prostate gland, passes through it, during which it receives additional envelopes, of a nature easily understood. Its next leap is to the prepared ovum, which it only reaches after taking refuge in a hollow, shell, attached to what is called the " head of a spermatozoa," which in itself is the half germ (the ovum being the other) of the physical structure.

Imagine, if you please, a monad just incarnated in many folds. Its color is a pearly white, approaching the hue of pure fire; its bulk, with its investments about one-tenth that of the head of a small pin ; without them, about so much less that probably a million might float without contact in a single drop of water. Its envelopes are the very incarnations and condensations of electricity and magnetism ; and so possess the power of repelling uncongenialities, and of attracting whatever is essential to its development, during and subsequent to its temporary home at the gestative centre. The essences and life of all that the parent may eat and drink, or breathe—as perfumes, odors, and so forth—are gravitative to the precious point ; and so the monad unfolds, and its envelopes grow ; the one destined to become a living, active soul—the other, the temple of flesh and blood, in which it will, for three score years and ten, more or less, exercise and improve its faculties and powers. Now, this process is exactly analogous to that whereby God Himself brings humans into being ; only that instead of having a female form to shield them (the monads), He made use of matter in other forms—worlds, and substantial things. It is easy to see how the first human being was brought into existence, albeit the full statement thereof belongs to another volume than the present—the first part of the present one merely giving an outline thereof.

Man's body is of the earth, earthy; it serves the

soul's purposes for a time, and when it can no longer do so, we die because it is the nature of matter to decay and change ; but soul being of God, the HONOVER, AUM, the SACRED, the HOLY, the GREAT MYSTERY, lives on forever and for evermore ; and in all human probability unfolds continually and incessantly.

Could you procure a microscopic view of a monad, you would behold a perfect resemblance of a human being of infinitesimal proportions, standing at full length, but with closed eyes, in the midst of a surrounding and protecting sphere, formed of something a myriad degrees more sublimated than the rarest imponderable known to science.*

Soul has two methods of increase : first, it feeds on notions, thoughts, sensations, ideas, emotions, hopes, joys, fears and anticipations, based on that which is external of itself. The experiences and discipline thus derived, constitute Progression. On the other hand, it creates, moulds, and fashions things *from* itself, and by the exercise, grows intuitive and strong. This is Development, or Unfolding. Souls are all of the same

---

* " Over the graves of the newly dead, may, on dark nights, be seen hovering the forms of those within them—strange, ghastly, ghostly forms they are. The exhalations of the decaying bodies assume the shape and proportions of the living being, and affright the passers by."—*Jung Stilling.*

" Burn a rose, and then mix its asheswith water in a bowl ; set it away in a still place, and in a few days a thin, glairy scum will rise upon the surface, and arrange itself in the exact form of the original flower."—*Report of Acad. Sci., Paris,* 1834.

The acorn, split in two and exposed to a strong light and high magnifying power, will disclose the perfect outlines of an oak tree. The germ of all things contains the likeness of what hereafter they are destined to become, and so also does the germ or monad of a man.

PUB.

genesis, but, like trees of the forest, there are vast differences between them. Men often speak of "full souls, big souls, weak souls, strong souls, lean and fat souls," and so on—thus leaping to a truth by a single bound of intuition. For no greater truths exist than those words convey. People grow weary by labor, that's physical exhaustion ; and of pleasure, that's sensational weariness ; and of thinking, hoping, cogitating on a single subject, that's soul-tiredness—for all of which rest is demanded, or rather a change of attention and occupation.

The body is a laboratory, wherein the most beautiful and useful chemical labors are carried on ; and it extracts and distils the finest essences from all things it manipulates. True it is, that a coarse man will only extract physical energy from beef and wine ; but it is also true that these things contain something far more rare, and so subtle that it requires a stomach of finer texture and more elevated order to extract the higher essences, that go to inspire genius, develope poets, and sustain philosophers in thinking.

Some persons manufacture bleaching salts and oil of vitriol ; others compouud the delicate odors which float upon the air of palaces, and radiate from the garments of refined women ; yet both are chemists. And so of human bodies ; they feed on the essences of food, and convert these essences into the most spiritual forms possible ; this last is duly laid away in numberless magazines, or store-houses, which we call the " Nervous Ganglia." When these·stores are distributed, the body grows strong. When the supply is exhausted, we become faint and weary, and finally fall *asleep*, whereupon the soul-sun sets for a while (vide the case of the stu-

dent), withdraws from the brain, passes down the vertebræ, enters the solar plexus, changes the refined essences
of the ganglia into pure fire, endows it with portions of
its own divine life, sends a supply to every point where
the communications are not cut off by disease ; and so
increases the vigor, life, and bulk of the body.

When this recuperative work is done, the soul sometimes rests awhile, and remains shut out from this world
for hours ; during which time our existence is vegetative only, and we are in a deathly slumber, so far as
outward consciousness is concerned.  At such times, the
soul is making itself familiar with the elements of that
lofty and transcendant knowledge which all good human
beings are destined to fully acquire after death.  It is
talking with God, and God is in turn conversing with
it.  It is perusing its volume of Reminiscences, and
these sometimes vaguely, dimly flash forth on the outward memory, causing men to doubt the story that they
have not pre-existed.  Sometimes it is intently listening
to the glorious melodies which the seraphim sing, or
drinking in the knowledge of archangels ; for it is indeed true that—

> "Sometimes the aerial synod bends,
> And the mighty choir descends,
> And the brains of men thenceforth
> Teem with unaccustomed thoughts."

The soul returns from the inner to the outer life, and,
in spite of philosophy or reasoning to the contrary, *will*
entertain vague memories, indistinct yet half-positive
assurances of having been aforetime in some other place
than earth, or hell, or heaven ; nor can it get rid of this
conviction, because it is *true !*  *We have existed* SOME-
WHERE ELSE !  We *have* lived and acted parts before,

11

long ages ago, before this world was ushered into being from the fiery vortex of the Sun of suns ; *we have lived* and moved and had a being in a strange and far-off world.

> A realm of mystery and wonder, memory-filled, sublime ;
> Not in this world, or hell, heaven, space or time !

And so we sleep.  At other times, without arousing the body, the soul cautiously re-ascends its daily throne, takes advantage of the physical quiescence and slumber, and plays many a fantastic trick with the materials in its magazines,—all for its own amusement and that of its phantasmal comrades and lookers on, who do not fail to gather round the bedside and join the spectral sport.

Sometimes it overhauls the sheets of memory, sportively, racily, jocundly, mixes them all together, puts incongruous events alongside of bitter remembrances ; takes a character here, and one there, and forces them to perform the most ridiculous and absurd dramas imaginable ; nor does imagination itself escape, for the soul touches it, and forthwith it produces, like a fecund mother, and the night-born offspring are forced to mingle themselves in one indescribable medley, along with things of pure memory and reminiscence, thus forming an *olla podrida* without order, system, head, foot, beginning or end.   We are dreaming !*

---

* An objection may be urged here, to the effect that animals dream, as well as human beings.  Dogs bark in their sleep, and manifest all the phenomena of dreaming.  Has the dog, therefore, got a soul that pernoctates, goes abroad, and so forth?  To this I reply : It is by no means certain that the sleep-barking of dogs and other beasts is anything more or less than a merely physical, nervous agitation.  I am not sure that they really do have dreams.  Still, on this point I am

At other times, having placed proper sentinels to guard the body and telegraph to itself on the least appearance of danger, the royal soul, feeling its high-born nature demanding a supply not to be found within itself always, leaves for a while the scene of its sojourn, and leaps upward to the starry vault, to hold converse with the stars and their holy tenants : Then we have visions !

Again, it takes journeys over the earth's surface, visits old, familiar, or new and unknown places, persons and things : Then we are clairvoyant.

These are moods and phases of the soul's existence and activities, but they are not the highest ; for, at still other times, it arrays itself in its most regal garb, and, marshaled by an army itself has called into being, solemnly marches forth to attend THE COUNCIL OF THE HOURS!—and here a holy awe steals over me, as this trait and power of the soul is revealed. At such times we PROPHECY and become familiar with events, persons, principles, and things yet unborn in time and space ;— we have receded behind the wall of consciousness, and bathed for a time in the sea of mystery, every billow and wavelet of which constitutes a destiny. For that all things that are yet to be, at this moment exist as monads and uncarnated thoughts in the Mind of Minds, there cannot be a shadow of doubt ; nether can there

---

open to conviction, and just as soon as any well-bred dog, not one of your mongrel hounds either, shall tell me what he dreamed, I will announce that highly interesting fact to the world ; but until one shall do so, I shall insist upon the hypothesis, above set forth, that these somnolent exhibitions are in some way connected with what I call the process of monad-gestation, and not to the dreaming of the beast as such.

be one that man has been, still is, and hereafter will be, intromitted to this sacred labyrinth of knowledge, under certain conditions yet unknown to us. And yet man is a free-acting being.

Bye-and-bye the sleep is ended, and we return to outer, every-day life. The soul's magazines have been stored full of the needful energies, both for itself and body; and it can at will, and sometimes by the action of a power lying back of volition, send forth these fiery elements to warm up and invigorate the outer self, as occasion may demand. Thus comes the blush of love, the inspiration of song, and acting, the fire and energy of speech and oratory, the flames of lust and passion, the brutal vigor of the athlete and pugilist, the blaze of anger, and the sudden and awful courage and ferocity of those who, at other times, are poltroons and errant cowards.

Of course, some people accumulate more of this fire than others, and some are more sensitive to its action— even when it is quiescent—than less fine organizations possibly could be ; and these very sensitive persons will, from the effect this accumulated power has upon them, tell you more of an individual's character from a half hour's association, than others could after a dozen years of intimacy, for they come in almost direct *rapport* with the soul itself, with something of which the "sphere" is charged ; whereas those who are not so sensitive must base their verdict on what they see and hear,—the others, on what they feel and know.

This fact is beginning to be well known ; but there is a consideration arising out of it of vast importance. It is this : Those who are most sensitive are the very ones who absorb deepest of those energies. They draw it in like sponges, and give it out the same, as may be daily seen on the platforms whence "spiritual mediums" fulminate their doctrines. There you will see a fine, sensitive, delicate woman speaking for hours in tones of thunder, and with an energy sufficient to rack a far stouter frame to pieces,—physically sustained by what she draws from the audience, and returns likewise,—with something added from herself. Such persons, sitting in "circles," either draw off the very life of those with whom they join hands or come in contact, or else themselves are sponged dry.* Now, one of these sensitives will so absorb the sphere of persons with whom they may chance to be, that they may be led to do many a naughty thing, even against their own inclinations and judgment;—especially is this true with reference to the tender passion. Their conduct may be very reprehensible, their hearts be very pure. Of course this condition is a morbid one, and should be sternly fought against and battled down.

The question is often asked, " Do spirits eat ?" Answer: In the Middle States, eating is a strong phantasy ; the inhabitants believe they eat. In the Soul-world stomachs are useless, as well as the organs of sex, but the soul absorbs nutriment spontaneously. *There is no waste !*

Having thus briefly replied to the objections likely to be raised, I now resume the narrative at the point where it was left incomplete. What further took place will be found in the next section.

As the splendid sentences of Thotmor, recorded in a previous section, fell upon the hearing of my soul, that

---

* For further light on this point see a book called " The Sexual Question," by the writer of this work, and shortly to be published.

soul involuntarily bowed itself in awe: and as the expression, "*the workshop of the Eternal God; the orchestra of the Symphonies, the ladder reaching from Nothing to the Great Dome, beneath which sits in awful majesty, the* GREAT I AM,"—reached my understanding, there went up from the soul's deepest profound a desire to know who, what, and where was this supreme Ruler of the starry skies.

Scarcely was this thought fairly formed, when a deep slumber gently but rapidly stole over me. How long it continued I know not, but when consciousness for a moment returned again, I found myself brushing the dust from my apparel, beneath the trees from which my first journey had commenced. This occupation could not have lasted more than a minute, when I started off mechanically toward a deeper nook, and more secluded spot among the trees and bushes, apparently guided by instinct, or directed by a power above myself. And I lay me down, as if wearied with undue physical labor, and soon a gentle buzzing sound, like unto that made by myriad insects when the Day-God hies him to his slumber, and all the great, big world is still, lulled me into a sweet and soft repose. And a deep sleep fell upon my eyelids; and in that strange, mysterious rest, I experienced that which was not *all* a dream. I hasten to present the result of this last display of power.

## The Flight.

LIGHTLY, as floats the atom on a sunbeam, swiftly as the bird flies, gaily as a laughing child, a spiritual form sailed stilly through the SPACE. Beneath it rolled the globe, its black mountains, deep valleys, and all its silvery seas ; above it twinkled the starry shield of Heaven ; and afar off, on either hand, great suns looked out to see the moving panoply.

And still the soul sped on ; until, at last, its earthly home was in the distance, and all around the mighty Silence reigned. And still the soul swept onward! No dizziness, no faltering, from the awful sense of height, alarmed it ; no fear beset its bounding, joyous, happy heart. That soul was not my own, for the reason that no man can possibly predicate ownership of a soul—the thinking-principle—Mind ; for soul *is himself*. He can speak of, and say, " my body, limbs, faculties, qualities," and so forth, with correctness and propriety ; for these are his incidents, but *soul* is himself—that of which these incidents obtain. They are, to coin a word, the *outsphering* of the inner being : the soul was me.

In a little while, the question, " What, and why is this ? and whither am I going ?" rose in my mind. A silvery voice breathed silently into my spirit this response : " *Whoso truly willeth to know, shall know, by reason of the relationship between himself and the other two members of the great Eternal Trine*, provided always that the *wish is good*, and its realization would be productive of Excellence and Use.

" No bad man can earnestly wish and will good, *while* he is bad ; if he does, his failure is certain : not so with the good and lofty soul ! It is always welcome to the banquet of knowledge ; nor is the gate of Wisdom ever closed to it. The good man can solve all mysteries ; the good woman sound the depths of all Music, Love, and Beauty. Thus the saying is literally, perfectly, absolutely true, which affirms that if ye ' Seek first the

Kingdom of God and his righteousness, all things else shall be added unto you !' "

The voice was that of the fair being, whom Thotmor called his own. Previously intent upon observing the rapid changes about me, I did not, until that moment, realize that both these auroral spirits attended on this, my third flight.

" Brother," continued the sweet being, " Forget not the first lesson ; the second, thou art now receiving."

For a little while, still pondering on what I had been taught, and still moving forward and upward, I made no mental response or observation. Soon recurred to me, the phrase used by the female teacher a little time before : " And the two other members of the great Eternal Trine." I longed to know the meaning ; and at that instant a clearness of perception, power of conception, and ability of comprehension, was given to me, such as I never knew before. I asked mentally, how *this* came about, and the answer came to my understanding, through the channel of a clear intuition, and shaped itself in the following form, as nearly as words will hold it.

" The earth is coarse, yet imprisons the refined. It is a dense, gross substance, a heavy rough body, but it has a soul. The soul of the world is spirit. Every atom of matter has a moving, living, active, spiritual centre. The matter enchains the spirit, and the spirit (the principles of Beauty, Use, Goodness, Music, Odor, Tone, Sound, Rhythm, Shape, Sympathy and Coherence, constitute the World-soul or spirit)—and the spirit ever struggles to free itself from its unwilling thraldom. It can only do so by working up the *material* of its prison house into forms of Excellence, Use, Beauty, Sound,

Tone, Shape and Rhythm. When it does so, it escapes its jail, and goes back to God, whence it originally came, through the human organization, and others less perfect, in the form of Odors, Music, Tone, Sound, Beauty (flowers, forests, &c.) Art, Color, and their cognates. A rose is that success in its struggle, which attends that amount and phase of spirit, working out its liberation, from and through matter, by means of its inherent self—the principles named.

There are two Realms : Matter, filled with spirit, and Spirit (above, beyond), free of material encumbrance— the great Spiritual Ocean, in which all the worlds are floating.* The World-soul is spirit, negative : the great Ocean is spirit, positive. In it floats, rained down from the Infinite, myriads of existences, in the form of MONADS—each one a particle of soul given off, so to speak, from the great Eternal Brain.

These monads are not spirit negative, such as is contained in and constitutes the soul of the world, of matter in all its million forms of beasts, birds, reptiles, and vegetation ; nor spirit positive, such as constitutes the Sea whereon the worlds do float, and whose finer breath is the sphere of disembodied souls ; but they are the original soul-germs of immortal beings—they are the sparks which fell, and fall from God himself—particles of the Deific brain, unique, *sui generis*, unparticled, ho-

---

* I realized this tremendous truth. The links of the chain are : Granite Rock, Water, Atmosphere, extending about one hundred and fifty miles upward ; Electrical Sea, above the air, one hundred miles ; Magnetic Ocean, one hundred more ; above that, each remove being as great as between the first two, the ocean of Electrime, one hundred miles (the figures are approximative only). Next an ocean of Magnetime, then Ether, then Ethyle, and then the great Ocean of Spirit positive. All the rest are CUSHIONS, as it were, to this, our world.

11*

mogeneous: old as Deity, young as the new-born in-
fant; always existed, ever will exist. They are Pha-
souls (Fay-souls,) or Monads.

I now realized this strange truth : that the conscious
soul that constituted *me* was now beyond, as it were, all
the circumvolving material atmospheres surrounding.
earth, and that it was rapidly approaching the awful
and vast Spiritual Ocean. Presently it ceased its
flight, turned earthward, and made the following discovery : first, the SPIRITUAL pervaded the Ethylic Sea :
this, in turn, the Etherial ; that, the Magnetimic ; that,
in turn, Electrimic ; that, the Magnetic ; that, the Electric ; and that, in turn, the Earth Sphere, or 'Odylic'
emanation, which in turn pervades the atmospheric or
Oxygenic ; so that man really breathes several, instead
of a single atmosphere—the highest of which quickens
the spirit, as the lower does the body.

Turning the gaze outward, a fine, glorious, soft, silvery sea was seen spreading away in all directions ;
and the eye had no difficulty in traversing space, as on
earth it has, through the corporeal structure and the
several earth-airs. In this clear expanse of Spirit floats
uncounted globular monads, infinite in number, infinitesimal in volume ; they are each enveloped in a fine
electric substance, which surrounds them perfectly. The
spiritual waves bear them on its bosom to the earth ;
they, by a mysterious power, are drawn to the human
male brain, through the lungs ; they enter it, become
lodged, remain till a certain physical work is completed,
and then descend and effect their mission through the
aid of the prostate gland. At *certain times*, they quit
this, pass into the uterus, enveloped in the prostatic

mulse ; are caught up—are carried to the womb, and—
the work of INCARNATION is effected.*

Here, in these aerial Kingdoms, beyond the domain of
matter and the sphere of what we call Nature, or Natural Law, which of course does not govern Spirit, it having a mode of its own, I found two sorts of monads—
the one perfectly globular, which constitutes the germ
of the man—the others ovoidal, which constitutes the
germ of the female.  There are always two together : in
couples they come from the Eternal God, in couples
they return.

Placed in the uterus, these come in loving relations
with a subtile spirit originally in the female monad,
subsequently energized in the woman, condensed in the
' ova,' and there is a blending of elements—the external of the monad, and the internal of the ova ; and from
this blending springs a third something, which is the
nucleus of the nervous body, so to speak.  This nucleus
robs all earthly things of their vital life—plants, flowers, food, drink, and so on—through the instrumentality of all the bodily organs.  This union produces an
improvement in both ; together, they attract the great
spiritual substance or atmosphere pervading our air,
and then the child is quickened, and rises in the pelvis ;
the very instant that the first spark of this great spiritual atmosphere passes into the babe, the monad increases in bulk, bursts its bonds or envelopes, passes
from the foetal lungs to its brain, locates in the pineal
gland, radiates through the *corpus collossum*, energizes
its body, and, lo ! a soul has entered upon a new career.

* My business is with *facts* here ; therefore, I shall briefly state what
I beheld, and leave others to theorize—satisfied, as I am, that I have
penetrated the GRAND SECRET.

As said before, the soul grows—grows in two ways : first, by development—unfolding and awakening ; second, by acquired knowledge and experience. The latter is of and for the *earth*, the former is of and for the soul itself. The one depends on circumstance and accident, the other is above and beyond both. There may never be much of the latter, but the former will, must go on to Infinity. Both may go on to a great extent on earth ; one certainly will in the Hereafter.

All these things I felt, I saw, and knew, as I floated there on the shores of the Spiritual Kingdoms.

Have you ever beheld the golden rain of a rocket, on a stilly summer night ? You have ? Well, just so God rains monads from Himself ! Spirit is the emanation from God's body ! Monads are corruscations from His Soul ! These truths can never be *demonstrated ;* all spiritual truth is real, and demonstration is effective only in reference to fleeting appearances. The logical faculty deals with what pertains to us on earth ; that which pertains to the Spiritual, requires some higher power of the soul. It has it—in the Intuitions. The logical faculty deals with Progress ; Intuition with Development—unfolding : organic the one—central-soul the other. Intuition will one day substantiate my discoveries—when I am dead, and this writing is a century old.

At present there is really no Spiritual Philosophy at all—scarcely an approximation thereto. We have not even a spiritual nomenclature, and it is exceedingly difficult to convey spiritual facts or ideas in terms notoriously adapted only to the expression of transitory earthly knowledge.

Swedenborg's ideas are worth all others on the great

subject, yet he even must be read in Latin or German, to be correctly understood. The English is the tongue of commerce—has too much ring of the dollar in it—to be used to express spiritual things. I shall try to convey my experiences so as to be understood ; yet how can I hope to be ?—how make the fact known, that one human soul is actually larger, deeper, greater, than this whole material globe ?—that it has a sun, within the cerebrum ; a moon, the solar plexus ; that its sun rises (when we wake), and sets, retires to the vertebral column, sinks within the great ganglion, behind the stomach, when we sleep ; that it has stars, the nerve-villi ; planets, the ganglia ; it has a milky way, the great nervous cord ; comets, and, in short, everything that the outer world has, and much beside. How shall I express these facts so as to be understood ? for the terms I use do not convey the exact meaning. Who can understand that the soul has hills, mountains, valleys, and so forth ? Yet it hath all these things in a higher and heavenly sense. Still more difficult will it be to prove or show that the Bible saying, that " the kingdom of heaven is within" every one, is a literal truth. The soul, *per se*, contains within itself the sum total of a dozen universes, each differing from the other, each one overlying that beneath it ; and just as fast as the soul outgrows, unfolds from, or ' vastates' either of these, new and higher ones become apparent, just as there dwells an appreciation of the refined and beautiful in every coarse man or woman ; but, in order that this esthetic sense shall come out and be active, a certain discipline is essential, the result of which is a vastation and throwing off of what impeded and obstructed this beauty-sense. This is the end and mission of education or discipline. Our principal life—for we lead several at the same time, is the life of Imagination. We form, in fact create, by a mystic power not yet understood, whole galleries of paintings, figures, adventures and circumstances, ' houses in Spain,' ' castles in the air.' These are our in-creations, because, while yet in the body, they loom up in the deep, distant depths of the mind, as images more or less vague and shadowy. They are as yet within us, pictured, as they are, upon the outer surfaces of the soul, yet within the radius of the spirit.

After death, these become the realities of our then existence, are the spontaneous out-births or out-creations of our souls, and in them we live, move, and have our being—happy, joyous, pleasant, provided our souls are beautiful, calm, and serene ; but if they be not so, then those out-creations are full of horrors—serpents, noisome things, reptiles and dead men's bones.

Few, very few clairvoyants have ever beheld the realities of the spiritual world. I know of but few, contemporaneous or historical, whom I believe to have ever beheld the mysteries of the other life. Amongst the few, Behmen, Swedenborg, and Harris stand pre-eminent. The others—some of them honest, doubtless, but often deluded—have beheld their own out-creations, or the spiritual photographs on the sky-surfaces of things and events pertaining to the earth. Every out-creation differs from all others ; hence arises the annoying discrepancies and diverse accounts of the same things, which we are constantly receiving—as, for instance, the spirit-land, the sun, moon, planets, and their occupants, as given by various so-called modern seers. The memory of man is internal to himself while here, but after death it is, as it were, the furniture of the parlor where-in he lives on the other side of time ; and these tableau-vivants, or living pictures, when seen by clairvoyants, are passed off upon men as the revelation of realities, when they are but the ephemera of existence. Spirits tell us of their legs, lungs, bodies, lands, parks, and so forth,—and of their gardens, houses, trees, forests, and the like. All this is very well, and are spiritual facts *to them*, yet are but the out-creations of the human soul, which really has no legs, arms, and so forth, because the soul is MIND, and can have no possible use for these things ; yet, for a long period, these very things are realities to the spirit and to clairvoyants.

The fact is, good spirits do not appear one-tenth as often as imagined ; the majority of spiritual appear-ances are but out-creations—subjective images of the seer, objectified—else are psychological projections of other minds—images impressed upon the susceptible person's brain.

The spiritual world, as it is generally mapped out to us, appears but a few degrees in advance of this one, on the same general plane, if we are to believe the tales told us concerning it ; while the fact is, that world is not like this in any respect. It is not a place, literally speaking, but is a condition—a single one of thousands that have been—of millions yet to be. Dream-life is a good illustration of my meaning. It is a condition of the soul. In it, we have a life actual, real, absolute ; not in far-off regions, because we are still in our bed-rooms ; but in the midst of our own private domain, our own out-creations, our personal universe.

The human soul, as said before, is a divine kaleides-cope, which forever changes, yet never exhausts its ca-

pacity, either *for* change, or for appreciation for the bliss
thence derived, or of trouble encountered.  So we have
no need of legs in the spirit-world, because our movements are not with reference to space—we have done
with roads and distances there ; but our changes are of
state or condition.  Illustration : Anna is a beautiful
girl—pious, good, pure, excellent ; sits beside her lover,
John—a polished scoundrel in every sense.  One bullet
kills both, instantly.  They die on the spot.  Both
awake in the other life—in the *same room*, yet are a
million miles apart, because their respective mental
states determine their relation to each other *there*, albeit
other things determine it here.

They may never not only not meet again, but never
know aught of each other, so vast is the real distance
(condition) between the twain.  The spiritual world of
the one will abound with forms of beauty, use, goodness :
that of the other will abound with toads, swamps,
snakes, bugs and unseemly things.  Why ?—because
each is surrounded with his or her personal out-creations.  Each communicating back to earth, will tell
what each beholds ; both will be true, yet both fail to
give even the ghost of a real notion about the absolute
supernal world.  Whatever we are, we see ; whatever
we want, is there before us—we have.  Thus we can
ascend in goodness, or sink away to the very depths of
hell—both our own, however. * * * * * And all these
things came to me there, as I floated on a wave of the
sea of knowledge.

Self-induced psycho-vision often passes as the product
of spirits.  The line is yet to be drawn between the
seeming and the real in this respect.  Spirits first are
monads—spiritual (psychal) atoms—God-existent from

all past eternity : Secondly, they are awakened beings, self-existent to all future states—not times merely : Thirdly, at physical birth they, as monads, cease to be ; at physical death a change as complete and great as the last occurs. And now they have passed through, and across three eternities ; that of monads, matter, and spirit ; and fourthly, they remain in no condition above a century (which accounts for the fact that no well-authenticated instance of intercourse with a spirit over a century dead, has yet been recorded) ; lastly, they ever pass onward, and each condition differs from the last, as does sleep from wakefulness. There are millions of these changes. It takes about a century to graduate and gravitate from one condition to another. When we pass from this world, we take some things with us which we are obliged to unlearn there. Thus, some want drink, others rest, fruit, land, houses, money, and so forth ; some want children and desire to cohabit as on earth. All have just what they want ; only that the children begotten there, are mere phasmas—just as by a powerful effort we can create a beautiful puppy dog, and hold it as an ideal before our eyes while here.

A crazy man's golden crown and throne, although to us nothing but straw and bits of stone, are to him gold and diamonds ; and flash forth the richest scintillations of the most precious jewels. It is a state of the mind. Millions of crazy people inhabit both worlds ; whence it follows that insanity *is* a disease of the mind, as well as a result of organic and chemical change and disturbance in the body.

It is hard to describe spiritual things in material language. Amongst all the flood of " Spiritual literature," I know of no single work that gives the faintest idea of spiritual actualities.* All that passes current, as such, is far more ideal and material than spiritual, and are referable, as to their origin, to excited ideality, and other peculiar mental states, rather than to the Supernal world. Amidst the three million speeches a year, delivered under professed spirit influence, it is my deliberate conviction, that not over ten in one thousand has its source in the pure Soul-realm, but many originate in the Middle-states of the spiritual world; very many of the vivid and beautiful descriptions of spirit life, scenery and so forth, which so please us to hear, are transcripts from the individuals' inner-self, or rather of the out-creations thereof. Of course, these are true to the individual, but to no one else : let it be once remembered that the man is as immortal in the past, as he is now, and will be ; and that during that state (as Monad or Pha-soul) of pre-carnate being, he had an experience as real to him *then*, as his present is to him now ; and we shall no longer marvel at genius, or at the stupendous powers of the human mind. During the sublime experiences of my soul, which I am endeavoring to recount, I became thoroughly satisfied, not as the medium, not from spiritual teaching, but from soul-observation, that man, like God, had no beginning, as did matter as we know it—and that like Him, he will never positively have an end ; albeit the modes of God, and those of man—for at bottom, they are ONE, continually change conditions. This brings us to the question, " What is God ?"  *  *  *  *  Up there,† upon

--------

* If we except Swedenborg, and a fugitive lecture or two, by persons not necessary to be named herein.

† I now discovered that " up" was a condition of soul and spirit—and that to both, time and space did not exist.

the beautiful ether, all was still and silent music, yet moving in Beauty, Order, and Form—which were out-creations of one Eternal Monad, self-conscious and awful—shone a sun of ineffable glory and majesty—the Omnipotent God.

This sun shines in the heaven of spirit, just as the comparatively tiny and material suns illuminate the material universe. The spiritual does not glide into the material, but is from and above it, just in the sense that the *meaning* of a sentence is above the sounds .or characters which convey it—and in no other. The grand procession of material universes constantly sweeps along the Eternities; receive Light, Life and Love thence; fructify; incarnate the monad's Beauty, Consciousness, Form, Order, Law, Music, and Number, in human souls; and then exhaustion prepares the self-same material universes—or rather, their bases for a new infiltration—of God-Od, so to speak, differing from the last; and so on forever. One procession is one Eternity—or rather, Cycle. Thus it will be seen, by those who can grasp this tremendous thought, that all matter—the amazing system of substance, is after all, but a mere fleck—a mote in the sun-rays—a mere grain on the awful shores of the stupendous SPIRITUAL OCEAN; nor does all the matter existing, bear a greater proportion to the spiritual, than an orange does in bulk to the Rocky Mountain Chain. The material systems move near its centre, and the spiritual waves flow on all sides into the Ineffable BEYOND.

The fountain, whence they flow is GOD! and this word "God" is a poor name. Men become "gods" in the great hereafter—gods for GOOD, USE and ORDER, or the opposite of these; but this, of which I speak, the

Eternal Secret, the awful, yet radiant MYSTERY, is as far beyond the Ideal Jehovah, as is the human beyond the analid.    Let us make a chain : Matter is the first link : Spirit is the second—I speak of UNIVERSES now, remember ; Soul—that which constitutes the Human THINK-principle, is the third ; well, this OVER-SOUL flows through all these, as man's spirit through his body.    Now man is conscious only partly ; he knows nothing just on the *other side* of himself, is ignorant of what life is, and of that august power which governs his involuntary self.    Well, the OVER-SOUL flows out into the All—into the universe of THINK, (I can use no other term,) into that of Soul, MONADS, Spirit, Matter ; and while pervading and being imminent in ALL, is self-conscious at every point ; in the THINK, the MONAD, the Soul, the Spirit, the Matter, in every particle that IS, or can ever BE.    I hold this, as the truest definition of the Deity yet given ; and in the radiant presence of such a thought, all human things must bow ; all human pride stand back, all human ideas pale and fade.    *    * And these things came to me, and I believe them true.

And God is not good, but beyond it ; is not truth, but its foundation ; is not power, nor Life, nor THINK, but beyond, beneath, above all these !    Spirit may be repre-sented as the soul of matter : Soul as the inmost of Spirit ; Monad as the base of Soul ; THINK, as the essence of Monad ; God as the SOUL OF THINK.    Here, let no man smile at these uncouth expressions ; they stand as symbols of mighty truths.    I have said that Monads were scintillations from God's brain : They are : That Matter was THE PROCEEDING from his body. Monads are forms of thought, and are the bubbles on His ever-rising tide of SOUL.    Hence, these monads are, so to speak, the *givings off* of his spirit. God's Spirit is the element, Soul ; but of THIS Soul, none but Himself knoweth.

And as I floated there on the sea of knowledge, an impulse sprung up to know more ; and these questions were fashioned in my soul, and that soul derived from out the mystery the answers appended to each question : " Is not man forever in the human form ?" In human form, YES ; in human shape, no : Man was once the monad—a finite sun. He still is so as to himself (see a previous section), and the body which he uses is but an out-creation, as are his mental pictures ; with the difference that the latter are volitional and circumstantial, while the former is constitutional. The shape,— organic, is the very best adapted to the purposes it serves, and it is the effect of a force lying behind the personal consciousness. Its use is for the material ; it could have none in the spiritual world, save as the effect of Soul-habit, or as a means of discipline in the lesser or "lower" departments or conditions thereof. " How of dead infants ?" Infants have spiritual bodies, and retain them till discipline places them beyond the necessity. In all cases, the bodily forms are attachments to the human, so long as the human is in the sphere of discipline,—hence moves within the possibilities of Good and Evil. When they leave this latter, and merge into the sphere of USES, the external of the soul corresponds to its new state. A soul is immaterial, as of the nature of THINK,—hence needs no stomach to digest food, lungs to breathe air, legs for locomotion, and so forth ; for all these are principles of the soul, with mere out-created organs. When it needs the organs no longer, it dispenses therewith, but the *principles* underlying them still remain,

> "Unhurt amid the rush of warring elements,
> The wreck of matter, and the crush of worlds."

A man sits in his study, and thinks of his father's house, many, many miles away. He sees it ;—well, brook, barn, trees, garden, flowers,—all, all just as they really exist. Now, the man's body, being a mere thing of circumstance, still remains in the study, but the man himself is gone ; his body and spirit are in the room, but himself is at the old homestead. Space, time, and flight are not to the soul,—only to forms and things of coarser nature and lesser majesty.

The soul thinks "I am there," and—*there it is.* Certain persons, gifted, can see things spiritual ; all persons can at times, and frequently are sensible of the presence of others, whose bodies are far away. They are made sensible of it by soul-contact. It is possible for a man to project an image of himself to any distance, which image shall be mistaken for himself. These images, being such, of course, cannot speak when questioned by whoever sees them. Whoever can picture the exact simulacrum of himself, can *will* this figure whither soever he may choose, and then persons who behold this declare they have seen his "spectre," "phantom," "ghost," "wraith," or "double." Again, the man of strong will and pure desires may quit the body spiritually, actually, and be perceptible to others at a distance ; may be spoken to, hold conversations, and move material objects, when his body lies scores of leagues away.

"Are there demons ?" Yes, two kinds : forms of

fear, corresponding to a man's bad moral state,—projected out-creations from the wicked self. Such are the fiends, snakes, toads, devils and horrid monsters seen by the victim of *delirium tremens.* Of the same order, but beautiful, instead of the reverse, are the angels, ghillim, houris, fairy-forms, peris and naiads, seen by the rapt enthusiasts of all ages and climes, but especially of the Orient, when inspired by opium, love, and religion ; out-creations of their inmost souls,—subjective images objectified. This species of out-projection pertains to all persons, while under the discipline of good and evil, virtue and vice, and all other material conditions and accidents. "What do you mean by virtue and vice, as material incidents ?" I mean that good and evil are but conditions environing man, while under the sway of his inevitable discipline.

---

There is such a thing as the spirit of Community. A mob is a fearful thing, a dreadful power, and it developes a ferocity which does not inhere in any one of the multitude composing it—a material energy of awful force. A reasoner can take aside, one by one, an entire audience, and convince them thus of the justice of the cause he advocates ; but, let them be combined, and he shall not be able to convince the general sense, nor succeed in evoking aught but derisive sneers at his "imbecility." Or conversely : he may not be able to convince the people, taken singly, yet, let him pour out his soul before them, *congregated,* and he shall sway them as the tempest sways the forest—material energy in both cases. Again : vice is frequently not considered in the act itself, but in the how society views it. Thus, adultery,

in France, is laughed at as " the mere affair of a sofa ;".
in England, its penalty is a black eye or so, and half a
crown a week ; in the Orient, it is a matter of course ;
in the Southern States, it is a legal and *very peculiar*
institution ; and in New England it is a fearful crime ;
and yet is, notwithstanding, a very fashionable vice, in
spite of bolts and bars ; one, too, that has lately stained
not a few preachers of the gospel.    Adultery, so far as
individuals are concerned, is, except in rare instances,
a thing of terrible moment ; but, alas ! the very ones
who make the most noise about it, denounce it the
loudest and prosecute the sinners most grievously, are
the very ones who are particularly weak in that direction themselves.    Many a judge has left the bench,
wherefrom he had just sentenced some weak one to long
years of penal servitude, to revel in a wanton's arms !
    Individuals are governed by personal laws and in-
fluences ; but society, community, the mob, develope an
" opinion" or "sentiment," before which all charitable, just, or personal considerations vanish and are
forgotten.    Many a jury, if individual preferences
were allowed scope, would free the culprit whom the
"twelve" consign to dungeon or the gibbet.    This is
material force!    Again : A fellow hires himself out as
a soldier, to commit homicide as often as he can ;—goes
out ; does so ; comes back, after making a dozen or
two,—perhaps a hundred orphans;—settles down in
life, beneath his " laurels," lives to a good old age, dies,
and goes to—hell,—I think, with ne'er a pang or qualm
of conscience.    Why ? Because the community smiles
on him and sustains, as a mass, the very thing—man-
killing—that every one of them, taken singly, condemns
and must ever disapprove.

This personal feeling is Common Sense. The other is Public Opinion. The last is always wrong; the other is always right. The individual is generally just, the community very seldom. Public opinion is, therefore, a mere physical power; and as such, eternally changes. Common sense, on the contrary, ever and always accretes and intensifies, spreads and grows stronger as the years and people pass away; the one is accidental and material; the other, personal, constitutional, and real. Now take a couple of other men, constituted precisely as was our soldier : let them, each for himself, commit a genteel murder ; one gets caught at it and is strung up and choked to death in a period of time, varying from four to twenty minutes; choked till his eyes bulge out, his tongue lolls thick and swollen from his mouth—by a fellow who gets paid for the job. Society says this is right *as* Society ; but take every one that composes it aside, and let him look on that blue-black throat, at those bulging eye-balls, contorted features, and ghastly carrion ; ten thousand to one, that every man of them will denounce this legal choking affair as a damnable piece of buisness, totally unworthy of a savage, much less civilized (?) men and women.

Here you see the thing is material—is the monstrous out-creation of the social body, and not at all related to man, as an individual. How happens this out-creation of the body-politic to be so terrible ? just go back a few pages and you will see that " the out-creation always corresponds to the condition of the being whence it emanates." The great mass is barbarous today ; and civilization, much less Spiritualization, is the exception to the general rule and order. Bye-and-bye

12

civilization will be the rule, and then we shall have a better "Public Opinion ;" therefore, less hanging, and things of that sort. Let us work for it.

Turn we now to the fellow that earned his ten dollars by performing the choking operation—the nice young gentleman who so gaily looped the rope and pulled the neat little spring which sent a soul to God on a yard of twisted hemp. How does he feel when the job is over? Why, not at all uneasy. The guilt of doing this wicked thing is not *his*, he feels—albeit, he and I disagree on this point. It is not his, and so he "don't care a fig." That's it exactly. He, like the choked-to-death, whose eyes bulge out, who bleeds at the ears, whose tongue is so largely swollen that it won't stay in his blood-slavered mouth—he, too, I say, has sent a soul prematurely cross-lots home; but feeleth he remorse ? No more than a good dram of sixpenny damnation will drown—but not forever ! Oh, no !—for just as sure as God reigns, he must come up to the bar for sentence, and must expiate his error somewhere, at some time.

The judge, the jury, the legislators—all, just as the executioner, feel that they are clear of even this judicial murder, and at last, we trace the responsibility home to a formless, brainless monster, without a body, yet with a great black soul, whose name is, "PUBLIC OPINION." Presently, you and I, sir and madam, will beget a better one—God speed the day !

Now for the other murderer. He has too much tact and *finesse* to be caught, caged, and strung up. Chemistry can't fasten the deed on him, nor can skilful detectives trip him up ; and so he goes along, happy as a lark in the day-time ! But somehow or other his dreams are devilishly unpleasant ! Why?—Because in the silence of the night, when deep sleep falleth upon men, a spirit passes before his face, bearing a very astonishing resemblance to a former acquaintance of his, now, alas! deceased ; and, although he is above the weakness of believing in " spirits," yet he often catches himself ex-claiming, " By God, I believe it's his ghost !"—an out-creation of his foul within.	From this day forward, the invisible fangs of Public Opinion, go deeper and deeper into his soul—a moral augur, sinking an artesian shaft into his very centre—until, at last, the waters are reached, and burst forth in one full, deep stream of agony—Remorse.	The executed suffered about ten deaths, in expiation of the one life he took ; but *this* wretch, whose crime is not known, suffers a dozen deaths a day.

Now, in a community where man-slaying don't count much against a citizen, this fellow would not have suffered one whit more than did the soldier, or Jack Ketch. * * * * I said that there were two kinds of demons.	Having described one, we will glance rapidly at the other ; the process is simple enough.	A man's elevation on the scale depends upon himself—if he loves disorder more than its opposite, hatred than love, the deformed than the lovely—why, the man, in so far forth as he departs from rectitude of his own purpose and will, just so far does he demonize himself. And as there is no limit to advancement or descension, so he may become guileful to an immense degree—be a demon.

There are myriads of such within the compass, and on the confines of the Material Realms, but none beyond them in the Divine City of Pure Spirit.	But *within* those limits exists a Badness, so awful, so vast, that the soul shrinks before the terrible reality. These beings cannot injure our souls, save by the voluntary co-operation of our own wills and loves.

I content myself with this brief outline now, promising to take up the subject hereafter. In this book I have touched only a few of the lesser truths of the Universe, and shall go deeper next time.

All these things came to me as I floated on the air. These practical lessons I received from Thotmor and his Cynthia, and from my own spontaneous reachings forth. Presently Thotmor looked lovingly upon the maiden at his side, and then upon myself. She turned to me, and said, "This lesson will do for the present. Return once more to, earth." * * * * Again, a deep sense of drowsiness fell upon me, and seemingly, I slept. When next I woke, I was beneath the tree, and the golden sun was setting.

This was not all I learned ; but my present task is finished. Patience, my reader ! Since these truths were written I have received a message from beyond the sea. I am going to cross it. I shall speedily return and relate to you and all my brethren the things I there have seen. Till then, ADIEU !

# CIRCULAR NOTICE.

## POSITIVE MEDICINE.

I take this method of informing my numerous friends and the public that I am still manufacturing my great curatives, but during the past eight years have, by the aid of the highest procurable chemical assistance, been enabled to bring them to a state of perfection that leaves nothing to be desired in that direction. Now, as in years past, I devote myself to one speciality, viz. : the treatment of NERVOUS and SCROFULOUS diseases. In addition to my own system, that of Dr. P. B. Randolph has been transferred to me by special deed, and the public well know that amongst the thousands of cases of an especial nature treated by him, not two per cent. out of the entire number but were perfectly cured. The combined system is the result of twenty years of profound study. The diseases I treat are those whose ravages are indeed fearful, but which are seldom understood, and still more seldom cured by ordinary medical practitioners. My system and my remedies are known only to myself, and, it is needless to state, have, for the last ten years, stood alone and unequalled, and are alike adapted to the wants of either sex. In accordance with my system of *Positive Medicine*, in every case I furnish just what Nature, the only great Physician, needs, in order to be enabled to effect a cure. There is no guess-work at all about the matter, but I proceed with geometrical precision to a certain and foreseen result, and that too, not by Herb teas, or deleterious compounds of any sort, but by means of an *Entirely New Class* of curative agents. Every one of these compounds is elegant in appearance, delicious to the taste, steady and uniform in its effects, and absolutely *Positive* in curative results, a desideratum never before attained in the history of medicine. For instance : Chemical research has enabled us to bring to light a hitherto supposed unattainable combination of proximate principles, with certain ultimate elements. The *First* of which is named

## PHYMYLLE.

It is the *only* remedy extant for SPERMATORRHEA or Seminal losses ; is the most efficient agent yet discovered in cases of Atony and morbidity of the *vital* apparatus in either sex. In Leucorrhea, it stands alone. It is the agent for the cure, not only of the HABIT, but of the disastrous effects of ignorance, even where insanity has resulted ; because it supplies that whereof the body has been drained, and therefore is indicated in all affections of the Brain, Nervous System and Heart.

There are those who prefer to have written formulas to prepare their own medicines. To such I send them at $5 per case. *The Second Medicine,* my

## IRON AND MANGANESE COMPOUND,

is a certain cure for Ovarian, Uterine, Prostatic and Vaginal Ulcerations, as well as for Ulcers in the Stomach, Liver and Intestines. There can be no question of the great medicinal value of the ferro-manganic preparations. This syrup is used with success in anæmic cases, scrofulous, syphilitic, and cancerous affections. Each fluid ounce of the syrup contains fifty grains of the mixed Iodides. Dose, from 10 drops to a fluid drachm.

The diseases herein named, which I treat, EXIST, and therefore ought to be cured. · It is my business to do this, and this is my only apology for advertising in this manner. Knowing my power over them, I feel religiously impelled to use it for the benefit of those who need my skill.

The two medicines, used conjointly with the third, is a certain and positive cure for Scrofula, Fits, Tape-Worm, Epilepsy, Consumption, Dropsy, Dyspepsia, Liver Disease, Gravel, Canker, Rheumatism, Insanity, Ulcers, Tumors, Salt Rheum, Spermatorrhea or Seminal Weakness, and the various affections of the Stomach, Brain, Lungs and Heart, Piles and Fistula, and all diseases of the blood, all of which morbid conditions can only be removed by vacating the body and blood of all deleterious substances and humors, and by supplying the elements whereof it stands in need. That physician is a fool who claims or expects to cure two men of opposite temperament of the same disease, with one medicine. It cannot be done, and never will be, else Science is at fault ; which cannot be the case, seeing that she absolutely demonstrates that each of the above diseases indicates the absence from the body of one, two, and, in certain cases, no less than *seven* of the prime elements of the body. My remedies supply these elements of the system, and thus effect the cure. Remedy No. 3 is the

## INVIGORANT.

Its name suggests its use and office, either alone or in combination with the others. It will, to quote the language of a patient, restored by its use, " Put life in hoary age, and fire in the veins of ice !" not by mere stimulations, but by permanent invigoration. Persons who have become exhausted by folly, study, over-working of the brain, sedentary habits and excess, have herein their only remedy. No. 4,

## THE EPILEPSY AND FITS CURE,

certain, positive and invaluable. No. 5,

## POWDERS,

for the cure of diseases of either sex, arising from colds and derangements of the natural system. They are prepared as ordered only, owing to the high cost of their materials. They are sent in courses at six, ten, twenty and twenty-five dollars—sufficient for one case—except desperate ones, and at these prices are the cheapest medicines in the world ; for they do their work, and do it thoroughly and well. In connection with this subject, allow me to state that these remedies are sure and certain ; they are not mere catch-pennies— are sold at high prices because they cost high to manufacture. One ingredient alone, in numbers one and three, is imported at the cost of 80 cents a drachm. In this connection also, let me state that all persons, sick or well, should read my pamphlet called :

## "LOVE, A PHYSICAL SUBSTANCE."
### A NEW AND STARTLING THEORY.

Diseases arising from perverted, inverted, retroverted, frozen and fevered love and passion, and how to cure them. Price 25 cents. The work will be re-written, improved and enlarged every six months.

Address,      M. J. RANDOLPH, Utica, New York.

---

## IMPORTANT PUBLICATIONS.

"IT ISN'T ALL RIGHT." A scorching review of Dr. A. B. Child's new theory that " Whatever is, is Right"—murder, robbery, rape, war, falsehood, and all the modern abominations included. The pamphlet rips the horrible fabric all to shreds. Price, 15 cents.

THE UNVEILING OF MODERN SPIRITUALISM. By the Converted Medium. No man ever had a more thrilling and terrific experience of certain phases of Spiritualism than the author of this pamphlet. It reveals the secret workings of the modern theurgy fuller and better than any work extant, besides a thorough refutation of the assertion that some men are not immortal. Price, 25 cents.

In preparation : HASHISH ; *Its Uses and Abuses.* Being the experience of three souls during their illumination by means of this terrible drug. The thrilling revelations of this pamphlet exceed anything of the kind ever written. It details the curious effects of Hashish—its clairvoyance power, and what several souls learned while under its wierd and awful influence—How a soul lives a thousand years in a moment of time—Where the Hashish world is. It will contain the *only solution* of this mystery ever attempted—and the true one. Sold to subscribers at 50 cents a copy. A limited number only will be printed. Issued Sept. 1, 1861. Address as above.

www.ingramcontent.com/pod-product-compliance
Lightning Source LLC
Chambersburg PA
CBHW021100030726
47496CB00006B/1919